CSS Mastery

Advanced Web Standards Solutions

Andy Budd
with Cameron Moll
and Simon Collison

friendsof

DESIGNER TO DESIGNER™

an Apress® company

CSS Mastery:
Advanced Web Standards Solutions

ISBN-13 (paperback): 978-1-59059-614-2
ISBN-13 (electronic): 978-1-4302-0123-6

Printed and bound in the United States of America 19 18 17 16 15

Trademarked names may appear in this book. Rather than use a trademark symbol with every occurrence of a trademarked name, we use the names only in an editorial fashion and to the benefit of the trademark owner, with no intention of infringement of the trademark.

Distributed to the book trade worldwide by Springer-Verlag New York, Inc., 233 Spring Street, 6th Floor, New York, NY 10013. Phone 1-800-SPRINGER, fax 201-348-4505, e-mail orders-ny@springer-sbm.com, or visit www.springeronline.com.

For information on translations, please contact Apress directly at 2855 Telegraph Avenue, Suite 600, Berkeley, CA 94705. Phone 510-549-5930, fax 510-549-5939, e-mail info@apress.com, or visit www.apress.com.

The information in this book is distributed on an "as is" basis, without warranty. Although every precaution has been taken in the preparation of this work, neither the author(s) nor Apress shall have any liability to any person or entity with respect to any loss or damage caused or alleged to be caused directly or indirectly by the information contained in this work.

The source code for this book is freely available to readers at www.friendsofed.com in the Downloads section.

Product numbers for the images used in Tuscany Luxury Resorts are as follows:
FAN1003579, FAN1003613, FAN1006983, and DVP0703035.

Credits

Lead Editor	**Copy Editor**
Chris Mills	Liz Welch
Technical Reviewer	**Assistant Production Director**
Molly Holzschlag	Kari Brooks-Copony
Editorial Board	**Production Editor**
Steve Anglin	Kelly Winquist
Dan Appleman	
Ewan Buckingham	**Compositor and Artist**
Gary Cornell	Diana Van Winkle, Van Winkle Design
Jason Gilmore	
Jonathan Hassell	**Proofreader**
Chris Mills	April Eddy
Dominic Shakeshaft	
Jim Sumser	**Indexer**
	John Collin
Project Manager	
Denise Santoro Lincoln	**Interior and Cover Designer**
	Kurt Krames
Copy Edit Manager	
Nicole LeClerc	**Manufacturing Director**
	Tom Debolski

CONTENTS AT A GLANCE

CONTENTS

FOREWORD

In our wonderful world of web design, there are 3,647 ways to accomplish the same goal. Approximately. And that absurdly fictitious number is increasing every day. Instead of one, correct way of solving a particular problem, we're both blessed and cursed by the abundant choices we have as web designers. It's these choices that make designing for the Web fun and interesting, while at the same time overwhelming. *CSS Mastery* will help cure that *overwhelmingitis* (a word that I've just invented).

Andy Budd has been writing, designing, and speaking about standards-based web design for years, and we're now lucky to see his clear, easy-to-follow way of teaching essential CSS techniques compiled in this very book. The result is a card catalog of indispensable solutions, tricks, and tips that a web professional such as yourself should not be without.

I've always frowned on publications that suggest a *single*, correct way of accomplishing a goal, and Andy does the complete opposite, offering multiple methods for tasks such as styling links, creating tabbed navigation, or creating columned layouts (to name but a few). Armed with these popular and stylish approaches to common design elements, you'll be better prepared to make your own *informed* decisions.

And as if that wasn't enough, Andy's gone ahead and enlisted the help of two imitable designers to help pull all the pieces together, showing how these essential techniques can work *together*. I've long been a fan of Cameron's and Simon's work, and to see two great case studies covering fluid, bulletproof designs as well as flexible style solutions, respectively... well, that's just a gigantic bonus.

So dig in and start chipping away at those 3,647 ways to master your CSS.

Dan Cederholm
Salem, Massachusetts
Author, Web Standards Solutions

ABOUT THE AUTHORS

 **Andy Budd** is a user experience designer and web standards developer living and working in Brighton, England. As the creative director of web design consultancy Clearleft (www.clearleft.com), Andy enjoys building attractive, accessible, and standards-compliant websites. His online home can be found at www.andybudd.com, where he writes about modern web design practices.

Andy is a regular speaker at international design conferences, workshops, and training events, and organized the UK's first web 2.0 conference (www.dconstruct.org). Passionate about the quality of education in the industry, Andy runs SkillSwap (www.skillswap.org), a free community training and networking project. Andy also helped set up the Web Standards Awards (www.webstandardsawards.com), a project that aims to recognize websites for their use of web standards.

When he's not building websites, Andy is a keen travel photographer. Never happier than when he's diving some remote tropical atoll, Andy is also a qualified PADI dive instructor and retired shark wrangler.

Cameron Moll, recognized as one of the industry's most balanced new media designers, is proficient in functional web design, elegant interfaces, and clean markup. Cameron has been involved in the design and redesign of scores of websites, and his influential techniques have found favor in circles across the Web. A marketing background and a keen eye for design lead him to merge form and function in the form of compelling visual experiences.

Cameron's work has been recognized by respected organizations and notable individuals such as National Public Radio (NPR), Communication Arts, and Veer. His personal site, CameronMoll.com, delivers design how-tos in the form of engaging conversation, on-topic banter, and downloadable artwork source files.

Simon Collison is Lead Web Developer at Agenzia (www.agenzia.co.uk), and has worked on numerous web projects for record labels, high-profile recording artists, and leading visual artists and illustrators, including The Libertines, Black Convoy, and Project Facade. Simon also oversees a production line of business, community, and voluntary sector websites, and passionately ensures everything he builds is accessible and usable, and complies with current web standards. Simon regularly reviews CSS-based websites for Stylegala, and does his best to keep his highly popular blog (www.collylogic.com) updated with noise about web standards, music, film, travels, and more web standards.

On those rare occasions away from the computer, Simon can be found in the pub, or trying to con free gig tickets out of his clients. A little too obsessed with music, he is very likely to bore you with his latest musical Top 100, or give you a potted history of the UK indie scene from 1979 to the present day. Simon has lived in many cities, including London and Reykjavik, but now lives happily in Nottingham with Emma and a cat called Ziggy.

ABOUT THE TECHNICAL REVIEWER

Molly E. Holzschlag is a well-known Web standards advocate, instructor, and author. A popular and colorful individual, she is Group Lead for the Web Standards Project (WaSP) and an invited expert to the GEO working group at the World Wide Web Consortium (W3C). Among her 30-plus books is the recent *The Zen of CSS Design*, coauthored with Dave Shea. The book artfully showcases the most progressive csszengarden.com designs. You can catch up with Molly's blog at—where else?—http://molly.com/.

ACKNOWLEDGMENTS

Andy Budd

Thanks to everybody who helped make this book possible, both directly and indirectly.

To Chris for guiding me through the writing process and helping turn my ideas into reality. And to everybody at Apress who worked tirelessly to get this book published on time. Your dedication and professionalism is much appreciated.

To my friends and colleagues at Clearleft (www.clearleft.com), Jeremy Keith (www.adactio.com) and Richard Rutter (www.clagnut.com), for providing encouragement and feedback throughout the book-writing process.

To Molly E. Holzschlag for lending your experience and breadth of knowledge to this book. Your support and guidance was invaluable, and I still don't know where you manage to find the time.

To Jamie Freeman and Jo Acres for providing the perfect environment in which to develop my skills. I'll pop around for tea and doughnuts soon. Thanks also to the Brighton web development community at large, and especially everybody on the BNM and SkillSwap mailing lists.

To all my colleagues who continue to share their wealth of knowledge in order to make the Web a better place. This book would not have been possible without the previous work of the following people, to name but a few: Cameron Adams, John Allsopp, Nathan Barley, Holly Bergevin, Douglas Bowman, The BritPack, Dan Cederholm, Tantek Çelik, Joe Clark, Andy Clarke, Simon Collison, Mike Davidson, Garrett Dimon, Derek Featherstone, Nick Fink, Patrick Griffiths, Jon Hicks, Shaun Inman, Roger Johansson, Ian Lloyd, Ethan Marcotte, Drew McLellan, Eric Meyer, Cameron Moll, Dunstan Orchard, Veerle Pieters, D. Keith Robinson, Jason Andrew Andrew Santa Maria, Dave Shea, Ryan Sims, Virtual Stan, Jeffrey Veen, Russ Weakley, Simon Willison, and Jeffrey Zeldman.

To all the readers of my blog and everybody I've met at conferences, workshops, and training events over the last year. Your discussions and ideas helped fuel the content of this book.

Big thanks to Mel, for proofreading each chapter and putting up with me over the last 9 months.

And lastly, thanks to you for reading. I hope this book helps you take your CSS skills to the next level.

Cameron Moll

I'd like to give gratitude to all the contributors to my case study. A big nod goes to Ryan Parman, whose TIMEDATE script was used to generate the day/month stamp in the upper-right corner of the Tuscany layout. Download a copy of his script here: www.skyzyx.com/scripts/.

And endless thanks to Veer for providing the gorgeous images used in this layout. Without their help, Tuscany Luxury Resorts may have otherwise been visually drab. Somehow, without fail, Veer always delivers unique, phenomenal visual elements—photography, type, merchandise, and more—that are far from commonplace. Access their collections here: www.veer.com/.

Simon Collison

I must thank the incredible Jon Burgerman (www.jonburgerman.com), Richard May (www.richard-may.com), and all my other Black Convoy (www.blackconvoy.com) friends for allowing me to use their images and names, and generally skim the cream off their talent for this case study. Huge thanks also to the cool Swede Roger Johansson (www.456bereastreet.com) for allowing me to use his rounded corners and for buying me a drink last summer. The More Than Doodles design was built quickly and efficiently thanks to the inspired templating system within the ExpressionEngine (www.expressionengine.com) publishing platform—a tool I could not live without. Finally, thanks to the Agenzia (www.agenzia.co.uk) boys for turning a blind eye to my fevered book writing of late. Much appreciated all around.

INTRODUCTION

There are an increasing number of CSS resources around, yet you only have to look at a CSS mailing list to see the same questions popping up time and again. "How do I center a design?" "What is the best rounded-corner box technique?" "How do I create a three-column layout?" If you follow the CSS design community, it is usually a case of remembering which website a particular article or technique is featured on. However, if you are relatively new to CSS, or don't have the time to read all the blogs, this information can be hard to track down.

Even people who are skilled at CSS run into problems with some of the more obscure aspects of CSS such as the positioning model or specificity. This is because most CSS developers are self-taught, picking up tricks from articles and other people's code without fully understanding the spec. And is it any wonder, as the CSS specification is complex and often contradictory, written for browser manufacturers rather than web developers?

Then there are the browsers to contend with. Browser bugs and inconsistencies are one of the biggest problems for the modern CSS developer. Unfortunately, many of these bugs are poorly documented and their fixes verge on the side of folk law. You know that you have to do something a certain way or it will break in one browser or another. You just can't remember which browser or how it breaks.

So the idea for a book formed. A book that brings together the most useful CSS techniques in one place, that focuses on real-world browser issues and that helps plug common gaps in people's CSS knowledge. A book that will help you jump the learning curve and have you coding like a CSS expert in no time flat.

Who is this book for?

CSS Mastery is aimed at anybody with a basic knowledge of (X)HTML and CSS. If you have just recently dipped your toes into the world of CSS design, or if you've been developing pure CSS sites for years, there will be something in this book for you. However, you will get the most out of this book if you have been using CSS for a while but don't consider yourself a master just yet. This book is packed full of practical, real-world advice and examples, to help you master modern CSS design.

How is this book structured?

This book eases you in gently, with two chapters on basic CSS concepts and best practices. You will learn how to structure and comment your code, the ins-and-outs of the CSS positioning model, and how floating and clearing really works. You may know a lot of this already, but you will probably find bits you've missed or not understood fully. As such, the first two chapters act as a great CSS primer as well as a recap on what you already know.

With the basics out of the way, the next five chapters cover core CSS techniques such as image, link, and list manipulation; form and data-table design; and pure CSS layout. Each chapter starts simply and then works up to progressively more complicated examples. In these chapters you will learn how to create rounded-corner boxes, images with transparent drop shadows, tabbed navigation bars, and flickr-style rollovers. If you want to follow along with the examples in this book, all the code examples can be downloaded from www.friendsofed.com.

Browser bugs are the bane of many a CSS developer, so all the examples in this book focus on creating techniques that work across browsers. What's more, this book has two whole chapters devoted to hacks, filters, bugs, and bug fixing. In these chapters you will learn about some of the most common filters, when to use them, and when not to use them. You will also learn about bug-hunting techniques and how to spot and fix common bugs before they start causing problems. You will even learn what really causes many of Microsoft Internet Explorer's seemingly random CSS bugs.

The last two chapters are the *piece de resistance*. Simon Collison and Cameron Moll, two of the best CSS designers around, have combined all of these techniques into two fantastic case studies. So you learn not only how these techniques work, but also how to put them into practice on a real-life web project.

This book can be read from cover to cover, or kept by your computer as a reference of modern tips, tricks, and techniques. The choice is up to you.

Conventions used in this book

This book uses a couple of conventions that are worth noting. The following terms are used throughout this book:

- (X)HTML refers to both the HTML and XHTML languages.
- Unless otherwise stated, CSS relates to the CSS 2.1 specification.
- IE 5.x/Win means Internet Explorer versions 5.0 and 5.5 for Windows.
- IE 6 and below on Windows refers to Internet Explorer 5.0 to 6.0 on Windows.

It is assumed that all the (X)HTML examples in this book are nested in the <body> of a valid document, while the CSS is contained in the <head> of the document for convenience. Occasionally, (X)HTML and CSS have been placed in the same code example for brevity. However, in a real document, these items need to go in their respective places to function correctly.

```
p {color: red;}

<p>I'm red</p>
```

Lastly, for (X)HTML examples that contain repeating data, rather than writing out every line, the ellipsis character (...) is used to denote code continuation:

```
<ul>
<li>Red</li>
<li>Yellow</li>
<li>Pink</li>
<li>Green</li>
...
</ul>
```

So, with the formalities out of the way, let's get started.

1 SETTING THE FOUNDATIONS

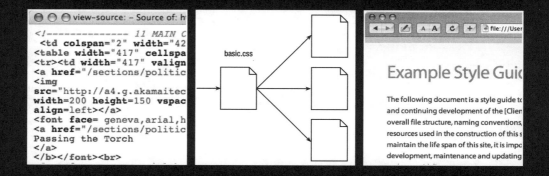

The human race is a naturally inquisitive species. We just love tinkering with things. When I recently bought a new iMac G5 I had it to bits within seconds, before I'd even read the instructions. We enjoy working things out ourselves, creating our own mental models about how we think things behave. We muddle through and only turn to the manual when something goes wrong or defies our expectations.

One of the best ways to learn Cascading Style Sheets (CSS) is to jump right in and start tinkering. However, if you're not careful you may end up misunderstanding an important concept or building in problems for later on. In this chapter, I am going to review some basic, but often misunderstood, concepts and show you how to keep your (X)HTML and CSS clear and well structured.

> *When we use the term XHTML, we are referring to Extensible Hypertext Markup Language, and when we use the term (X)HTML, we are referring to both XHTML and HTML.*

In this chapter you will learn about

- The importance of a well-structured and meaningful document
- Coding best practices
- Common coding mistakes
- Document types, DOCTYPE switching, and browser modes
- Ways to target your styles
- The cascade, specificity, and inheritance

Structuring your code

Most people don't think about the foundations of a building. However, without solid foundations, the majority of the buildings around us wouldn't exist. While this book is about advanced CSS techniques, much of what we are going to do would not be possible (or would be very difficult) without a well-structured and valid (X)HTML document to work with.

In this section you will learn why well-structured and meaningful (X)HTML is important in CSS development. You will also learn how you can add more meaning to your documents, and by doing so, make your job as a developer easier.

Use meaningful markup

The early Web was little more than a series of interlinked research documents using HTML to add basic formatting and structure. However, as the World Wide Web increased in popularity, HTML started being used for presentational purposes. Instead of using heading elements for page headlines, people would use a combination of font and bold tags to create the visual effect they wanted. Tables got co-opted as a layout tool rather than a way of displaying data, and people would use blockquotes to add whitespace rather than to indicate quotations. Very quickly the Web lost its meaning and became a jumble of font and table tags (see Figure 1-1).

```
<!--------------- 11 MAIN CONTENT------------------->
  <td colspan="2" width="425" valign="top" bgcolor=#eeeee3>
<table width="417" cellspacing="0" cellpadding="4" border=0>
<tr><td width="417" valign="top">
<a href="/sections/politics/DailyNews/DEMCVN_open000813.html"  >
<img
src="http://a4.g.akamaitech.net/7/4/622/001/abcnews.go.com/media/FrontPage/i
width=200 height=150 vspace=0 hspace=3 border=0 alt="Not Looking Back"
align=left></a>
<font face= geneva,arial,helvetica size=5><b>
<a href="/sections/politics/DailyNews/DEMCVN_open000813.html" >
Passing the Torch
</a>
</b></font><br>
<font face=geneva,arial,helvetica size=2>Bill Clinton gave a spirited
defense of his eight years in office and touted the qualifications of his
vice president, Al Gore, who wants to take Clinton&#0146;s place in the
White House. Get full coverage and <a href
="http://abcnews.go.com/sections/politics/DailyNews/DEMCVN_trans_clinton0008
a transcript</a>.</font>
```

Figure 1-1. The markup for the lead story from abcnews.com on August 14, 2000, uses tables for layout and large, bold text for headings. The code lacks structure and is difficult to understand.

HTML was intended to be a simple and understandable markup language. However, as web pages became more and more presentational, the code became almost impossible to understand. As such, complicated WYSIWYG (What You See Is What You Get) tools were needed to handle this mass of meaningless tags. Unfortunately, rather than making things simpler, these tools added their own complicated markup to the mix. By the turn of the millennium, the average web page was so complicated it was almost impossible to edit by hand for fear of breaking the code. Something needed to be done.

Then along came Cascading Style Sheets. With CSS it became possible to control how a page looked externally and to separate the presentational aspect of a document from its content. Presentational tags like the font tag could be ditched, and layout could be controlled using CSS instead of tables. Markup could be made simple again, and people began to develop a newfound interest in the underlying code.

Meaning started to creep back into documents. Browser default styles could be overridden so it became possible to mark something up as a heading without it being big, bold, and ugly. Lists could be created that didn't display as a series of bullet points, and blockquotes could be used without the associated styling. Developers started to use (X)HTML elements because of what they meant rather than how they looked (see Figure 1-2).

```
view-source: - Source of: http://abcnews.go.com/

<div id="main_story" class="clearthis">
<div id="main_photo" align="right">
<a href="/International/wireStory?id=947057"><img width="126"
src="http://a.abcnews.com/images/International/BAG12007171046.jpeg"
id="BAG12007171046.jpeg" height="188" /></a></div>

<div id="main_headline">

<h2 class="replace">
<a href="/International/wireStory?id=947057">Iraq Bomb Toll Grows; New
Attacks Kill 22</a>
</h2>
<p>New suicide bombings killed at least 22 people in the Baghdad area on
Sunday, while relatives struggled to identify charred bodies from a fiery
suicide attack near a Shiite mosque in Musayyib that...</p>

</div>
</div>
```

Figure 1-2. The markup for the lead story on abcnews.com from earlier this year is well structured and easy to understand. While it does contain some presentational markup, the code is a significant improvement on the code in Figure 1-1.

Meaningful markup provides the developer with several important benefits. Meaningful pages are much easier to work with than presentational ones. For example, say you need to change a quotation on a page. If the quotation is marked up correctly, it is easy to scan through the code until you find the first blockquote element. However, if the quotation is just another paragraph element tag, it will be a lot harder to find.

As well as being easy for humans to understand, meaningful markup—otherwise known as semantic markup—can be understood by programs and other devices. Search engines, for instance, can recognize a headline because it is wrapped in h1 tags and assign more importance to it. Screenreader users can rely on headings as supplemental page navigation.

Most importantly for the context of this book, meaningful markup provides you with a simple way of targeting the elements you wish to style. It adds structure to a document and creates an underlying framework to build upon. You can style elements directly without needing to add other identifiers, and thus avoid unnecessary code bloat.

(X)HTML includes a rich variety of meaningful elements, such as

- h1, h2, etc.
- ul, ol, and dl
- strong and em

- blockquote and cite
- abbr, acronym, and code
- fieldset, legend, and label
- caption, thead, tbody, and tfoot

As such, it is always a good idea to use an appropriate meaningful element where one exists.

IDs and class names

Meaningful elements provide an excellent foundation, but the list of available elements isn't exhaustive. (X)HTML was created as a simple document markup language rather than an interface language. Because of this, dedicated elements for things such as content areas or navigation bars just don't exist. You could create your own elements using XML, but for reasons too complicated to go into, it's not very practical at this time.

The next best thing is to take existing elements and give them extra meaning with the addition of an ID or a class name. This adds additional structure to your document, and provides useful hooks for your styles. So you could take a simple list of links, and by giving it an ID of mainNav, create your own custom navigation element.

```
<ul id="mainNav">
  <li><a href="#">Home</a></li>
  <li><a href="#">About Us</a></li>
  <li><a href="#">Contact</a></li>
</ul>
```

An ID name is used to identify an individual element on a page, such as the site navigation, and must be unique. IDs are useful for identifying persistent structural elements such as the main navigation or content areas. They are also useful for identifying one-off elements—a particular link or form element, for example.

Across a site, ID names should be applied to conceptually similar elements in order to avoid confusion. Technically, you could give both your contact form and your contact details the ID name of contact, assuming they were on separate pages. However, you would then need to style each element based on its context, which could be problematic. Instead, it would be much simpler to use distinct ID names such as contactForm and contactDetails.

While a single ID name can only be applied to one element on a page, the same class name can be applied to any number of elements on a page. Classes are very useful for identifying types of content or similar items. For instance, you may have a news page that contains the date of each story. Rather than giving each date a separate ID, you could give all of them a class name of date.

When naming your IDs and classes, it is important that you keep the names as meaningful and "un-presentational" as possible. For instance, you could give your section navigation an ID of rightHandNav as that is where you want it to appear. However, if you later choose to position it on the left, your CSS and (X)HTML will go out of sync. Instead, it would make more sense to name the element subNav or secondaryNav. These names explain what the element is rather than how it is presented. The same is true of class names. Say you want all your error messages to be red. Rather than using the class name red, choose something more meaningful like error or feedback (see Figure 1-3).

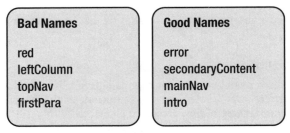

Figure 1-3. Good and bad ID names

When writing class and ID names, you need to pay attention to case sensitivity. CSS is generally a case-insensitive language. However, the case-sensitivity of things that appear in the markup, such as class and ID names, depends on the case sensitivity of the markup language. If you are using XHTML, class and ID names are case sensitive, whereas with regular HTML they are case insensitive. The best way to handle this issue is simply to be consistent with your naming conventions. So, if you use camel case in your (X)HTML class names, carry this through to your CSS as well.

Due to the flexibility of classes, they can be very powerful. At the same time, they can be overused and even abused. Novice CSS authors often add classes to nearly everything in an attempt to get fine-grained control over their styles. Early WYSIWYG editors also had the tendency to add classes each time a style was applied. Many developers picked up this bad habit when using generated code to learn CSS. This affliction is described as *classitis* and is, in some respects, as bad as using table-based layout because it adds meaningless code to your document.

```
<h3 class="newsHead">Zeldman.com turns 10</h3>
<p class="newsText">
Another milestone for Jeffrey as zeldman.com turns 10 today
</p>
<p class="newsText"><a href="news.php" class="newsLink">More</a></p>
```

In the preceding example, each element is identified as being part of a news story by using an individual news-related class name. This has been done to allow news headlines and text to be styled differently from the rest of the page. However, you don't need all these extra classes to target each individual element. Instead, you can identify the whole block as a news item by wrapping it in a division with a class name of news. You can then target news headlines or text by simply using the cascade.

```
<div class="news">
<h3>Zeldman.com turns 10</h3>
<p>Another milestone for Jeffrey as zeldman.com turns 10 today</p>
<p><a href="news.php">More</a></p>
</div>
```

Removing extraneous classes in this way will help simplify your code and reduce page weight. I will discuss CSS selectors and targeting your styles shortly. However, this overreliance on class names is almost never necessary. I usually only apply a class to an element if an ID isn't suitable, and I try to use them sparingly. Most documents I create usually only need the addition of a couple of classes. If you find yourself adding lots of classes, it's probably an indication that your (X)HTML document is poorly structured.

Divs and spans

One element that can help add structure to a document is a div element. Many people mistakenly believe that a div element has no semantic meaning. However, div actually stands for *division* and provides a way of dividing a document into meaningful areas. So by wrapping your main content area in a div and giving it an ID of mainContent, you are adding structure and meaning to your document.

To keep unnecessary markup to a minimum, you should only use a div element if there is no existing element that will do the job. For instance, if you are using a list for your main navigation, there is no need to wrap it in a div.

```
<div id="mainNav">
  <ul>
    <li>Home</li>
    <li>About Us</li>
    <li>Contact</li>
  </ul>
</div>
```

You can remove the div entirely and simply apply the ID to the list instead:

```
<ul id="mainNav">
  <li>Home</li>
  <li>About Us</li>
  <li>Contact</li>
</ul>
```

Using too many divs is often described as *divitus* and is usually a sign that your code is poorly structured and overly complicated. Some people new to CSS will try to replicate their old table structure using divs. But this is just swapping one set of extraneous tags for another. Instead, divs should be used to group related items based on their meaning or function rather than their presentation or layout.

Whereas divs can be used to group block-level elements, spans can be used to group or identify inline elements:

```
<h2>Where's Durstan?</h2>
<p>Published on <span class="date">March 22nd, 2005</span>
by <span class="author">Andy Budd</span></p>
```

It's generally less common to need to group or identify inline elements, so spans are seen less frequently than divs. Where you will see spans used are effects such as image replacement, which use them as extra hooks to hang additional styles on.

Although the goal is to keep your code as lean and meaningful as possible, sometimes you cannot avoid adding an extra nonsemantic div or span to display the page the way you want. If this is the case, don't fret too much over it. We live in a transitional period and hopefully CSS 3 will give us much greater control of our documents. In the meantime, real-world needs often have to come before theory. The trick is knowing when you have to make a compromise and if you are doing it for the right reasons.

CSS comes in various versions, or "levels," so it's important to know which version to use. CSS 1 became a recommendation at the end of 1996 and contains very basic properties such as fonts, colors, and margins. CSS 2 built on this and added advanced concepts such as floating and positioning to the mix, as well as advanced selectors such as the child, adjacent sibling, and universal selectors. At the time of writing, CSS 2 was still the latest version of CSS, despite becoming a recommendation as long ago as 1998.

Time moves very slowly at the World Wide Web Consortium (W3C), so while work on CSS 3 started before the turn of the millennium, the final release is still a long way off. To help speed development and browser implementation, CSS 3 has been broken down into modules that can be released and implemented independently. CSS 3 contains some exciting new additions, including a module for multicolumn layout. However, the selectors module is nearest completion and could possibly become a recommendation as early as 2006.

Because of the expected length of time between the release of CSS 2 and CSS 3, work started in 2002 on CSS 2.1. This revision of CSS 2 intends to fix some errors and provide a much more accurate picture of CSS browser implementation. CSS 2.1 is slowly nearing completion but probably won't be finished until late 2006. But it does provide a much more accurate representation of the current state of CSS and is the version I currently use.

Document types, DOCTYPE switching, and browser modes

A document type definition (DTD) is a set of machine-readable rules that define what is and isn't allowed in a particular version of XML or (X)HTML. Browsers will use these rules when parsing a web page to check the validity of the page and act accordingly. Browsers know which DTD to use, and hence which version of (X)HTML you are using, by analyzing the page's DOCTYPE declaration.

A DOCTYPE declaration is a line or two of code at the start of your (X)HTML document that describes the particular DTD being used. In this example, the DTD being used is for XHTML 1.0 Strict:

```
<!DOCTYPE html PUBLIC "-//W3C//DTD XHTML 1.0 Strict//EN"
"http://www.w3.org/TR/xhtml1/DTD/xhtml1-strict.dtd">
```

DOCTYPE declarations will typically, but not always, contain a URL to the specified DTD file. Browsers tend to not read these files, choosing instead to recognize common DOCTYPE declarations.

Validation

As well as being semantically marked up, an (X)HTML document needs to be written using valid code. If the code is invalid, browsers will try to interpret the markup themselves, sometimes getting it wrong. Worse still, if an XHTML document is being sent with the correct MIME type, browsers that understand XML simply won't display an invalid page. Because browsers need to know which DTD to use in order to process the page correctly, a DOCTYPE declaration is required for the page to validate.

You can check to see if your (X)HTML is valid by using the W3C validator, a validator bookmarklet, or a plug-in like the Firefox Developer Extension. Many (X)HTML editors now have validators built in, and you can even install a copy of the W3C validator locally on your computer. The validator will tell you if your page validates, and if not, why not.

Validation is important because it can help you track down bugs in your code. As such, it is a good idea to get into the habit of validating early and often. However, validation isn't an end unto itself, and many otherwise good pages fail to validate due to small errors such as unencoded ampersands, or because of legacy content. So although validation is important, in the real world, a degree of common sense is required.

> *Various code validation tools are available. You can validate your site online by going to* http://validator.w3.org/ *and entering your URL. However, if you are going to validate often—which is a good idea—typing your URL each time can become a little tedious. Instead, I use a handy validation bookmarklet, or favelet, which is a small piece of JavaScript that can be stored in the bookmarks or favorites folder in your browser. Clicking the bookmark will trigger the JavaScript action. In the case of the validator bookmarklet, it runs the page you are currently on through the W3C validator and displays the results. You can find the validator bookmarklet along with many other handy web development bookmarklets on my personal site at* www.andybudd.com/bookmarklets/.*
>
> *If you use Firefox, you can download and install a wide variety of plug-ins. Among the numerous validator plug-ins available, my personal favorite is the Web Developers Extension plug-in. As well as allowing you to validate your (X)HTML and CSS, it enables you to do a wide variety of other useful tasks like outlining various (X)HTML elements, turning off stylesheets, and even editing styles in the browser. The Web Developers Extension can be downloaded from* http://chrispederick.com/work/firefox/webdeveloper/ *and is a must-have for any CSS developer using Firefox.*
>
> *There is now also a developer toolbar for Internet Explorer 6 and above. You can download this toolbar from* http://tinyurl.com/7mnyh. *Although it is not as feature rich as the Firefox toolbar, it is still extremely useful.*

As well as being important for validation, browsers have started to use DOCTYPE declarations for another purpose.

Browser modes

When browser manufacturers started to create standards-compliant browsers, they wanted to ensure backward compatibility. To accomplish this, they created two rendering modes: standards mode and quirks mode. In standards mode the browser renders a page according to the specifications, and in quirks mode pages are displayed in a looser, more backward-compatible fashion. Quirks mode typically emulates the behavior of older browsers such as Microsoft Internet Explorer 4 and Netscape Navigator 4 to prevent older sites from breaking.

The most obvious example of the difference between these modes revolves around the Internet Explorer on Windows proprietary box model. When Internet Explorer 6 debuted, the correct box model was used in standards mode, while the older, proprietary box model was used in quirks mode. To maintain backward compatibility with sites built for IE 5 and below, Opera 7 and above also uses IE's faulty box model in quirks mode.

Other differences in rendering are subtler and specific to certain browsers. However, they include things like not requiring the # symbol for hex color values, assuming lengths without units in CSS are pixels, and increasing the font size by one step when using keywords.

Mozilla and Safari have a third mode called "almost standards mode," which is the same as standards mode, except for some subtle differences in the way tables are handled.

DOCTYPE switching

The browser chooses which rendering method to use based on the existence of a DOC-TYPE declaration and the DTD being used. If an XHTML document contains a fully formed DOCTYPE, it will normally be rendered in standards mode. For an HTML 4.01 document, a DOCTYPE containing a strict DTD will usually cause the page to render in standards mode. A DOCTYPE containig a transitional DTD and URI will also cause the page to render in standards mode, while a transitional DTD without a URI willcause the page to render in quirks mode. A badly formed or nonexistent DOCTYPE will cause both HTML and XHTML documents to be rendered in quirks mode.

The effect of choosing a rendering mode based on the existence of a DOCTYPE is known as DOCTYPE switching, or DOCTYPE sniffing. Not all browsers follow these exact rules, but they give you a good idea of how DOCTYPE switching works. Eric Meyer has done some further research on this subject and has created a chart (http://meyerweb.com/eric/dom/dtype/dtype-grid.html) that shows the various rendering modes different browsers use depending on the DOCTYPE declaration in use.

DOCTYPE switching is a hack used by browsers to distinguish legacy documents from more standards-compliant ones. Despite writing valid CSS, if you choose the wrong DOCTYPE, your pages will be rendered in quirks mode and behave in a buggy and unpredictable way. As such, it is important to include a fully formed DOCTYPE declaration on every page of your site and choose a strict DTD when using HTML.

```
<!DOCTYPE HTML PUBLIC "-//W3C//DTD HTML 4.01//EN"
    "http://www.w3.org/TR/html4/strict.dtd">

<!DOCTYPE html PUBLIC "-//W3C//DTD XHTML 1.0 Transitional//EN"
"http://www.w3.org/TR/xhtml1/DTD/xhtml1-transitional.dtd">

<!DOCTYPE html PUBLIC "-//W3C//DTD XHTML 1.0 Strict//EN"
    "http://www.w3.org/TR/xhtml1/DTD/xhtml1-strict.dtd">
```

Many HTML editors will automatically add a DOCTYPE declaration for you. If you are creating an XHTML document they may also add an XML declaration before the DOCTYPE declaration:

```
<?xml version="1.0" encoding="utf-8"?>
```

An XML declaration is an optional declaration used by XML files to define things such as the version of XML being used and the type of character encoding. Unfortunately, IE 6 automatically switches to quirks mode if the DOCTYPE declaration is not the first element on a page. Therefore, unless you are serving your pages as XML documents, it is best to avoid using an XML declaration.

Getting your styles to hit the target

A valid and well-structured document provides the framework to which your styles are applied. To be able to style a particular (X)HTML element using CSS, you need to have some way of targeting that element. In CSS the part of a style rule that does this is called the *selector*.

Common selectors

The most common kinds of selectors are type and descendant selectors. Type selectors are used to target a particular type of element, such as a paragraph, an anchor, or a heading element. You do this by simply specifying the name of the element you wish to style. Type selectors are sometimes also referred to as *element* or *simple* selectors.

```
p {color: black;}
a {text-decoration: underline;}
h1 {font-weight: bold;}
```

Descendant selectors allow you to target the descendants of a particular element or group of elements. A descendant selector is indicated by a space between two other selectors. In this example, only anchor elements that are descendants of a list item will be styled, so anchors within a paragraph will be unaffected.

```
li a {text-decoration: none;}
```

These two types of selector are great for applying generic styles that apply across the board. To be more specific and target selected elements, you can use ID and class selectors. As the names suggest, these selectors will target elements with the corresponding ID or class name. ID selectors are identified using a hash character; class selectors are identified with a period. The first rule in this example will make the text in the introductory paragraph bold, and the second rule will make the date green:

```
#intro {font-weight: bold;}
.datePosted {color: green;}

<p id="intro">Some Text</p>
<p class="datePosted">24/3/2006</p>
```

As I mentioned previously, many CSS authors develop an overreliance on class and, to a lesser extent, ID selectors. If they want to style headlines one way in the main content area and another way in the secondary content area, there is the tendency to create two classes and apply a class to each headline. A much simpler approach is to use a combination of type, descendant, ID, and/or class selectors:

```
#mainContent h1 {font-size: 1.8em;}
#secondaryContent h1 {font-size: 1.2em;}

<div id="mainContent">
<h1>Welcome to my site</h1>
...
</div>
<div id="secondaryContent">
<h1>Latest news</h1>
...
</div>
```

This is a very simple and obvious example. However, you will be surprised how many elements you can successfully target using just the four selectors discussed so far. If you find yourself adding lots of extraneous classes to your document, it is probably a warning sign that your document is not well structured. Instead, think about how these elements differ from each other. Often you will find that the only difference is where they appear on the page. Rather than give these elements different classes, think about applying a class or an ID to one of their ancestors, and then targeting them using a descendant selector.

Pseudo-classes

There are instances where you may want to style an element based on something other than the structure of the document—for instance, the state of a form element or link. This can be done using a pseudo-class selector.

```
/* makes all unvisited links blue */
a:link {color:blue;}
```

```
/* makes all visited links green */
a:visited {color:green;}

/* makes links red when hovered or activated */
a:hover, a:active {color:red;}

/* makes table rows red when hovered over */
tr:hover {background-color: red;}

/* makes input elements yellow when focus is applied */
input:focus {background-color:yellow;}
```

:link and :visited are known as *link* pseudo-classes and can only be applied to anchor elements. :hover, :active, and :focus are known as *dynamic* pseudo-classes and can theoretically be applied to any element. Unfortunately, only a few modern browsers such as Firefox support this functionality. IE 6 and below only pays attention to :active and :hover selectors if applied to an anchor link, and ignores :focus completely.

The universal selector

The universal selector is possibly one of the most powerful and least used of all the selectors. The universal selector acts like a wildcard, matching all the available elements. Like wildcards in other languages, the universal selector is denoted by an asterisk. The universal selector is normally used to style every element on a page. For instance, you can remove the default browser padding and margin on every element using the following rule:

```
* {
  padding: 0;
  margin: 0;
}
```

When combined with other selectors, the universal selector can be used to style all the descendants of a particular element, or skip a level of descendants. You will see how this can be put to practical effect a little later in this chapter.

Advanced selectors

CSS2 has a number of other useful selectors. Unfortunately, while modern browsers such as Firefox and Safari support these advanced selectors, IE 6 and below do not. Luckily, CSS was created with backward compatibility in mind. If a browser doesn't understand a selector, it ignores the whole rule. That way, you can apply stylistic and usability embellishments in more modern browsers, and not worry about it causing problems in older browsers. Just remember to avoid using these more advanced selectors for anything critical to the functioning of your site.

Child and adjacent sibling selectors

The first of these advanced selectors is the child selector. Whereas a descendant selector will select all the descendants of an element, a child selector only targets the element's immediate descendants, or "children." In the following example, the list items in the outer list will be given a custom icon while list items in the nested list will remain unaffected:

```
#nav > li {background: url(folder.png) no-repeat left top;}

<ul id="nav">
<li>Home</li>
<li>Services
<ul>
<li>Design</li>
<li>Development</li>
<li>Consultancy</li>
</ul>
</li>
<li>Contact Us </li>
</ul>
```

It is possible to "fake" a child selector that works in IE 6 and below by using the universal selector. To do this you first apply to all of the descendants the style you want the children to have. You then use the universal selector to override these styles on the children's descendants. So to fake the previous child selector example you would do this:

```
#nav li {background: url(folder.png) no-repeat left top;}
#nav li * {background-image: none;}
```

You may also want to style an element based on its proximity to another element. The adjacent sibling selector allows you to target an element that is preceded by another element that shares the same parent. Using the sibling selector, you could make the first paragraph following a top-level heading bold, while leaving other paragraphs unaffected:

```
h1 + p {font-weight: bold;}

<h1>Main Heading</h1>
<p>First Paragraph</p>
<p>Second Paragraph</p>
```

Attribute selectors

As the name suggests, the attribute selector allows you to target an element based on the existence of an attribute or the attribute's value. This allows you to do some very interesting and powerful things.

For example, when you hover over an element with a `title` attribute, most browsers will display a tooltip. You can use this behavior to expand the meaning of things such as abbreviations:

```
<abbr title="Cascading Style Sheets">CSS</abbr>
```

However, there is no way to tell that this extra information exists without hovering over the element. To get around this problem, you can use the attribute selector to style abbr elements with titles differently from other elements—in this case, by giving them a dotted bottom border. You can provide more contextual information by changing the cursor from a pointer to a question mark when the cursor hovers over the element, indicating that this element is different from most.

```
abbr[title] {border-bottom: 1px dotted #999;}
abbr[title]:hover {cursor: help;}
```

In addition to styling an element based on the existence of an attribute, you can apply styles based on a particular value. For instance, sites that are linked to using a rel attribute of nofollow gain no added ranking benefit from Google. The following rule displays an image next to such links, possibly as a way of showing disapproval of the target site:

```
a[rel="nofollow"] {
  background-image: url(nofollow.gif);
  padding-right: 20px;
}
```

One clever way of using the attribute selector is to capitalize on the fact that IE 6 and below does not support it. You can then apply one style to IE and another style to more standards-compliant browsers. For instance, IE has problems displaying 1-pixel dotted borders, choosing to render them dashed instead. Using an attribute selector, you could choose to apply your dotted-border style only to browsers you know will render it correctly. This is done by targeting the class attribute rather than using a class selector.

```
.intro {border-style: solid;}
[class="intro"] {border-style: dotted;}
```

Some attributes can have more than one value, separated by spaces. The attribute selector allows you to target an element based on one of those values. For instance, a group of developers have suggested using predefined keywords in the attribute of links to define the relationship one site owner has with another. You can use this information to apply an image to any links that contain the keyword friend in the rel attribute.

```
a[rel~="friend"] {background-image: url(friend.gif);}
```

```
<a href="http://www.hicksdesign.com/" rel="friend met colleague" >
John Hicks
</a>
```

> *Using the rel attribute with friend values is known as the XHTML Friends Network, or XFN for short, and is one of several new "microformats" to have developed recently. You can find out more about XFN at http://gmpg.org/xfn/ and about the concept of microformats in general at http://microformats.org.*

Once these advanced CSS 2 selectors are widely supported, the need to add extra divs or classes to your code will be greatly reduced.

The cascade and specificity

With even a moderately complicated stylesheet, it is likely that two or more rules will target the same element. CSS handles such conflicts through a process known as the *cascade*. The cascade works by assigning an importance to each rule. Author stylesheets are considered the most important, followed by user stylesheets, and finally the default stylesheets used by your browser or user agent. To give users more control, they can override any rule by specifying it as !important—even a rule flagged as !important by the author.

So the cascade works in the following order of importance:

- User styles flagged as !important
- Author styles flagged as !important
- Author styles
- User styles
- Styles applied by the browser/user agent

Rules are then ordered by how specific the selector is. Rules with more specific selectors override those with less specific ones. If two rules are equally specific, the last one defined takes precedence.

Specificity

To calculate how specific a rule is, each type of selector is assigned a numeric value. The specificity of a rule is then calculated by adding up the value of each of its selectors. Unfortunately, specificity is not calculated in base 10 but a high, unspecified, base number. This is to ensure that a highly specific selector, such as an ID selector, is never overridden by lots of less specific selectors, such as type selectors. However, if you have fewer than 10 selectors in a specific selector, you can calculate specificity in base 10 for simplicity's sake.

The specificity of a selector is broken down into four constituent levels: a, b, c, and d.

- If the style is an inline style, then a = 1.
- b = the total number of ID selectors.
- c = the number of class, pseudo-class, and attribute selectors.
- d = the number of type selectors and pseudo-element selectors.

Using these rules it is possible to calculate the specificity of any CSS selector. Table 1-1 shows a series of selectors, along with their associated specificity.

Table 1-1. Specificity example

Selector	Specificity	Specificity in base 10
`Style=""`	1,0,0,0	1000
`#wrapper #content {}`	0,2,0,0	200
`#content .datePosted {}`	0,1,1,0	110
`div#content {}`	0,1,0,1	101
`#content {}`	0,1,0,0	100
`p.comment .dateposted {}`	0,0,2,1	21
`p.comment{}`	0,0,1,1	11
`div p {}`	0,0,0,2	2
`p {}`	0,0,0,1	1

At first glance, all this talk of specificity and high but undefined based numbers may seem a little confusing, so here's what you need to know. Essentially, a rule written in a style attribute will always be more specific than any other rule. A rule with an ID will be more specific than one without an ID, and a rule with a class selector will be more specific than a rule with just type selectors. Finally, if two rules have the same specificity, the last one defined prevails.

Using specificity in your stylesheets

Specificity is very useful when writing CSS as it allows you to set general styles for common elements and then override them for more specific elements. For instance, say you want most of the forms on your site to be 30em wide but your search form needs to be only 15em wide:

```
form {width: 30em;}
form#search {width: 15em;}
```

Whenever you want to create a new form you do not have to worry about changing anything in the CSS, as you know it will be styled correctly. However, on larger sites you will find more and more exceptions will start to creep in. Maybe you will have a login form that you want to be 20em wide or a larger application form that needs to be 40em wide. Each time you create a more specific style, you will probably need to override some of the general rules. This can lead to quite a bit of extra code. It can also start to get very complicated as one element may be picking up styles from a variety of places.

To avoid too much confusion, I try to make sure my general styles are very general while my specific styles are as specific as possible and never need to be overridden. If I find that I have to override general styles several times, it's simpler to remove the declaration that needs to be overridden from the more general rules and apply it explicitly to each element that needs it.

Adding a class or an ID to the body tag

One interesting way to use specificity is to apply a class or an ID to the body tag. By doing this, you can then override styles on a page-by-page or even a site-wide basis. For instance, if you wanted your homepage to have a different layout from the rest of your site, you could add a class name to the body element on your home page and use it to override your styles:

```
#content {
  float: left;
}

.homepage #content {
  float: right;
}

#nav {
  float: right;
}

.homepage #nav {
  float: left;
}
```

You will see later on how this technique can be used to highlight the current page a visitor is on in your site navigation.

Adding an ID to every page of your site gives users the ability to override your stylesheets with their own user stylesheets. Site-wide IDs, known colloquially as CSS signatures, tend to take the format id="www-sitename-com". At a simple level the users may want to override your font sizes or color scheme to make the site easier to read. They could do so by adding the following rule to their user stylesheet:

```
body#www-andybudd-com {
  font-size: 200%;
  background-color: black;
  color: white;
}
```

However, it doesn't need to stop there. CSS signatures give your users the power to completely restyle your site. They could hide elements they don't like, change the layout, or come up with a completely new design.

Inheritance

People often confuse inheritance with the cascade. Although they seem related at first glance, the two concepts are actually quite different. Luckily, inheritance is a much easier concept to grasp. Certain properties, such as color or font size, are inherited by the descendants of the elements those styles are applied to. For instance, if you were to give the body element a text color of black, all the descendants of the body element would also have black text. The same would be true of font sizes. If you gave the body a font size of 14 pixels, everything on the page should inherit that font size. I say *should* because IE for Windows and Netscape have problems inheriting font sizes in tables. To get around this, you will either have to specify that tables should inherit font sizes or set the font size on tables separately.

If you set the font size on the body, you will notice that this style is not picked up by any headings on the page. You may assume that headings do not inherit text size. But it is actually the browser default stylesheet setting the heading size. Any style applied directly to an element will always override an inherited style. This is because inherited styles have a null specificity.

Inheritance is very useful as it lets you avoid having to add the same style to every descendant of an element. If the property you are trying to set is an inherited property, you may as well apply it to the parent element. After all, what is the point of writing this:

```
p, div, h1, h2, h3, ul, ol, dl, li {color: black;}
```

when you can just write this:

```
body {color: black;}
```

Just as sensible use of the cascade can help simplify your CSS, good use of inheritance can help to reduce the number and complexity of the selectors in your code. It you have lots of elements inheriting various styles, though, determining where the styles originate can become confusing.

Planning, organizing, and maintaining your stylesheets

The larger, more complicated, and graphically rich your sites become, the harder your CSS is to manage. In this section, I will look at ways to help you manage your code, including splitting up your files into multiple stylesheets, grouping your styles into logical sections, and adding comments to make your code easier to read.

Applying styles to your document

You can add styles directly to the head of a document by placing them between style tags; however, this is not a very sensible way to apply styles to a document. If you want to create another page using the same styles, you would have to duplicate the CSS on the new page. If you then wanted to change a style, you would have to do it in two places rather than one. Luckily, CSS allows us to keep all our styles in one or more external stylesheets. There are two ways to attach external stylesheets to a web page. You can link to them or you can import them:

```
<link href="/css/basic.css" rel="stylesheet" type="text/css" />
<style type="text/css">
<!--
@import url("/css/advanced.css");
-->
</style>
```

Older browsers such as Netscape 4 do not understand importing. Therefore, you can use import to hide complicated styles from older browsers, which they may not understand. In the previous example I linked to a simple stylesheet that contained basic typographic styles most browsers will understand. I then imported a more advanced stylesheet that contained more complicated styles like floated or positioned layouts. Using this method you can even create one design for older browsers and another for more modern versions.

You do not have to confine importing to an (X)HTML document. You can also import one stylesheet from another stylesheet. This allows you to link to your basic stylesheet from the (X)HTML page and then import your more complicated styles into that stylesheet (see Figure 1-4):

```
@import url(/css/layout.css);
@import url(/css/typography.css);
@import url(/css/color.css);
```

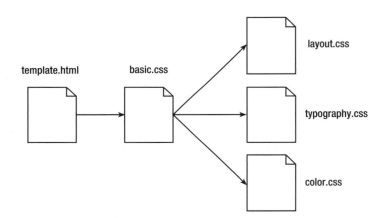

Figure 1-4. Multiple stylesheets can be imported into a single stylesheet that is then linked to your HTML page.

This helps to remove some complexity from your (X)HTML documents and allows you to manage all your stylesheets in one place. Import rules need to be the first rules in a stylesheet or they may not work properly. Because imported stylesheets are considered to come before linked stylesheets, it's important to remember that the rules in your linked stylesheets will be overriding your imported rules and not the other way around.

While it is theoretically possible to import one stylesheet into a stylesheet that is itself being imported, this type of daisy chaining or multilevel nesting is not well supported. As such, you should probably avoid nesting imports more than two levels deep.

Very few people use Netscape 4 these days, so you probably do not need to worry too much about this browser. You could forget the simple linked stylesheet and import your styles instead. However, IE 5/6 for Windows have a strange quirk that affects pages using only the import rule. When an affected page loads, it is temporarily displayed unstyled, before the styles are finally rendered. The bug is called the "Flash of Unstyled Content" bug, or FOUC for short. Having a link or script element in the head of your document prevents this bug, so even if you are not too worried about supporting Netscape 4, it may still be worth linking to a basic stylesheet and then importing your styles from there.

Commenting your code

When writing your own stylesheets, you will have a good idea how they are structured, what problems you have encountered, and why things have been done a certain way. But if you come back to that stylesheet in 6 months, there is a good chance you will have forgotten much of this. Additionally, you may need to hand your CSS to somebody else for implementation, or another developer may have to edit your code in the future. It is therefore a good idea to comment your code.

Adding comments in CSS is very simple. A CSS comment starts with /* and ends with */. This type of commenting is known as C style commenting as it is the type of comment used in the C programming language. Comments can be single or multiline and can appear anywhere within the code.

```
/* Body Styles */
body {
  font-size: 67.5%; /* Set the font size */
}
```

Adding structural comments

The first thing I do when creating a new stylesheet is add a comment block at the top to describe what the stylesheet is for, the creation date or version number, who created it, and how to get in touch with them:

```
/*-------------------------------------------------------------------
Basic Style Sheet (for version 4 browsers)

version:   1.1
author:    andy budd
email:     info@andybudd.com
website:   http://www.andybudd.com/
------------------------------------------------------------------*/
```

This gives other developers a good overview of the file, allows them to see if it is current, and gives them a means of tracking down the original author if something doesn't make sense.

I then break the stylesheet down into sensible chunks. I usually start with general rules such as typography, headlines, and links. Next I tackle the major sections of a page based on how they appear in the flow of the document. This will typically include a branding section, main content, secondary content, main nav, secondary nav, and a footer section. Lastly, I deal with general elements that appear intermittently throughout the site. These are usually things like box styles, form styles, and graphical buttons. Similar to the introductory comment, I use a large stylized comment header to help visually separate each section:

```
/* Typography
------------------------------------------------------------------*/
```

Not everything naturally falls into a well-defined block, so some judgment is required. Keep in mind that the more you can break up and objectify your code, the easier it is to understand and the quicker you can find the rules you are looking for.

If your CSS files become very long, finding the style you want can be difficult. One way to speed things up is to add a *flag* to each of your comment headers. A flag is simply an extra character preceding your header text that does not naturally appear in your CSS files. A search for your flag followed by the first couple of letters in your comment header will take you right to the part of the file you're looking for. So in this example, a search for "=typ" will take you straight to the typography section of your stylesheet:

```
/* =Typography
-----------------------------------------------------------------*/
```

Because many CSS files tend to have a similar structure, you can save time by creating your own pre-commented CSS templates to use on all your projects. You can save even more time by adding a few common rules that you use in all of your sites, to create a sort of prototype CSS file. That way, you will not have to reinvent the wheel each time you start a new project. A sample prototype CSS file can be found in the code download for this book at www.friendsofed.com.

Note to self

Sometimes you may need to use a hack or workaround to solve a particular problem. In these cases it is a good idea to document the problem, the workaround you used, and, if available, a URL explaining the fix:

```
/*
Use the star selector hack to give IE a different font size
http://www.info.com.ph/~etan/w3pantheon/style/starhtmlbug.html
*/

* html body {
  font-size: 75%;
}
```

To make your comments more meaningful, you can use keywords to distinguish important comments. I use TODO as a reminder that something needs to be changed, fixed, or revisited later on; BUG to document a problem with the code or a particular browser; and KLUDGE to explain a nasty workaround:

```
/* :TODO: Remember to remove this rule before the site goes live */
/* :KLUDGE: I managed to fix this problem in IE by setting a small
negative margin but it's not pretty */
/* :BUG: Rule breaks in IE 5.2 Mac  */
```

You could also use the keyword TRICKY to alert other developers about a particularly complicated piece of code. In programming terms, these keywords are called *gotchas* and can prove very helpful in the later stages of development.

Removing comments and optimizing your stylesheets

Comments can increase the size of your CSS files quite considerably. Therefore, you may want to strip comments from your live stylesheets. Many HTML/CSS and text editors have a search and replace option, making it pretty easy to remove comments from your code. Alternatively, you could use one of several online CSS optimizers such as the one found at www.cssoptimiser.com/. Not only does an optimizer remove comments but it also strips out whitespace, helping to shave off a few extra bytes from your code.

Some people have experimented with writing comments in PHP format and then serving their stylesheets up as PHP. The stylesheets will get sent to the PHP parser, which will strip out all the comments, before being sent to the browser. You can do this by setting the MIME type for CSS files in an .htaccess file:

```
addtype application/x-httpd-php .css
```

However, you need to make sure that your CSS files are being cached or this approach will slow down rather than increase the speed of your site. This can be done using PHP, but it does start to get complicated—therefore, it is probably best avoided unless you are confident that you know what you are doing.

The best option is probably to enable server-side compression. If you are using an Apache server, talk to your hosts about installing mod_gzip or mod_deflate. Many modern browsers can handle files compressed with GZIP, and decompress them on the fly. These Apache modules will detect whether your browser can handle such files, and if it can, send a compressed version. Server-side compression can reduce your (X)HTML and CSS files by around 80 percent, reducing your bandwidth and making your pages much faster to download. If you don't have access to these Apache modules, you still may be able to compress your files by following the tutorial found at http://tinyurl.com/8w9rp.

Style guides

Most websites will have more than one person working on them, and larger sites can involve several teams all working on different aspects of the site. It is possible that programmers, content managers, and other front-end developers may need to understand how elements of your code and design function. Therefore, it is a very good idea to create a style guide.

A style guide is a document, web page, or microsite that explains how the code and visual design of a site are pieced together. A good style guide should start with an overview of the site structure, file structure, and naming conventions used. It should contain detailed information about the coding standards that designers, developers, and content editors need to adhere to in order to maintain the quality of the site. This could include things like the versions of XHTML/CSS to use, the chosen accessibility level, browser support details, and general coding best practices. The style guide should detail layout and stylistic elements such as the dimensions of various elements, the size of gutters, the color palette used, and the associated hex values. The style guide should also give details and examples of any special CSS styles used. For instance, if you were using a class to denote feedback, you would show what elements the class could be applied to and how those elements would look.

Style guides are a great way of handing a project over to those responsible for maintaining or implementing the site. By setting down some simple guidelines, you can help ensure the site develops in a controlled way, and help lessen the fragmentation of your styles over time. To help you create your own style guide, an example style guide is available in this book's code download (see Figure 1-5).

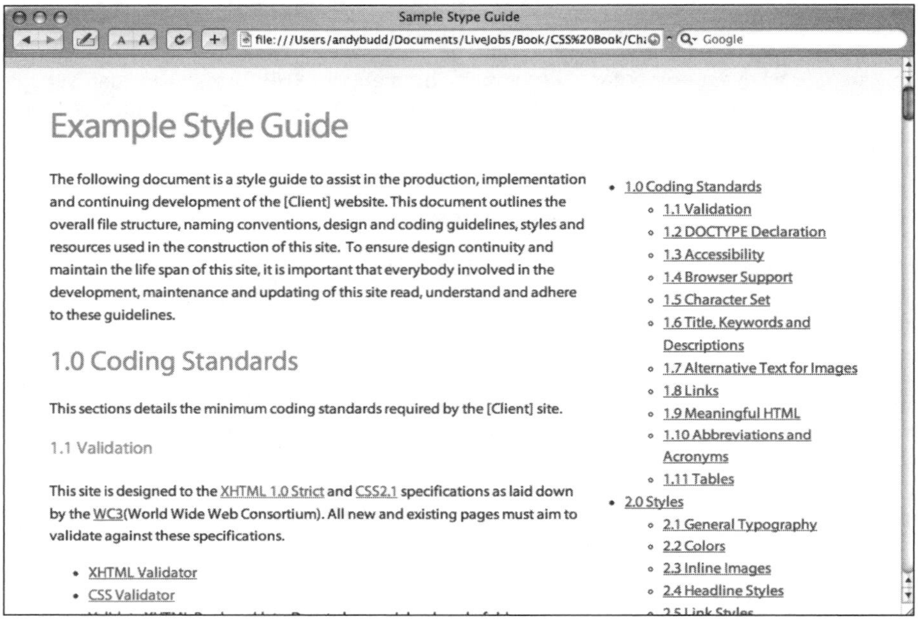

Figure 1-5. An example style guide

Organizing your stylesheets for easy maintenance

For a simple website, you can get away with using a single CSS file. With larger and more complicated sites, it can be a good idea to separate your styles for ease of maintenance. How you separate your styles is a matter of choice. I generally have one CSS file for the basic layout and another for typography and design embellishment. This way, once the layout is set, I rarely have to go back and change the layout stylesheet. This also protects my layout stylesheet from accidentally being altered and breaking.

You can abstract things further by creating a separate CSS file for color. Then, if you want to offer different color themes, it is easy to create a new color stylesheet. If you have lots of forms on your site, you may want to create a separate CSS file for all of your form styles. You can then link to that file only when it is needed, thus reducing the initial download overhead. If you have some pages on your site that are very distinct from the rest of your site, you may want to consider splitting these off into their own CSS files. For instance, if your homepage layout is very different from the rest of the site, you may want to create a separate CSS file just for the homepage.

It's worth bearing in mind that every CSS file means an extra call to the server. This can cause a performance hit, so some developers prefer to have one large CSS file rather than several smaller ones. The final choice really depends on the situation and is, to some degree, a matter of personal preference. I tend to favor flexibility and ease of maintenance whenever possible.

Summary

In this chapter you've seen how a well-structured and meaningful document can help provide a solid framework for applying your styles. You've learned about some of the more advanced CSS selectors and how CSS handles conflicting rules. You've also seen how well-structured and well-commented CSS files can make your life easier and increase your productivity.

In the next chapter, you will learn about the CSS box model, how and why margins collapse, and how floating and positioning really works.

Without Margin Collapsing

No boxes floated

SПООК.Са

Home
About
Topics
Resume
Contact

Site Updates
February 13, 2005 | Other

Just a heads up that I've updated the site a little so if anything is a
sure to let me know.

Updates include:

- Updated the styles on the comments
- Added an intro paragraph to the home page
- E-mail notification checkbox state is maintained in preview
  should make you happy, Mark)
- You can now use <code> in comments
- Moved MovableType database from Berkeley to MySQL (v
  went fairly smoothly except when it entir'd out the first time
  login to MySQL and delete the tables in order to restart the
  process)

COI
4 cou

Jonathan Snook
February 13, 2005
05:27 PM

Actually, just noticed one small glitch as a result of changing datab
all notification subscriptions have been lost! Sorry folks.

Three of the most important CSS concepts to grasp are floating, positioning, and the box model. These concepts control the way elements are arranged and displayed on a page, forming the basis of CSS layout. If you are used to controlling layout with tables, these concepts may seem strange at first. In fact, most people will have been developing sites using CSS for some time before they fully grasp the intricacies of the box model, the difference between absolute and relative positioning, and how floating and clearing actually work. Once you have a firm grasp of these concepts, developing sites using CSS becomes that much easier.

In this chapter you will learn about

- The intricacies and peculiarities of the box model
- How and why margins collapse
- The difference between absolute and relative positioning
- How floating and clearing work

Box model recap

The box model is one of the cornerstones of CSS and dictates how elements are displayed and, to a certain extent, how they interact with each other. Every element on the page is considered to be a rectangular box made up of the element's content, padding, border, and margin (see Figure 2-1).

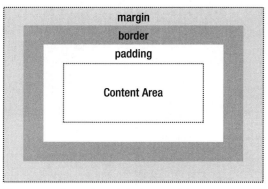

Figure 2-1. Illustration of the box model

Padding is applied around the content area. If you add a background to an element, it will be applied to the area formed by the content and padding. As such, padding is often used to create a gutter around content so that it does not appear flush to the side of the background. Adding a border applies a line to the outside of the padded area. These lines come in various styles such as solid, dashed, or dotted. Outside the border is a margin. Margins are transparent and cannot be seen. They are generally used to control the spacing between elements.

Padding, borders, and margins are optional and default to zero. However, many elements will be given margins and padding by the user-agent stylesheet. You can override these browser styles by setting the element's `margin` or `padding` back to zero. You can do this on a case-by-case basis or for every element by using the universal selector:

```
* {
  margin: 0;
  padding: 0;
}
```

In CSS, `width` and `height` refer to the width and height of the content area. Adding padding, borders, and margins will not affect the size of the content area but will increase the overall size of an element's box. If you wanted a box with a 10-pixel margin and a 5-pixel padding on each side to be 100 pixels wide, you would need to set the width of the content to be 70 pixels (see Figure 2-2):

```
#myBox {
  margin: 10px;
  padding: 5px;
  width: 70px;
}
```

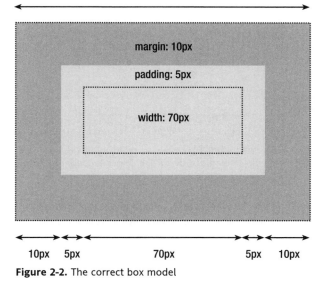

Figure 2-2. The correct box model

Padding, borders, and margins can be applied to all sides of an element or individual sides. Margins can also be given a negative value and can be used in a variety of techniques.

IE/Win and the box model

Unfortunately, IE 5.x and IE 6 in quirks mode use their own, nonstandard box model. Instead of measuring just the width of the content, these browsers take the width property as the sum of the width of the content, padding, and borders. This actually makes a lot of sense because in the real world boxes have a fixed size and the padding goes on the inside. The more padding you add, the less room there would be for the content. However, despite the logic, the fact that these versions of IE disregard the specification can cause significant problems. For instance, in the previous example the total width of the box would only be 90 pixels in IE 5.x. This is because IE 5.x will consider the 5 pixels of padding on each side as part of the 70-pixel width, rather than in addition to it (see Figure 2-3).

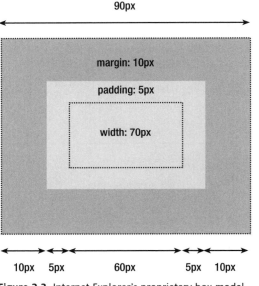

Figure 2-3. Internet Explorer's proprietary box model can cause elements to be smaller than intended.

Luckily, there are several ways you can tackle this issue, the details of which can be found in Chapter 9. However, by far the best solution is to avoid the problem altogether. You can do this by never adding padding to an element with a defined width. Instead, try adding padding or margins to the element's parent or children.

Margin collapsing

Margin collapsing is a relatively simple concept. In practice, however, it can cause a lot of confusion when you're laying out a web page. Put simply, when two or more vertical margins meet, they will collapse to form a single margin. The height of this margin will equal the height of the larger of the two collapsed margins.

When two elements are above one another, the bottom margin of the first element will collapse with the top margin of the second element (see Figure 2-4).

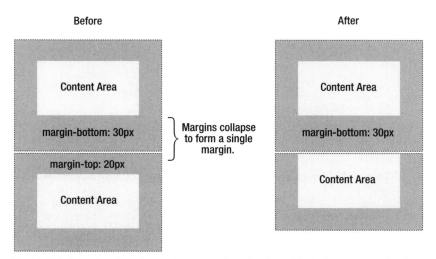

Figure 2-4. Example of an element's top margin collapsing with the bottom margin of the preceding element

When one element is contained within another element, assuming there is no padding or border separating margins, their top and/or bottom margins will also collapse together (see Figure 2-5).

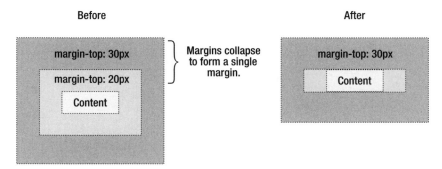

Figure 2-5. Example of an element's top margin collapsing with the top margin of its parent element

It may seem strange at first, but margins can even collapse on themselves. Say you have an empty element with a margin, but no border or padding. In this situation the top margin is touching the bottom margin and they collapse together (see Figure 2-6).

Figure 2-6. Example of an element's top margin collapsing with its bottom margin

If this margin is touching the margin of another element, it will itself collapse (see Figure 2-7).

Figure 2-7. Example of an empty element's collapsed margin collapsing with another empty element's margins

This is why a series of empty paragraph elements take up very little space, as all their margins collapse together to form a single small margin.

Margin collapsing may seem strange at first, but it actually makes a lot of sense. Take a typical page of text made up of several paragraphs (see Figure 2-8). The space above the first paragraph will equal the paragraph's top margin. Without margin collapsing, the space between all subsequent paragraphs will be the sum of their two adjoining top and bottom margins. This means that the space between paragraphs will be double the space at the top of the page. With margin collapsing, the top and bottom margins between each paragraph collapse, leaving the spacing the same everywhere.

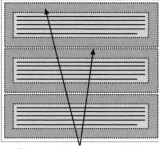

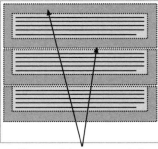

Figure 2-8. Margins collapse to maintain consistent spacing between elements.

Margin collapsing only happens with the vertical margins of block boxes in the normal flow of the document. Margins between inline boxes, floated, or absolutely positioned boxes never collapse.

Positioning recap

Now that you are familiar with the box model, let's take a look at the visual formatting and positioning models. Understanding the nuances of both of these models is vitally important as together they control how every element is arranged on a page.

The visual formatting model

People often refer to elements such as p, h1, or div as block-level elements. This means they are elements that are visually displayed as blocks of content, or "block boxes." Conversely, elements such as strong and span are described as inline elements because their content is displayed within lines as "inline boxes."

It is possible to change the type of box generated by using the display property. This means you can make an inline element such as an anchor behave like a block-level element by setting its display property to block. It is also possible to cause an element to generate no box at all by setting its display property to none. The box, and thus all of its content, is no longer displayed and takes up no space in the document.

There are three basic positioning schemes in CSS: normal flow, floats, and absolute positioning. Unless specified, all boxes start life being positioned in the normal flow. As the name suggests, the position of an element's box in the normal flow will be dictated by that element's position in the (X)HTML.

Block-level boxes will appear vertically one after the other; the vertical distance between boxes is calculated by the boxes' vertical margins.

Inline boxes are laid out in a line horizontally. Their horizontal spacing can be adjusted using horizontal padding, borders, and margins (see Figure 2-9). However, vertical padding, borders, and margins will have no effect on the height of an inline box. The horizontal box formed by a line is called a line box, and a line box will always be tall enough for all the line boxes it contains. There is another caveat, though—setting the line height can increase the height of this box.

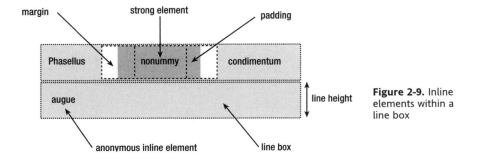

Figure 2-9. Inline elements within a line box

In the same way that (X)HTML elements can be nested, boxes can contain other boxes. Most boxes are formed from explicitly defined elements. However, there is one situation where a block-level element is created even if it has not been explicitly defined. This occurs when you add some text at the start of a block-level element like a div. Even though you have not defined the text as a paragraph, it is treated as such:

```
<div>
some text
<p>Some more text</p>
</div>
```

In this situation, the box is described as an anonymous block box since it is not associated with a specifically defined element.

A similar thing happens with the lines of text inside a block-level element. Say you have a paragraph that contains three lines of text. Each line of text forms an anonymous line box. You cannot style anonymous block or line boxes directly as there is nothing to hook on to. However, it is useful to understand that everything you see on your screen creates some form of box.

Relative positioning

Relative positioning is a fairly easy concept to grasp. If you relatively position an element, it will stay exactly where it is. You can then shift the element "relative" to its starting point by setting a vertical or horizontal position. If you set the top position to be 20 pixels, the box will appear 20 pixels below the top of its original position. Setting the left position to 20 pixels will create a 20-pixel space on the left of the element, moving the element to the right (see Figure 2-10).

```
#myBox {
  position: relative;
  left: 20px;
  top: 20px;
}
```

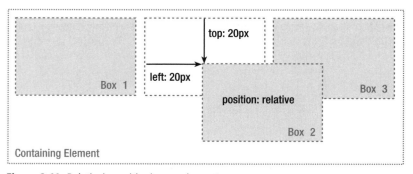

Figure 2-10. Relatively positioning an element

With relative positioning, the element continues to occupy the original space, whether or not it is offset. As such, offsetting the element can cause it to overlap other boxes.

Absolute positioning

Relative positioning is actually considered part of the normal flow positioning model, as the position of the element is relative to its position in the normal flow. By contrast, absolute positioning takes the element out of the flow of the document, thus taking up no space. Other elements in the normal flow of the document will act as though the absolutely positioned element was never there (see Figure 2-11).

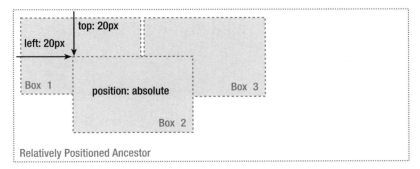

Figure 2-11. Absolutely positioning an element

An absolutely positioned element is positioned in relation to its nearest positioned ancestor. If the element has no positioned ancestors, it will be positioned in relation to the initial containing block. Depending on the user agent, this will either be the canvas or the HTML element.

As with relatively positioned boxes, an absolutely positioned box can be offset from the top, bottom, left, or right of its containing block. This gives you a great deal of flexibility. You can literally position an element anywhere on the page.

> *The main problem people have with positioning is remembering which type of positioning is which. Relative positioning is "relative" to the element's initial position in the flow of the document, whereas absolute positioning is "relative" to nearest positioned ancestor or, if one doesn't exist, the initial container block.*

Because absolutely positioned boxes are taken out of the flow of the document, they can overlap other elements on the page. You can control the stacking order of these boxes by setting a property called the z-index. The higher the z-index, the higher up the box appears in the stack.

Positioning an absolutely positioned element in relation to its nearest positioned ancestor allows you to do some very interesting things. For instance, say you wanted to align a paragraph of text at the bottom right of a large box. You could simply give the container box a relative position and then absolutely position the paragraph in relation to this box:

```
#branding {
  width: 700px;
  height: 100px;
  position: relative;
}

#branding .tel {
  position: absolute;
  right: 10px;
  bottom: 10px;
  text-align: right;
}

<div id="branding">
<p class="tel">Tel: 0845 838 6163</p>
</div>
```

Absolutely positioning a box in relation to a relatively positioned ancestor works well in most modern browsers. However, there is a bug in IE 5.5 and IE 6 on Windows. If you try to set the position of the absolutely positioned box relative to the right or bottom of the relatively positioned box, you need to make sure the relatively positioned box has some dimensions set. If not, IE will incorrectly position the box in relation to the canvas instead. You can read more about this bug and possible fixes in Chapter 9. The simple solution is to set the width and height of your relative box to avoid this problem.

Absolute positioning can be a useful tool when laying out a page, especially if it is done using relatively positioned ancestors. It is entirely possible to create a design solely using absolute positioning. For this to work, these elements need to have fixed dimensions so you can position them where you want without the risk of overlapping.

Because absolutely positioned elements are taken out of the flow of the document, they have no effect on boxes in the normal flow. If you were to enlarge an absolutely positioned box—by increasing the font size, for instance—the surrounding boxes wouldn't reflow. As such, any change in size can ruin your finely tuned layout by causing the absolutely positioned boxes to overlap.

Fixed positioning

Fixed positioning is a subcategory of absolute positioning. The difference is that a fixed element's containing block is the viewport. This allows you to create floating elements that always stay at the same position in the window. An example of this can be seen at snook.ca (see Figure 2-12). The weblog comment form has been given a fixed position to keep it anchored at the same place on screen when the page is scrolled. This really helps improve usability and you don't have to scroll all the way to the bottom of the page to leave a comment.

Figure 2-12. At snook.ca, the comment field on the right side of the screen uses a fixed position to stay at the same position in the viewport.

Unfortunately, IE 6 and below do not support fixed positioning. To get around this problem, Jonathan Snook uses JavaScript to replicate the effect in IE.

Floating

The last positioning model is the float model. A floated box can either be shifted to the left or the right until its outer edge touches the edge of its containing box, or another floated box. Because floated boxes aren't in the normal flow of the document, block boxes in the regular flow of the document behave as if the floated box wasn't there.

As shown in Figure 2-13, when you float Box 1 to the right, it's taken out of the flow of the document and moved to the right until its right edge touches the right edge of the containing block.

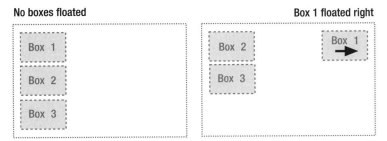

Figure 2-13. Example of an element being floated right

In Figure 2-14, when you float Box 1 to the left, it is taken out of the flow of the document and moved left until its left edge touches the left edge of the containing block. Because it is no longer in the flow, it takes up no space and actually sits on top of Box 2, obscuring it from view. If you float all three boxes to the left, Box 1 is shifted left until it touches its containing box, and the other two boxes are shifted left until they touch the preceding floated box.

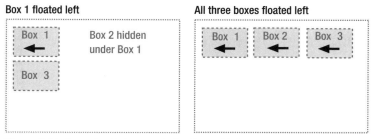

Figure 2-14. Example of elements being floated left

If the containing block is too narrow for all of the floated elements to fit horizontally, the remaining floats will drop down until there is sufficient space (see Figure 2-15). If the floated elements have different heights, it is possible for floats to get "stuck" on other floats when they drop down.

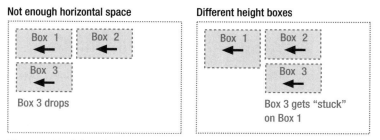

Figure 2-15. If there is not enough available horizontal space, floated elements will drop down until there is.

Line boxes and clearing

Line boxes next to a floated box are shortened to make room for the floated box, and flow around the float. In fact, floats were created to allow text to flow around images (see Figure 2-16).

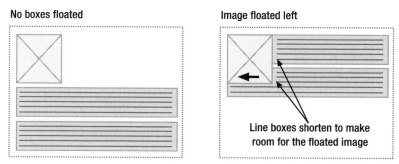

Figure 2-16. Line boxes shorten when next to a float.

To stop line boxes flowing around the outside of a floated box, you need to apply a clear to that box. The clear property can be left, right, both, or none, and indicates which side of the box should not be next to a floated box. To accomplish this, enough space is added above the cleared element's top margin to push the element's top border edge vertically down, past the float (see Figure 2-17).

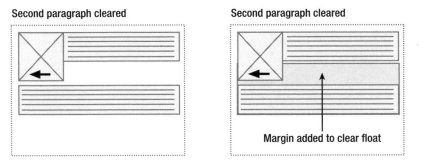

Figure 2-17. Clearing an element's top margin to create enough vertical space for the preceding float

As you've seen, floated elements are taken out of the flow of the document and have no effect on surrounding elements. However, clearing an element essentially clears a vertical space for all the preceding floated elements.

This can be a useful layout tool as it allows surrounding elements to make space for floated elements. This solves the problem we saw earlier with absolute positioning where changes in vertical height do not affect surrounding elements and can break your design.

Let's have a look at floating and clearing in a little more detail. Say you have a picture that you want to float to the left of a block of text. You want this picture and text to be contained in another element with a background color and border. You would probably try something like this:

```
.news {
  background-color: gray;
  border: solid 1px black;
}

.news img {
  float: left;
}

.news p {
  float: right;
}

<div class="news">
<img src="news-pic.jpg" />
<p>Some text</p>
</div>
```

However, because the floated elements are taken out of the flow of the document, the wrapper div takes up no space. How do you visually get the wrapper to enclose the floated element? You need to apply a clear somewhere inside that element (see Figure 2-18).

Unfortunately, no existing element is available that we can clear so you need to add an empty element and clear that.

```
.news {
  background-color: gray;
  border: solid 1px black;
}

.news img {
  float: left;
}

.news p {
  float: right;
}

.clear {
  clear: both;
}

<div class="news">
<img src="news-pic.jpg" />
<p>Some text</p>
<div class="clear"></div>
</div>
```

This gets the result we want, but at the expense of adding extraneous code to our markup. Often there will be an existing element you can apply the clear to, but sometimes you may have to bite the bullet and add meaningless markup for the purpose of layout.

Instead of clearing the floated text and image, you could choose to float the container div as well:

```
.news {
  background-color: gray;
  border: solid 1px black;
  float: left;
}

.news img {
  float: left;
}
```

Container does not enclose floats

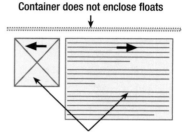

Floats take up no space

Container now encloses floats

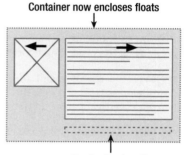

Empty clearing div

Figure 2-18. Because floats take up no space, they are not enclosed by container elements. The addition of an empty clearing element forces the container element to enclose the floats.

```
.news p {
  float: right;
}

<div class="news">
<img src="news-pic.jpg" />
<p>Some text</p>
</div>
```

This creates the desired result. Unfortunately, the next element is now going to be affected by the float. To solve this problem, some people choose to float nearly everything in a layout and then clear those floats using an appropriate meaningful element, often the site footer. This helps reduce or eliminate the need for extraneous markup. However, floating can be complicated and some older browsers may choke on heavily floated layouts. As such, many people prefer to add that extra bit of markup.

Applying an overflow property of hidden or auto will automatically clear any contained floats without the addition of extra markup. This method is not appropriate in all situations, since setting the box's overflow property will affect how it behaves.

Lastly, some people have taken to clearing floats using CSS-generated content or JavaScript. The basic concept for both methods is the same. Rather than add a clearing element directly to the markup, you add it to the page dynamically. For both methods you need to indicate where the clearing element goes, and this is usually done with the addition of a class name:

```
<div class="news clear">
<img src="news-pic.jpg" />
<p Some text</p>
</div>
```

Using the CSS method, you use the :after pseudo-class in combination with the content declaration to add new content at the end of the specified existing content. In this case I'm adding a full stop as it is a fairly small and unobtrusive character. You don't want the new content to take up any vertical space or be displayed on the page, so you need to set height to 0 and visibility to hidden. Because cleared elements have space added to their top margin, the generated content needs to have its display property set to block. Once this is done, you can then clear your generated content:

```
.clear:after {
  content: ".";
  height: 0;
  visibility: hidden;
  display: block;
  clear: both;
}
```

> *This method works in most modern browsers but fails in Internet Explorer 6 and below. Various workarounds are available, many of which are documented at* `www.positioniseverything.net/easyclearing.html`*. The most common of these involves using the Holly Hack (see chapter 8) to trick IE 5-6 into applying "Layout" (see chapter 9) and incorrectly clearing the floats.*
>
> ```
> .clear {
> display: inline-block;
> }
> /* Holly Hack Targets IE Win only \*/
> * html .clear {height: 1%;}
> .clear {display: block;}
> /* End Holly Hack */
> ```
>
> *However, due to its complexity this method may not be suitable for everybody.*

An explanation of the JavaScript method is beyond the scope of this book but is worth a brief mention. Unlike the previous method, the JavaScript method works on all major browsers when scripting is turned on. However, if you use this method, you need to make sure that the content is still readable when scripting is turned off.

Summary

In this chapter you have learned about some of the peculiarities of the box model. You have seen how vertical adjacent margins collapse to form a single margin, and how IE 5.*x* on Windows interprets the width property differently from other browsers. You now understand the difference between absolute and relative positioning and how useful absolute positioning in a relative container can be. Lastly, you have seen how floats behave in various circumstances and learned that clearing works by increasing the cleared element's top margin.

Now that you are armed with this knowledge, let's start putting it to good use. In the next section of this book, you will be introduced to a number of core CSS concepts and you'll see how they can be used to create a variety of useful and practical techniques. So open your favorite text editor, and let's get coding.

3 BACKGROUND IMAGES AND IMAGE REPLACEMENT

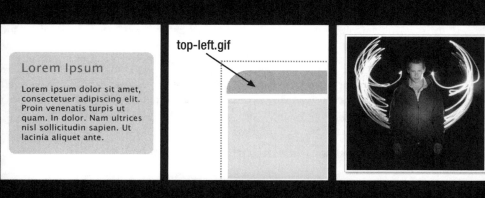

Now that you are all up to speed with the theory, let's start putting this into practice. Today's Web is a very visual medium. The humble image tag has allowed web designers to turn dull and uninspiring documents into graphically rich experiences. Graphic designers quickly seized on the image tag (originally intended as a way to add visual content to a website) as a way of visually embellishing a page. In fact, if it wasn't for the invention of the image tag, the profession of web designer may never have evolved.

Unfortunately, we've used the image tag to clutter our pages with purely presentational images. Luckily, CSS gives us the ability to display an image on a page without it being part of the markup. This is achieved by adding an image as a background to an existing element. Through a series of practical examples, this chapter will show you how background images can be used to create a variety of interesting and useful techniques.

In this chapter you will learn about

- Fixed- and flexible-width rounded-corner boxes
- The sliding doors technique
- Mountaintop corners
- CSS drop shadows
- PNG transparency support for Internet Explorer 5.*x* and above
- Image replacement

Background image basics

Applying a background image is easy. Say you want your website to have a nice tiled background. You can simply apply the image as a background to the body element:

```
body {
  background:url(pattern.gif);
}
```

The default browser behavior is to repeat background images horizontally and vertically so that the image tiles across the whole of the page. For more control you can choose whether your background image tiles vertically, horizontally, or not at all.

Gradients are very fashionable at the moment so you may want to apply a vertical gradient to your page instead. To do this, create a tall but narrow gradient graphic. You can then apply this graphic to the body of the page and let it tile horizontally:

```
body {
  background: #ccc url(gradient.gif) repeat-x;
}
```

Because the gradient has a fixed height, it will stop abruptly if the content of the page is longer than the height of the image. You could choose to create a really long image, possibly one that fades to a fixed color. However, it is always difficult to predict how long a page will become. Instead, simply add a background color as well. Background images always sit on the top of the background color, so when the image runs out the color will be displayed. If you choose a background color that is the same as the bottom of the gradient, the transition between image and background color will be seamless.

Tiling images can be useful in some situations. However, most of the time, you will want to add non-tiled images to your page. For instance, say you want your web page to start with a large branding image. You could simply add the image directly into the page, and in many situations this would be the correct thing to do. Yet if the image contains no information and is purely presentational, you may want to separate the image from the rest of your content. You can do this by creating a hook for the image in your HTML and applying the image using CSS. In the following example I have added an empty div to the markup and given it an ID of branding. You can then set the dimensions of the div to be the same as the branding image, apply it as a background, and tell it not to repeat.

```
#branding {
  width: 700px;
  height: 200px;
  background:url(/images/branding.gif) no-repeat;
}
```

Lastly, it is possible to set the position of your background image. Say you want to add a bullet to every headline on your site, as shown in Figure 3-1. You could do something like this:

```
h1 {
  padding-left: 30px;
  background: url(/images/bullet.gif) no-repeat left center;
}
```

Figure 3-1. Creating a bullet using a background image

The last two keywords indicate the positioning of the image. In this case, the image will be positioned to the left of the element and vertically centered. As well as using keywords, you can set a background image's position using units such as pixels or percentages.

If you set a background position using pixels, the top-left corner of the image is positioned from the top-left corner of the element by the specified number of pixels. So if you were to specify a vertical and horizontal position of 20 pixels, the top-left corner of the image will appear 20 pixels from the top-left corner of the element. However, background positioning using percentages works slightly differently. Rather than positioning the top-left corner of the background image, percentage positioning uses a corresponding point on the image. So if you set a vertical and horizontal position of 20 percent, you are actually positioning a point 20 percent from the top left of the image, 20 percent from the top left of the parent element (see Figure 3-2).

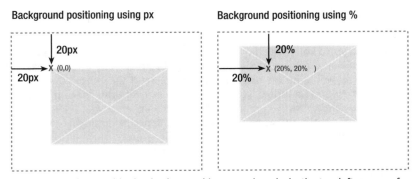

Figure 3-2. When positioning background images using pixels, the top-left corner of the image is used. When positioning using percentages, the corresponding position on the image is used.

If you want to position the previous bullet example using percentages instead of keywords, setting the vertical position to 50 percent would vertically center the bullet image:

```
h1 {
   padding-left: 30px;
   background: url(/images/bullet.gif) no-repeat 0 50%;
}
```

The specification says that you are not supposed to mix units such as pixels or percentages with keywords. This seems like a nonsensical rule and one that many modern browsers deliberately ignore. However, mixing units and keywords fails to work on certain browsers and will most likely invalidate your page. As such, it is best not to mix units with keywords at this time.

While background images are a simple concept to grasp, they form the basis of many advanced CSS techniques.

Rounded-corner boxes

One of the first criticisms leveled against CSS-based designs was that they were very square and boxy. To get around this, people started creating designs that incorporated more organic curved shapes. Rounded-corner boxes very quickly became one of the most sought-after CSS techniques around. There are various ways of creating rounded-corner boxes. Each approach has its strengths and weaknesses, and the one you choose depends largely on your circumstances.

Fixed-width rounded-corner boxes

Fixed-width rounded-corner boxes are the easiest to create. They require only two images: one for the top of the box and one for the bottom. For example, say you want to create a box style like the one in Figure 3-3.

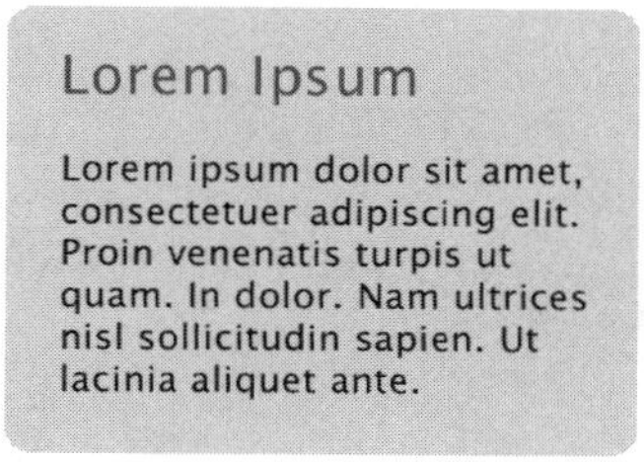

Figure 3-3. A simple rounded-corner box style

The markup for the box looks something like this:

```
<div class="box">
  <h2>Headline</h2>
  <p>Content</p>
</div>
```

In your favorite graphics package you need to create two images like those in Figure 3-4: one for the top of the box and one for the bottom. The code and images for this and all the other examples in this book can be downloaded from www.friendsofed.com.

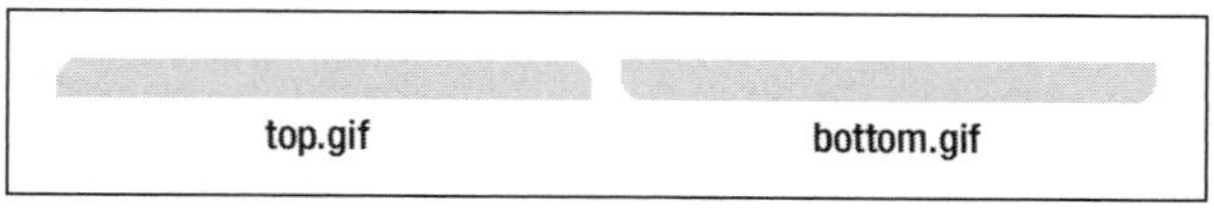

top.gif   bottom.gif

Figure 3-4. The top and bottom curve graphics

You then apply the top image to the heading element and the bottom image to the bottom of the box div. Because this box style just has a solid fill, you can create the body of the box by adding a background color to the box div.

```
.box {
  width: 418px;
  background: #effce7 url(images/bottom.gif) no-repeat  left bottom;
}

.box h2 {
  background: url(images/top.gif) no-repeat left top;
}
```

You will not want your content to butt up against the sides of the box, so you also need to add some padding to the elements inside the div:

```css
.box h2 {
  padding: 10px 20px 0 20px;
}

.box p {
  padding: 0 20px 10px 20px;
}
```

This is great for a simple box with a solid color and no borders. But what if you want to create a fancier style, such as the one in Figure 3-5?

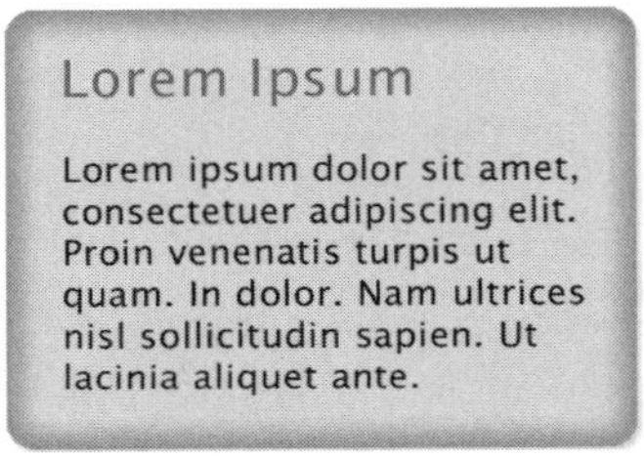

Lorem Ipsum

Lorem ipsum dolor sit amet,
consectetuer adipiscing elit.
Proin venenatis turpis ut
quam. In dolor. Nam ultrices
nisl sollicitudin sapien. Ut
lacinia aliquet ante.

Figure 3-5. Example of a stylized rounded-corner box

You can actually use the same approach, but this time, instead of setting a background color on the box, you can set a repeating background image. For this to work you will need to apply the bottom curve image to another element. In this case, I used the last paragraph element in the box:

```css
.box {
  width: 424px;
  background: url(images/bg-tile.gif) repeat-y;
}

.box h2 {
  background: url(images/bg-top.gif) no-repeat left top;
  padding-top: 20px;
}

.box .last {
  background: url(images/bg-bottom.gif) no-repeat left bottom;
  padding-bottom: 20px;
}

.box h2, .box p {
  padding-left: 20px;
  padding-right: 20px;
}
```

```
<div class="box">
  <h2>Headline</h2>
  <p class="last">Content</p>
</div>
```

Figure 3-6 shows the resulting styled box. Because no height has been given to the box, it will expand vertically as the text size is increased.

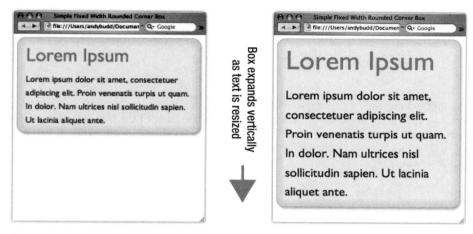

Figure 3-6. Styled fixed-width box. The height of the box expands as the text size is increased.

Flexible rounded-corner box

The previous examples will all expand vertically if you increase your font size. However, they do not expand horizontally as the width of the box has to be the same as the width of the top and bottom images. If you want to create a flexible box, you will need to take a slightly different approach. Instead of the top and bottom curves consisting of a single image, they need to be made up of two overlapping images (see Figure 3-7).

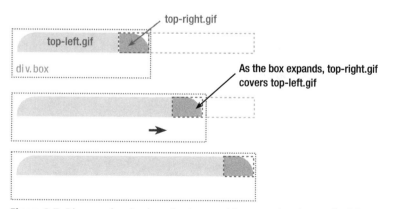

Figure 3-7. Diagram showing how the top graphics expand to form a flexible rounded-corner box

As the box increases in size, more of the larger image will be revealed, thus creating the illusion that the box is expanding. This concept is sometimes referred as the *sliding doors technique* because one image slides over the other, hiding it from view. More images are required for this method to work, so you will have to add a couple of extra, nonsemantic elements to your markup.

```
<div class="box">
  <div class="box-outer">
    <div class="box-inner">
    <h2>Headline</h2>
    <p>Content</p>
    </div>
  </div>
</div>
```

This method requires four images: the top two images make up the top curve, and the bottom two images make up the bottom curve and the body of the box (see Figure 3-8). As such, the bottom images need to be as tall as the maximum height of the box. We will name these images top-left.gif, top-right.gif, bottom-left.gif, and bottom-right.gif.

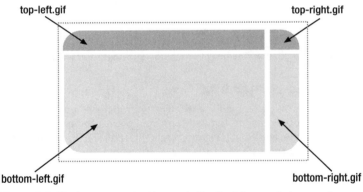

Figure 3-8. The images required to create the flexible rounded-corner box

First you apply the bottom-left.gif to the main box div and bottom-right.gif to the outer div. Next you apply top-left.gif to the inner div and finally top-right.gif to the heading. Lastly, it is a good idea to add some padding to space out the contents of the box a little.

```
.box {
  width: 20em;
  background: #effce7 url(images/bottom-left.gif) ➥
  no-repeat left bottom;
}
```

```
.box-outer {
  background: url(images/bottom-right.gif) no-repeat right bottom;
  padding-bottom: 5%;
}

.box-inner {
  background: url(images/top-left.gif) no-repeat left top;
}

.box h2 {
  background: url(images/top-right.gif) no-repeat right top;
  padding-top: 5%;
}

.box h2, .box p {
  padding-left: 5%;
  padding-right: 5%;
}
```

In this example I have set the width of the box in ems, so increasing the text size in your browser will cause the box to stretch (see Figure 3-9). You could, of course, set the width in percentages, and have the box expand or contract depending on the size of the browser window. This is one of the main principles behind elastic and flexible layouts, something I will be covering later in the book.

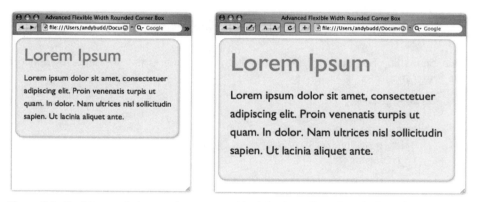

Figure 3-9. Flexible rounded-corner boxes expand both horizontally and vertically as the text is resized.

The addition of a couple of extra nonsemantic elements is not ideal. If you only have a couple of boxes it is probably something you can live with. But if you are concerned you could always add the extra elements using JavaScript (and the DOM) instead. For more details on this topic, see the excellent article by Roger Johansson of 456 Berea Street at http://tinyurl.com/82y8l.

Mountaintop corners

Mountaintop corners are a simple yet very flexible concept, first coined by Dan Cederholm of www.simplebits.com, author of the best-selling friends of ED book *Web Standards Solutions* (friends of ED, 2004). Suppose you want to create a variety of different-colored rounded-corner boxes. Using the previous methods you'd have to create different corner graphics for each color theme. This may be okay if you only had a couple of themes, but say you wanted to let your users create their own themes? You'd probably have to create the corner graphics dynamically on the server, which could get very complicated.

Fortunately, there is another way. Instead of creating colored corner graphics, you can create curved, bitmap corner masks (see Figure 3-10). The masked area maps to the background color you are using while the actual corner area is transparent. When placed over a colored box, they give the impression that the box is curved (see Figure 3-11).

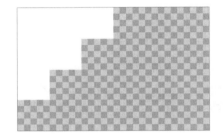

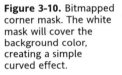

Figure 3-10. Bitmapped corner mask. The white mask will cover the background color, creating a simple curved effect.

As these corner masks need to be bitmapped, subtle curves work best. If you try to use a large curve, it will appear jagged and unsightly.

The basic markup is similar to the previous method; it requires four elements to apply the four corner masks to:

```
<div class="box">
  <div class="box-outer">
    <div class="box-inner">
    <h2>Headline</h2>
    <p>Content</p>
    </div>
  </div>
</div>
```

The CSS is also very similar:

```
.box {
  width: 20em;
  background: #effce7 url(images/bottom-left.gif) ➥
  no-repeat left bottom;
}
```

```css
.box-outer {
  background: url(images/bottom-right.gif) no-repeat right bottom;
  padding-bottom: 5%;
}

.box-inner {
  background: url(images/top-left.gif) no-repeat left top;
}

.box h2 {
  background: url(images/top-right.gif) no-repeat right top;
  padding-top: 5%;
}

.box h2, .box p {
  padding-left: 5%;
  padding-right: 5%;
}
```

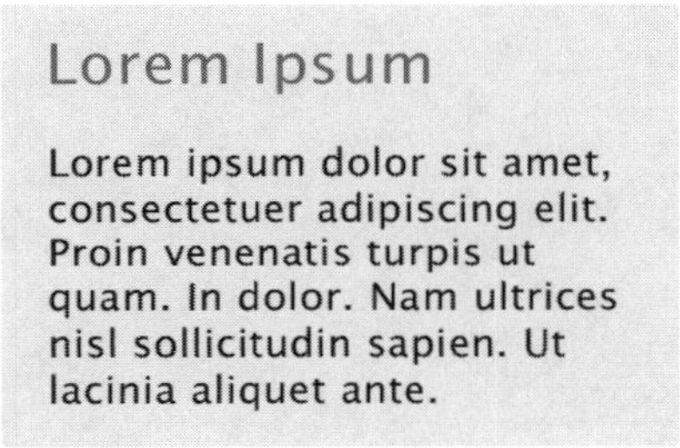

Lorem Ipsum

Lorem ipsum dolor sit amet, consectetuer adipiscing elit. Proin venenatis turpis ut quam. In dolor. Nam ultrices nisl sollicitudin sapien. Ut lacinia aliquet ante.

Figure 3-11. Mountaintop corner box

The main difference, apart from using different images, is the addition of a background color on the main box div. If you want to change the color of the box, you can simply change the color value in the CSS without having to re-create any new graphics. This method is only suitable for creating very simple boxes; however, it provides a great deal of flexibility and can be used over and over again on different projects.

Drop shadows

Drop shadows are a popular and attractive design feature, adding depth and interest to an otherwise flat design. Most people use a graphics package like Photoshop to add drop shadows directly to an image. However, using the power of CSS it is possible to apply simple drop shadow effects without altering the underlying image.

There are various reasons you may want to do this. For instance, you may allow nontechnical people to administer your site who have no experience using Photoshop, or you may simply be uploading images from a location where you do not have access to Photoshop, such as an Internet cafe. By having a predefined drop shadow style, you can simply upload a regular image and have it displayed on your site with a drop shadow.

One of the nicest benefits of using CSS is that it is nondestructive. If you decide that you want to remove the drop shadow effect later on, you can simply alter a couple of lines in your CSS files rather than having to reprocess all of your images.

Easy CSS drop shadows

This very simple drop shadow method was first described by Dunstan Orchard of www.1976design.com. It works by applying a large drop shadow graphic to the background of a wrapper div. The drop shadow is then revealed by offsetting the image using negative margins.

The first thing you need to do is create the drop shadow graphic. I created my drop shadow graphic using Adobe Photoshop. Create a new Photoshop file, the dimensions of which are as large as the maximum size of your image. I created a file that's 800 pixels by 800 pixels just to be on the safe side. Unlock the background layer and fill it with the color you want your shadow to sit on. In my case I simply kept the background layer white. Create a new layer and fill it with white. Now move this layer up and left by 4 or 5 pixels and then apply a 4- or 5-pixel-wide drop shadow to this layer. Save this image for web and call it shadow.gif (see Figure 3-12).

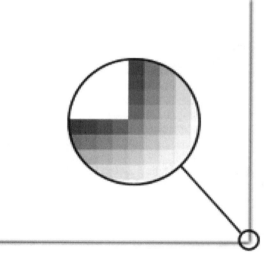

Figure 3-12. The 800×800 shadow.gif zoomed in so you can see the 5-pixel drop shadow

The markup for this technique is very simple:

```
<div class="img-wrapper"><img src="dunstan.jpg" width="300"➥
height="300" alt="Dunstan Orchard" /></div>
```

> *It is important to keep the code on one line and not separate the* div *and the image using whitespace. IE 5.5 has a whitespace bug that will cause a gap between the image and the drop shadow if your code is on separate lines.*

To create the effect, you first need to apply your shadow graphic to the background of the wrapper div. Because divs are block-level elements, they stretch horizontally, taking up all the available space. In this situation we want the div to wrap around the image. You can do this by explicitly setting a width for the wrapper div, but doing so reduces the useful-ness of this technique. Instead, you can float the div, causing it to "shrink-wrap" on mod-ern browsers, with one exception: IE 5.x on the Mac. You may want to hide these styles from IE 5.x on the Mac. For more information on hiding rules from various browsers, see Chapter 8, which discusses hacks and filters.

```
.img-wrapper {
  background: url(images/shadow.gif) no-repeat bottom right;
  clear: right;
  float: left;
}
```

To reveal the shadow image and create the drop shadow effect (see Figure 3-13), you need to offset the image using negative margins:

```
.img-wrapper img {
  margin: -5px 5px 5px -5px;
}
```

Figure 3-13. Image with drop shadow applied

You can create a good, fake photo border effect by giving the image a border and some padding (see Figure 3-14):

```
.img-wrapper img {
  background-color: #fff;
  border: 1px solid #a9a9a9;
  padding: 4px;
  margin: -5px 5px 5px -5px;
}
```

Figure 3-14. The final result

This works for most modern, standards-compliant browsers. However, we need to add in a couple of simple rules to get it working correctly in IE 6:

```
.img-wrapper {
  background: url(images/shadow.gif) no-repeat bottom right;
  clear: right;
  float: left;
  position: relative;
}

.img-wrapper img {
  background-color: #fff;
  border: 1px solid #a9a9a9;
  padding: 4px;
  display: block;
  margin: -5px 5px 5px -5px;
  position: relative;
}
```

The drop shadow effect now works in IE 6. The padding on the image does not show up in IE 5.x, but this is a relatively minor, presentational issue and one you can safely ignore.

Drop shadows a la Clagnut

Richard Rutter of www.Clagnut.com came up with a similar method for creating drop shadows. Instead of using negative margins, his technique uses relative positioning to offset the image:

```
.img-wrapper {
  background: url(images/shadow.gif) no-repeat bottom right;
  float:left;
  line-height:0;
}

.img-wrapper img {
  background:#fff;
  padding:4px;
  border:1px solid #a9a9a9;
  position:relative;
  left:-5px;
  top:-5px;
}
```

The padding on the image still does not display in IE 5.x, but in general browser support for this method is good.

Fuzzy shadows

The preceding methods provide a simple way to create a drop shadow effect. However, the one major criticism is the drop shadow's hard edge. If we were creating the effect in a graphics package like Photoshop the edges would fade into the background, creating a much more natural look. You can see a comparison of these two effects in Figure 3-15.

Figure 3-15. Some people don't like the hard edge the preceding techniques create, preferring a more photorealistic technique.

Luckily you can re-create this effect with the clever use of PNGs, masking, and the addition of a nonsemantic div. This method works by creating a PNG with alpha transparency to mask the edges of the drop shadow graphic.

First you need to make the masking PNG. Create a new Photoshop file that's 800 pixels by 800 pixels. Delete the contents of the background layer and then make a 5-pixel-wide selection at the right edge of the screen. Fill this with a gradient from white to transparent. Make a 5-pixel-high selection at the top of the page and again, fill this with your gradient. You should end up with a white, fuzzy border along the top and left of your document, as shown in Figure 3-16. Now save this as a 24-bit PNG and name the file mask.png.

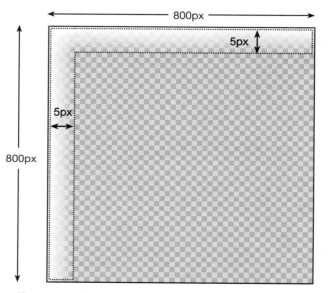

Figure 3-16. The transparent edges of this PNG will mask the corners of the shadow graphic, creating nice soft corners.

Unfortunately, older versions of IE do not support PNG alpha transparency. To deal with these browsers, you need to create an alternative graphic. In this case I have created a simple GIF mask that has a solid white 5-pixel left and top fill.

The markup for this technique looks like this:

```
<div class="img-wrapper">
 <div>
  <img src="dunstan.jpg" width="300" height="300" alt="Dunstan" />
 </div>
</div>
```

To create this effect, you first need to apply the shadow graphic to the `img-wrapper` div, aligning it to the bottom right:

```
.img-wrapper {
  background: url(images/shadow.gif) no-repeat right bottom;
  float: left;
}
```

Next you apply the masking image to the top right of the inner div. This lays the mask image over the top of the shadow image, masking the hard left and top edges, and creating a nice soft edge. At the moment both of these background images are covered by the main image. To create the offset you simply apply some padding to the bottom and right of the inner div:

```
.img-wrapper div {
  background: url(images/mask.png) no-repeat left top !important;
  background: url(images/mask.gif) no-repeat left top;
  padding: 0 5px 5px 0;
}
```

You will notice that I have applied both the PNG and the GIF to this rule. This is to accommodate both newer browsers that support PNG alpha transparency, as well as versions of IE that do not. Using a hack called the `!important` hack, the PNG will be displayed by more modern browsers, while IE users will be presented with the GIF. For more information on this hack, refer to Chapter 8.

IE 5.2 on the Mac doesn't "shrink-wrap" floated elements if they contain a block-level element. To get around this problem, we can simply float the second div as well as the first:

```
.img-wrapper div {
  background: url(images/mask.png) no-repeat left top !important;
  background: url(images/mask.gif) no-repeat left top;
  padding: 0 5px 5px 0;
  float: left; /* :KLUDGE: Fixes problem in IE5.2/Mac */
}
```

Lastly, we add the border effect to the image element:

```
.img-wrapper img {
  background-color: #fff;
  border: 1px solid #a9a9a9;
  padding: 4px;
}
```

Bringing all these steps together, the complete CSS looks like this:

```css
.img-wrapper {
  background: url(images/shadow.gif) no-repeat right bottom;
  float: left;
}

.img-wrapper div {
  background: url(images/mask.png) no-repeat left top !important;
  background: url(images/mask.gif) no-repeat left top;
  padding: 0 5px 5px 0;
  float: left; /* :KLUDGE: Fixes problem in IE5.2/Mac */
}

.img-wrapper img {
  background-color: #fff;
  border: 1px solid #a9a9a9;
  padding: 4px;
}
```

And the final effect should look like Figure 3-17.

Figure 3-17.
The final effect

If you wanted, you could leave this effect here, serving up a PNG to good browsers and a GIF to everything else. Unfortunately, as we all know, Internet Explorer has a pretty big market share, so very few people would actually get to see your fuzzy drop shadow.

Luckily, IE 5.5 and above has some proprietary CSS that forces PNG transparency:

```
filter:progid:DXImageTransform.Microsoft.AlphaImageLoader➡
(src='images/mask.png', sizingMethod='crop');
```

You could add this code to the existing CSS file and hide it from good browsers using an IE-specific hack. However, it would invalidate your CSS file. Also, you should try to avoid using hacks unless absolutely necessary. Instead, it makes more sense to put your rule in a separate CSS file and then hide it from everything other than IE. To do this, create a new CSS file called ie55.css and add the following code:

```
.img-wrapper div {
  filter:progid:DXImageTransform.Microsoft.AlphaImageLoader➥
  (src='img/shadow2.png', sizingMethod='crop');
  background: none;
}
```

The first rule uses IE's proprietary AlphaImageLoader filter to display the PNG with alpha transparency in IE 5.5 and above. The original background image will still be displayed, so the second rule simply hides the original background image.

Internet Explorer has another piece of proprietary code called a *conditional comment* that will let you serve up a particular stylesheet to specific versions of IE. In this case, you only want IE 5.5 and higher to see the new stylesheet, so you can place the following code in the head of the page:

```
<!--[if gte ie 5.5000]>
<link rel="stylesheet" type="text/css" href="ie55.css"/>
<![endif]-->
```

> *Don't worry too much about conditional comments at this stage; you will learn all about them in detail in Chapter 8.*

And that is it. All modern browsers as well as IE 5.5 and above will display a nice, faded-corner drop shadow. Everything else will be presented with a hard-corner drop shadow.

The concept of creating a basic page that works in all browsers, and then adding advanced styling or functionality for more modern browsers, is known as *progressive enhancement*. Conversely, ensuring that a page's style or functionality doesn't cause adverse effects in older browsers is known as *graceful degradation*. These are two very important concepts in standards-based design.

Onion skinned drop shadows

The last drop shadow method I am going to demonstrate uses a very similar technique to the rounded-corner box methods covered earlier. However, instead of using a mask to cover the ends of the shadow, you create two end shadow GIFs and lay them over the top of the hard ends of the main shadow graphic. To achieve this, you will need to add two extra nonsemantic divs to your markup to act as hooks for these images.

The basic HTML will look like this:

```
<div class="img-wrapper">
 <div class="img-outer">
  <div class="img-inner">
   <img src="images/dunstan.jpg" width="300" height="300" ➥
       alt="Dunstan" />
  </div>
 </div>
</div>
```

As before, you apply the main shadow image as a background of the main div:

```
.img-wrapper {
  background:url(images/shadow.gif) no-repeat right bottom;
  float: left;
}
```

And as before, you float the div so that it shrink-wraps.

Now you can apply the bottom-left corner to the bottom left of the outer div and the top-right corner to the top right of the inner div. The addition of some bottom and left padding to the inner div creates the drop effect. To make sure that the main image wrapper shrink-wraps in IE 5.2 on the Mac, you also need to float both these divs:

```
.img-outer {
  background:url(images/bottom-left2.gif) no-repeat left bottom;
  float: left; /* :KLUDGE: Fixes problem in IE5.2/Mac */
}

.img-inner {
  background:url(images/top-right2.gif) no-repeat top right;
  padding: 0 5px 5px 0;
  float: left; /* :KLUDGE: Fixes problem in IE5.2/Mac */
}
```

And lastly, as before, you can add a border and some padding to the image to create a nice photo-style frame:

```
.img-wrapper img {
  background-color: #fff;
  border: 1px solid #a9a9a9;
  padding: 4px;
  display: block;
}
```

The final CSS looks like this:

```
.img-wrapper {
  background:url(images/shadow.gif) no-repeat right bottom;
  float: left;
}
```

```
.img-outer {
    background:url(images/bottom-left2.gif) no-repeat left bottom;
    float: left; /* :KLUDGE: Fixes problem in IE5.2/Mac */
}

.img-inner {
    background:url(images/top-right2.gif) no-repeat top right;
    padding: 0 5px 5px 0;
    float: left; /* :KLUDGE: Fixes problem in IE5.2/Mac */
}

.img-wrapper img {
    background-color: #fff;
    border: 1px solid #a9a9a9;
    padding: 4px;
    display: block;
}
```

This method is very simple to understand and creates drop shadows that work on a wide range of browsers. The downside is the addition of two extra, nonsemantic divs. These are needed because CSS does not currently allow you to apply multiple background images to an element. CSS 3 will provide us with this ability in the future, so the use of multiple elements is just a transitional approach, and it should be quite easy to strip this extra markup out of your documents in the future. If you are concerned with the purity of your markup, you could always add these extra elements using JavaScript or generated content.

Image replacement

HTML text is great. Search engines can read it, you can copy and paste it, and it enlarges if you increase the text size in your browser. It is therefore a good idea to use HTML text instead of text as images wherever possible. Unfortunately, web designers have only a limited selection of fonts to play with. Also, while you can control your typography to a certain extent using CSS, some things just are not possible with live text. Because of this, there are occasions, usually for branding reasons, when you will want to use images of text instead.

Rather than embed these images directly in the page, CSS authors came up with the idea of *image replacement*. Essentially you add your text to the document as normal, and then, using CSS, you hide the text and display a background image in its place. That way, search engines still have the HTML text to find, and the text will be available if you disable CSS.

This seemed like a great idea for a while, until various flaws emerged. Some of the more popular methods are inaccessible to screen readers, and most do not work with images turned off but CSS turned on. As a result, many CSS authors have stopped using image replacement methods and have reverted to using plain text. While I advocate avoiding image replacement where possible, I still believe there can be situations where it is appropriate, such as when you need to use a particular font because of corporate branding guidelines. To do this, you should have a good grasp of the various techniques available and understand their limitations.

Fahrner Image Replacement (FIR)

Created by Todd Fahrner, FIR is the original, and probably the most popular, image replacement technique. I am going to explain this method because of its historical significance and because it is one of the easiest methods to understand. However, this method has some serious accessibility implications, which I will come to in a moment, and should thus be avoided.

The basic concept is very simple. You wrap the text you want to replace in a span tag:

```
<h2>
  <span>Hello World</span>
</h2>
```

You then apply your replacement image as a background image to the heading element:

```
h2 {
  background:url(hello_world.gif) no-repeat;
  width: 150px;
  height: 35px;
}
```

and hide the contents of the span by settings its display value to none:

```
span {
  display: none;
}
```

This method works like a charm, but it is this last rule that causes problems. Many of the most popular screenreaders ignore elements that have their display value set to none or hidden. Therefore, they will completely ignore this text, causing a huge accessibility problem. So a technique intended to improve the accessibility of a site actually has the opposite effect. For this reason it is best not to use this technique.

Phark

Mike Rundle of www.phark.net invented a screenreader-friendly image replacement technique that has the added benefit of dropping the extra, nonsemantic div:

```
<h2>
  Hello World
</h2>
```

Instead of using the display property to hide the text, the Phark method applies a very large, negative text indentation to the headline:

```
h2 {
  text-indent: -5000px;
  background:url(hello_world.gif) no-repeat;
  width: 150px;
  height:35px;
}
```

This method works well and solves the screenreader issue. However, as with the FIR method, this method does not work when images are turned off but CSS is turned on. This is an edge case and probably only applicable to people on very slow connections or those using their cell phones as a modem. There is an argument that site visitors do have the ability to turn images on and they just choose not to. However, it is worth bearing in mind that certain people may not see the replaced text so it is best to avoid using this method for crucial information or navigation.

Gilder/Levin method

This method, created jointly by Tom Gilder and Levin Alexander, is probably the most robust method available. It works well with screenreaders and allows the text to show up when images are off but CSS is on. It does this by layering an image over the text rather than hiding the text. That way, when images are turned off, you simply see the underlying text.

To use this technique, you need to add an additional, empty span inside the element you wish to replace:

```
<h2>
  <span></span>Hello World
</h2>
```

You then set the dimensions of the element to equal the dimensions of your image, and set the position of the element to relative:

```
h2 {
  width: 150px;
  height: 35px;
  position: relative;
}
```

This sets up a new positioning context for the enclosed span element, allowing you to position it absolutely over the text. When you set the dimensions to be 100 percent of the parent element, and apply your replacement image as a background on the span, the replaced text will be completely covered by the image:

```
h2 span {
  background: url(hello_world.gif) no-repeat;
  position: absolute;
  width: 100%;
  height: 100%;
}
```

When using this technique, you have to use an image with a solid background; otherwise the text will show through. The downside of this technique is the addition of a nonsemantic span.

Inman Flash Replacement (IFR)
and Scalable Inman Flash Replacement (sIFR)

One of the main problems image replacement tries to solve is the lack of fonts available on most computers. Rather than swap the text out with images of text, Mike Davidson and Shaun Inman took an altogether more inventive approach.

Flash allows you to embed fonts into a SWF file, so instead of swapping the text out for an image, they decided to swap the text out and replace it with a Flash file. The swapping is done using JavaScript by looping through the document and grabbing any text within a particular element or with a particular class name. The JavaScript then swaps the text for a small Flash file. The really clever part comes next. Rather than creating a separate Flash file for each chunk of text, this technique places the swapped text back into a single, duplicated Flash file. Thus, all you need to do to trigger your image replacement is add a class, and the combination of Flash and JavaScript will do the rest. Another benefit is that the text in Flash files can be made selectable, meaning that it can be copied and pasted with ease.

Shaun Inman released his Flash image replacement method and dubbed it "Inman Flash Replacement," or IFR for short. IFR is a very lightweight method. Details about this method, including the source code, can be found at www.shauninman.com/plete/2004/04/ifr-revisited-and-revised.

Mike Davidson built extensively on this method, creating the Scalable Inman Flash Replacement (sIFR) method. This method extends IFR by allowing things such as multiline text replacement and text resizing.

To use sIFR on your site, you first need to download the latest version from www.mikeindustries.com/sifr. Installing sIFR on your site is fairly simple, although it's worth reading through the documentation first. The first thing you need to do is open the Flash file, embed the font you want to use, and export the movie. For sIFR to work properly, you next need to apply the enclosed print and screen styles, or create your own. Now add the sifr.js JavaScript file to every page you want sIFR to work on. This file is highly configurable and allows you to specify which elements to replace, the text color, padding, case, and a variety of other stylistic elements. Once you are done, upload all the files to your server and watch your tired old fonts be replaced with dynamic Flash content.

The main problem with these techniques involves load times. The pages have to load fully before JavaScript can replace the text. Consequently, there is usually a brief flicker before all the text has been replaced with the Flash equivalent (see Figure 3-18).

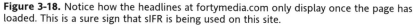

Figure 3-18. Notice how the headlines at fortymedia.com only display once the page has loaded. This is a sure sign that sIFR is being used on this site.

Although it is not a huge problem, it is noticeable and can give the impression that the page is loading slowly. Also, some pages can feel a little sluggish if there is a lot of Flash replacement going on. It's a good idea to keep any replacement to a minimum and limit this technique to main headlines only.

Summary

In this chapter you have learned how background images can be applied to elements to produce a variety of interesting techniques, such as flexible rounded-corner boxes and pure CSS drop shadows. You have seen how to force PNG support in Internet Explorer along with several methods of image replacement.

In the next chapter, you will learn how background images and links can be combined to create some interesting interactive effects.

4 STYLING LINKS

The humble anchor link is the foundation of the World Wide Web. It is the mechanism that allows web pages to interconnect and people to explore and navigate. The default styling for anchor links is fairly uninspiring, but with a little sprinkling of CSS you can do some amazing things.

In this chapter you will learn about

- Ordering your link selectors based on the cascade
- Creating stylized link underlines
- Styling external links using attribute selectors
- Making links behave like buttons
- Creating visited-link styles
- Creating pure CSS tooltips

Simple link styling

The easiest way to style a link is to use the anchor type selector. For instance, this rule will make all anchors red:

```
a {color: red;}
```

However, anchors can act as internal references as well as external links, so using a type selector is not always ideal. Take this situation, for example. The first anchor contains a fragment identifier, and when the user clicks that anchor, the page will jump to the second named anchor:

```
<p><a href="#mainContent">Skip to main content</a></p>
...
<h1><a name="mainContent">Welcome</a></h1>
```

While you probably only want the link to be styled red, the contents of the headline will be styled red also. To avoid this, CSS has two special selectors called link pseudo-class selectors. The :link pseudo-class selector is used to target links that have not been visited, and the :visited pseudo-class selector is used to target visited links. So in this example all unvisited links will be blue and all visited links will be green:

```
a:link {color: blue;}      /* Makes unvisited links blue */
a:visited {color: green;}  /* Makes visited links green */
```

The other two selectors you can use for styling links are the :hover and :active dynamic pseudo-class selectors. The :hover dynamic pseudo-class selector is used to target elements when they are hovered over, and the :active dynamic pseudo-class selector targets elements when they are activated. In the case of links, activation occurs when the link is clicked. So in this example, links will turn red when hovered over or clicked:

```
a:hover, a:active { color: red;}
```

One of the first things most people learn to use these selectors for is turning off the underline for links, and then turning them back on when they are hovered over or clicked. This can be done by setting the text-decoration property to none for unvisited and visited links, and to underline for hovered or active links:

```
a:link, a:visited {text-decoration: none;}
a:hover, a:active {text-decoration: underline;}
```

In the previous example the order of the selectors is very important. If the order is reversed, the hover and active styles won't work:

```
a:hover, a:active {text-decoration: underline;}
a:link, a:visited {text-decoration: none;}
```

The reason for this is the cascade. In Chapter 1 you learned that when two rules have the same specificity, the last rule to be defined wins out. In this situation, both rules have the same specificity so the :link and :visited styles will override the :hover and :active styles. To make sure this doesn't happen, it's a good idea to apply your link styles in the following order:

```
a:link, a:visited, a:hover, a:active
```

An easy way to remember this order is the phonetic LoVe:HAte, where *L* stands for link, *V* stands for visited, *H* stands for hover, and *A* stands for active.

Fun with underlines

From a usability and accessibility standpoint, it is important that your links are distinguishable by some means other than color. The reason for this is that many people with visual impairments find it difficult to distinguish between poorly contrasting colors, especially at small text sizes. For instance, people with color blindness cannot distinguish between certain color combinations with similar levels of brightness or saturation. Because of this, links are underlined by default.

Designers tend to dislike link underlines as they add too much weight and visual clutter to a page. If you decide to remove link underlines, you could choose to make links bold instead. That way your page will look less cluttered, but the links will still stand out:

```
a:link, a:visited {
  text-decoration: none;
  font-weight: bold;
}
```

You can then reapply the underlines when the links are hovered over or activated, reinforcing their interactive status:

```
a:hover, a:active {
  text-decoration: underline;
}
```

However, it is possible to create a low-impact underline using borders instead. In the following example, the default underline is removed and replaced with a less obtrusive dotted line. When the link is hovered over or clicked, this line turns solid to provide the user with visual feedback that something has happened:

```
a:link, a:visited {
  text-decoration: none;
  border-bottom: 1px dotted #000;
}

a:hover, a:active {
  border-bottom-style: solid;
}
```

Fancy link underlines

You can create some very interesting effects by using images to create your link underlines. For instance, I have created a very simple underline graphic comprised of diagonal lines (Figure 4-1).

Figure 4-1. Simple underline graphic

You can then apply this image to your links using the following code:

```
a:link, a:visited {
  color:#666;
  text-decoration: none;
  background: url(images/underline1.gif) repeat-x left bottom;
}
```

You can see the resulting styled link in Figure 4-2.

This is a link

Figure 4-2. Custom link underline

You do not have to stop with link and visited styles. In this example, I have created an animated GIF for the hover and active states, which I apply using the following CSS:

```
a:hover, a:active {
  background-image: url(images/underline1-hover.gif);
}
```

When you hover over or click the link, the diagonal lines appear to scroll from left to right, creating an interesting pulsing or poling effect. Not all browsers support background image animations, but those that do not will usually display the first frame of the animation, ensuring that the effect degrades nicely in older browsers.

Remember to use animation carefully as it can cause accessibility problems for some users. If in doubt, always remember to check the Web Content Accessibility Guidelines (WCAG 1.0) at www.w3.org/TR/WAI-WEBCONTENT/.

Highlighting different types of link

On many sites it is difficult to tell if a link points to another page on that site or to a different site altogether. We have all clicked a link expecting it to go to another page in the current site, only to be whisked away somewhere different and unexpected. To combat this problem, many sites will open external links in a new window. However, this is not a good idea as it is taking control away from the user and potentially littering their desktops with unwanted windows.

The best solution is to indicate external links somehow, and let the user decide whether they want to leave the site, open the link in a new window, or more probably these days, in a new tab. You can do this by adding a small icon next to any external links. Sites like wikipedia.com already do this and an icon convention for offsite links has started to appear: a box with an arrow (Figure 4-3).

Figure 4-3. External link icon

The easiest way to do this is to add a class to any external links, and then apply the icon as a background image. In this example I have created space for the icon by giving the link a small amount of right padding, and then applied the icon as a background image at the top right of the link (see Figure 4-4).

```
.external {
  background: url(images/externalLink.gif) no-repeat right top;
  padding-right: 10px;
}
```

This is an external link

Figure 4-4. External link styling

Although this method works, it is not a particularly smart or elegant way of doing things, as you have to manually add your class to each external link. What if there was a way to get CSS to determine whether something was an external link for you? Well, in fact there is: using attribute selectors.

As you learned in Chapter 1, attribute selectors allow you to target an element based on the existence or value of an attribute. CSS 3 extends the ability with substring matching attribute selectors. As the name suggests, these selectors allow you to target an element by matching part of the attribute's value to your chosen text. CSS 3 is not an official specification yet, so using these advanced selectors will probably invalidate your code. However, a number of standards-compliant browsers such as Firefox and Safari already support these CSS 3 selectors, so the chance of them being dropped from the final spec is pretty slim.

This technique works by first targeting any links that start with the text http: using the [att^=val] attribute selector:

```
a[href^="http:"] {
   background: url(images/externalLink.gif) no-repeat right top;
   padding-right: 10px;
}
```

This should highlight all external links. However, it will also pick up internal links using absolute rather than relative URLs. To avoid this, you need to reset any links to your own site by removing the external link icon. This is done by matching links that point to your domain name, removing the external link icon, and resetting the right padding (see Figure 4-5).

```
a[href^="http://www.yoursite.com"], a[href^="http://yoursite.com"]  {
   background-image: none;
   padding-right: 0;
}
```

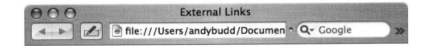

Figure 4-5. A page showing external links styled differently from internal ones

Most standards-compliant browsers support this technique, but older browsers such as IE 6 and below will simply ignore it.

If you like, you could extend this technique to highlight email links as well. In this example I am adding a small email icon to all mailto links:

```
a[href^="mailto:"] {
  background: url(images/email.png) no-repeat right top;
  padding-right: 10px;
}
```

You could even highlight nonstandard protocols such as the AIM instant messaging protocol, with a little AIM buddy icon (see Figure 4-6):

```
a[href^="aim:"] {
  background: url(images/im.png) no-repeat right top;
  padding-right: 10px;
}
```

```
<a href="aim:goim?screenname=andybudd">instant message</a>
```

Contact me by email ✉

Send me an instant message ♟ using AIM/iChat.

Figure 4-6. Email and instant message link styles

Highlighting downloadable documents and feeds

Another common frustration is clicking on a link thinking it is going to take you to a page, only for it to start downloading a PDF or Microsoft Word document. Luckily, CSS can help us distinguish these types of links as well. This is done using the [att$=val] attribute selector, which targets attributes that end in a particular value, such as .pdf or .doc:

```
a[href$=".pdf"] {
  background: url(images/pdfLink.gif) no-repeat right top;
  padding-right: 10px;
}
```

```
a[href$=".doc"] {
  background: url(images/wordLink.gif) no-repeat right top;
  padding-right: 10px;
}
```

So in a similar way to the previous examples, you can highlight links to word documents or PDFs with their own separate icon, warning people that they are downloads rather than links to another page.

Lastly, many people have RSS feeds on their website. The idea is for people to copy these links into their feed readers. However, inadvertently clicking one of these links may take you to a page of seemingly meaningless data. To avoid possible confusion, you could high-light RSS feeds using a similar method, with your own RSS icon:

```css
a[href$=".rss"], a[href$=".rdf"] {
    background: url(images/feedLink.gif) no-repeat right top;
    padding-right: 10px;
}
```

All these techniques can help to improve the user experience on your site. By warning users about offsite links or downloadable documents, you let them know exactly what to expect when they click a link, and avoid unnecessary backtracking and frustration.

> *Unfortunately, IE 6 and below doesn't support the attribute selector. Luckily, you can create a similar effect by adding a class to each element using JavaScript and the DOM. One of the best ways to do this is with Simon Willison's excellent* getElementBySelector *function; you can find more details at* http://tinyurl.com/dmao4.

Creating buttons and rollovers

Anchors are inline elements, which means they only activate when you click on the content of the link. However, there are instances when you want to create more of a button-like effect with a larger clickable area. You can do this by setting the display property of the anchor to block, and then changing the width, height, and other properties to create the style and hit area you want.

```css
a {
    display: block;
    width: 6em;   /* dimensions needed for IE5.x/Win */
    padding: 0.2em;
    line-height: 1.4;
    background-color: #94B8E9;
    border: 1px solid black;
    color: #000;
    text-decoration: none;
    text-align: center;
}
```

The resulting link should now look like Figure 4-7.

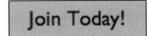

Figure 4-7. Link styled like a button

With the link now displaying as a block-level element, clicking anywhere in the block will activate the link.

If you look at the CSS, you'll see that the width has been explicitly set in ems. By their nature, block-level elements expand to fill the available width, so if the width of their parent elements were greater than the required width of the link, you would need to apply the desired width to the link. This would likely be the case if you wanted to use such a styled link in the main content area of your page. However, if your styled links were going in a sidebar, for example, you would probably just set the width of the sidebar, and not worry about the width of the links.

Unfortunately, IE 5.x on Windows has a bug whereby, if no width or height is defined, only the link text becomes active, even though the display property has been set to block. In the previous example I control the height of the button using line-height, so an explicit width is necessary to make the whole area clickable in IE 5.x for Windows.

You may wonder why I am using line-height to control the height of the button instead of height. Well, this is actually a handy little trick for centering the text in the button vertically. If you were to set a height, you would probably have to use padding to push the text down and fake vertical centering. However, text is always vertically centered in a line box, so by using line-height instead, the text will always sit in the middle of the box. There is one downside, though. If the text in your button wraps onto two lines, the button will be twice as tall as you want it to be. The only way to avoid this is to size your buttons and text in such a way that the text won't wrap, or at least won't wrap until your text size has been increased beyond a reasonable amount.

Simple rollovers

In the bad old days, people used large and overly complicated JavaScript functions to create rollover effects. Thankfully, using the :hover pseudo-class allows us to create rollover effects without the need of JavaScript. You can extend the previous example to include a very simple rollover effect simply by setting the background and text color of the link when hovered over (Figure 4-8):

```
a:hover {
  background-color: #369;
  color: #fff;
}
```

Figure 4-8. Hover style showing active area

Rollovers with images

Changing background colors works well for simple buttons, but for more complicated buttons it is best to use background images. For the next example I have created two button images, one for the up state and one for the hover state (see Figure 4-9). If you wanted, you could also add an active state, which would be triggered using the :active dynamic pseudo-class.

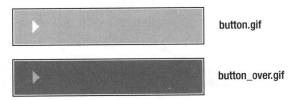

Figure 4-9. Images for the normal and hover button states

The code for this example is similar to the preceding example. The main difference is that background images are being used instead of background colors.

```
a:link, a:visited {
    display: block;
    width: 200px;
    height: 40px;
    line-height: 40px;
    color: #000;
    text-decoration: none;
    background: #94B8E9 url(images/button.gif) no-repeat left top;
    text-indent: 50px;
}

a:hover {
    background: #369 url(images/button_over.gif) no-repeat left top;
    color: #fff;
}
```

This example uses fixed-width and -height buttons, which is why I have set explicit pixel dimensions in the CSS. However, there is nothing to stop you from creating oversized button graphics, or using a combination of background colors and images to create a fluid or an elastic button.

Pixy-style rollovers

The main drawback with the multiple image method is a slight delay as browsers load the hover image for the first time. This can cause an undesirable flickering effect and make your buttons feel a little unresponsive. It is possible to preload the hover images by applying them as a background to the parent element. However, there is another way. Instead of swapping in multiple background images, use a single image and switch its background position instead. Using a single image has the added benefit of reducing the number of server requests as well as allowing you to keep all your button states in one place. This method is known as the Pixy method after the nickname of its creator, Petr Staníček.

Begin by creating your combined button image (see Figure 4-10). In this case I am only using an up state and an over state, but you could also have an active and a visited state if you desired.

Figure 4-10. Both button states as a single image

The code is almost identical to the previous example. However, this time you align the rollover image to the left for the normal link state, and then shift it to the right for the hover state.

```
a:link, a:visited {
  display: block;
  width: 200px;
  height: 40px;
  line-height: 40px;
  color: #000;
  text-decoration: none;
  background: #94B8E9 url(images/pixy-rollover.gif) no-repeat left top;
  text-indent: 50px;
}

a:hover {
  background-color: #369;
  background-position: right top;
  color: #fff;
}
```

Unfortunately, IE on Windows still makes a round-trip to the server to request a new image, even though all you are doing is changing the alignment of the image. This causes a slight flicker, which can be a little annoying. To avoid the flicker you need to apply the rollover state to the link's parent element, for example, its containing paragraph.

```
p {
  background: #94B8E9 url(images/pixy-rollover.gif)➥
  no-repeat right top;
}
```

The image will still disappear for an instant while it is being reloaded. However, during this time, the same image will be revealed underneath, hiding the flicker.

4

Visited-link styles

Designers and developers often forget about the visited-link style and end up styling visited links the same as unvisited ones. However, a separate visited-link style can help orientate users, showing them which pages or sites they have already visited and avoiding unnecessary backtracking. Visited-link styles can add clutter to the main content area of your site, so use them wisely. However, they come into their own when used in sidebars or subnavigation.

You can create a very simple visited-link style by adding a check box to every visited link:

```
a:visited {
  padding-right: 20px;
  background: url(check.gif) right middle;
}
```

Taking this a step further, say you had a list of links in your sidebar to external sites:

```
<ul>
  <li><a href="http://www.andybudd.com/">Andy Budd's Blogography</a></li>
  <li><a href="http://allthatmalarkey.co.uk/">Stuff and Nonsense</a></li>
  <li><a href="http://www.hicksdesign.co.uk/">Hicks Design</a></li>
  <li><a href="http://www.clagnut.com/">Clagnut</a></li>
  <li><a href="http://www.htmldog.com/">HTML Dog</a></li>
  <li><a href="http://adactio.com/journal/">Adactio</a></li>
  <li><a href="http://www.allinthehead.com/">All In The Head</a></li>
  <li><a href="http://www.markboulton.co.uk/">Mark Boulton</a></li>
  <li><a href="http://www.ian-lloyd.com/">Ian Lloyd</a></li>
</ul>
```

Using the Pixy rollover method you learned about earlier, you could create a single image for the unvisited and visited states (see Figure 4-11). If you wanted, you could add hover and active states as well.

Figure 4-11. Unvisited- and visited-link graphics in a single image

You would then apply your background image much in the same way as before. Do not worry about the list styling here, as I will be covering lists in depth in the next chapter. The most important thing to note is the background image styling on the anchor and the visited state.

```
ul {
  list-style:none;
}

li {
  margin: 5px 0;
}
```

```
li a {
  display: block;
  width: 300px;
  height: 30px;
  line-height: 30px;
  color: #000;
  text-decoration: none;
  background: #94B8E9 url(images/visited.gif) no-repeat left top;
  text-indent: 10px;
}

li a:visited {
  background-position: right top;
}
```

You can see the resulting links list in Figure 4-12. Each site you have visited will show up as a check next to the site name, providing valuable feedback that you've already been there. Simon Collison demonstrates how this concept can be put to practical use in his Chapter 10 case study.

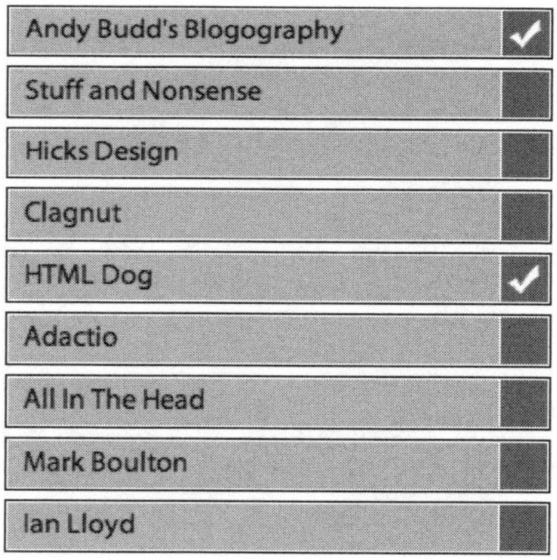

Figure 4-12. External link list showing visited sites with a check

Pure CSS tooltips

Tooltips are the little yellow text boxes that pop up in some browsers when you hover over elements with title tags. Several developers have created their own custom, stylized tooltips using a combination of JavaScript and CSS. However, it is possible to create pure CSS tooltips by using CSS positioning techniques. This technique requires a modern, standards-compliant browser like Firefox to work properly. As such, it is not a technique you would add to your day-to-day arsenal. However, it does demonstrate the power of advanced CSS and gives you a hint of what will be possible when CSS is better supported.

As with all of the examples in this book, you need to start with well-structured and meaningful (X)HTML:

```
<p>
<a href="http://www.andybudd.com/" class="tooltip">
Andy Budd<span> (This website rocks) </span></a>
is a web developer based in Brighton England.
</p>
```

I have given the link a class of tooltip to differentiate it from other links. Inside the link I have added the text I wish to display as the link text, followed by the tooltip text enclosed in a span. I have wrapped my tooltip text in brackets so that the sentence still makes sense with styles turned off.

The first thing you need to do is set the position property of the anchor to relative. This allows you to position the contents of the span absolutely, relative to the position of its parent anchor. You do not want the tooltip text to display initially, so you should set its display property to none:

```
a.tooltip {
    position: relative;
}

a.tooltip span {
    display: none;
}
```

When the anchor is hovered over, you want the contents of the span to appear. This is done by setting the display property of the span to block, but only when the link is hovered over. If you were to test the code now, hovering over the link would simply make the span text appear next to the link.

To position the contents of the span below and to the right of the anchor, you need to set the position property of the span to absolute and position it 1em from the top of the anchor and 2ems from the left.

> Remember, an absolutely positioned element is positioned in relation to its nearest positioned ancestor, or failing that, the root element. In this example, we have positioned the anchor, so the span is positioned in relation to that.

```
a.tooltip:hover span {
    display: block;
    position: absolute;
    top: 1em;
    left: 2em;
}
```

And that's the bulk of the technique. All that is left is to add some styling to make the span look more like a tooltip. You can do this by giving the span some padding, a border, and a background color:

```
a.tooltip:hover span {
  display:block;
  position:absolute;
  top:1em;
  left:2em;
  padding: 0.2em 0.6em;
  border:1px solid #996633;
  background-color:#FFFF66;
  color:#000;
}
```

Previewing the technique in Firefox, it should look something like Figure 4-13.

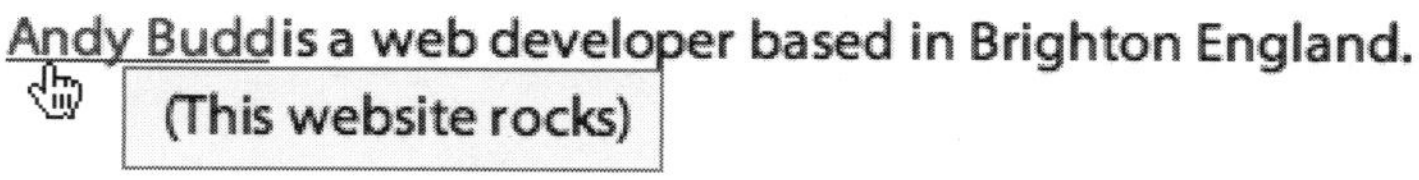

Andy Budd is a web developer based in Brighton England.

(This website rocks)

Figure 4-13. Pure CSS tooltip

Unfortunately, this technique does not work properly in IE 5.x on Windows as it stands. It would seem that IE has problems styling elements inside anchor links using a dynamic pseudo-class. However, there is a fix:

```
a.tooltip:hover {
  font-size: 100%; /* Fixes bug in IE5.x/Win */
}
```

Setting the font size as 100% on the hovered anchor somehow triggers Internet Explorer on Windows into correctly styling the contained span. Strange I know, but that's IE for you.

Sadly this technique breaks in Safari, and I have not managed to find a fix as I've done for Internet Explorer on Windows.

Summary

In this chapter you have learned how to style links in a variety of ways. You now know how to style links depending on the site or file they link to, and you can make links behave like buttons and create rollover effects using colors or images. You can even create advanced effects such as pure CSS tooltips.

In the next chapter you will learn how to manipulate lists, and using the information you have learned in this chapter, create navigation lists, pure CSS image maps, and remote rollovers. Let the fun begin.

4

5 STYLING LISTS AND CREATING NAV BARS

It is in our nature to try to organize the world around us. Scientists create lists of animals, plants, and chemical elements. Magazines create lists of the top 10 movies, the latest fashion trends, or the worst-dressed celebrities. People write shopping lists, to-do lists, and lists to Santa. We just love making lists.

Lists provide us with a way of grouping related elements and, by doing so, we give them meaning and structure. Most web pages contain some form of list, be it a list of the latest news stories, a list of links to your favorite web pages, or a list of links to other parts of your site. Identifying these items as lists and marking them up as such can help add structure to your HTML documents, providing useful hooks with which to apply your styles.

In this chapter you will learn about

- Styling lists with CSS
- Using background images as bullets
- Creating vertical and horizontal nav bars
- Using sliding doors tabbed navigation
- Creating CSS image maps
- Creating remote rollovers
- Using definition lists

Basic list styling

Basic list styling is very simple. Say you start with this simple to-do list:

```
<ul>
<li>Read emails</li>
<li>Write book</li>
<li>Go shopping</li>
<li>Cook dinner</li>
<li>Watch Scrubs</li>
</ul>
```

To add a custom bullet you could use the `list-style-image` property. However, this doesn't give you much control over the position of your bullet image. Instead, it is more common to turn list bullets off and add your custom bullet as a background image on the list element. You can then use the background image positioning properties to accurately control the alignment of your custom bullet.

Internet Explorer and Opera control list indentation using left margin, whereas Safari and Firefox choose to use left padding. As such, the first thing you will want to do is remove this indentation by zeroing down the `margin` and padding on the list. To remove the default bullet, you simply set the list style type to none:

```
ul {
   margin: 0;
   padding: 0;
   list-style-type: none;
}
```

Adding a custom bullet is very straightforward. Adding padding to the left side of the list item creates the necessary space for your bullet. The bullet is then applied as a background image on the list item. If the list item is going to span multiple lines, you will probably want to position the bullet at or near the top of the list item. However, if you know the contents of the list items won't span more than one line, you can vertically center the bullet by setting the vertical position to either middle or 50%:

```
li {
  background: url(bullet.gif) no-repeat 0 50%;
  padding-left: 30px;
}
```

The resulting styled list can be seen in Figure 5-1.

Read emails
Write book
Go shopping
Cook dinner
Watch Scrubs

Figure 5-1. Simple styled list with custom bullets

Creating a vertical nav bar

Combining the previous example with the link styling techniques you learned in Chapter 4, you can create graphically rich vertical navigation bars complete with CSS rollovers, like the one in Figure 5-2.

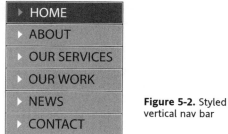

▸ HOME
▸ ABOUT
▸ OUR SERVICES
▸ OUR WORK
▸ NEWS
▸ CONTACT

Figure 5-2. Styled vertical nav bar

As always, you need to start with a good HTML framework:

```
<ul>
  <li><a href="home.htm">Home</a></li>
  <li><a href="about.htm">About</a></li>
  <li><a href="services.htm">Our Services</a></li>
  <li><a href="work.htm">Our Work</a></li>
  <li><a href="news.htm">News</a></li>
  <li><a href="contact.htm">Contact</a></li>
</ul>
```

The first thing you want to do is remove the default bullets and zero down the `margin` and padding:

```
ul {
    margin: 0;
    padding: 0;
    list-style-type: none;
}
```

Rather than style the list items, you are going to be styling the enclosed anchors. To create a button-like hit area, you need to set the `display` property of the anchors to block, and then specify the anchor's dimensions. In this example my navigation buttons are 200 pixels wide and 40 pixels high. The line height has also been set to 40 pixels in order to center the link text vertically. The last couple of rules are just stylistic, setting the color of the link text and turning off the underlines.

```
ul a {
    display: block;
    width: 200px;
    height: 40px;
    line-height: 40px;
    color: #000;
    text-decoration: none;
}
```

Using the Pixy rollover technique you learned about in Chapter 4, the rollover graphic (Figure 5-3) is applied as a background image to the anchor link.

Figure 5-3. A single image composed of both the up and hover state images

The background image is aligned left in order to reveal the up state. The anchor text is given a 50-pixel indent so that it is not sitting directly over the arrow in the background image.

```
ul a {
    display: block;
    width: 200px;
    height: 40px;
    line-height: 40px;
    color: #000;
    text-decoration: none;
    background: #94B8E9 url(images/pixy-rollover.gif)  no-repeat ➥
    left center;
    text-indent: 50px;
}
```

If you look at the rollover image in Figure 5-3, you will notice that it has a solid border all the way around the image. When these images are stacked vertically, the top and bottom borders will double up. However, you only want a single, 1-pixel black line between each nav bar item. To get around this problem, clip the top line off by aligning the background images to the bottom of the anchor and then reducing the height of the links by 1 pixel:

```
ul a {
   display: block;
   width: 200px;
   height: 39px;
   line-height: 39px;
   color: #000;
   text-decoration: none;
   background: #94B8E9 url(images/pixy-rollover.gif) no-repeat ➥
   left bottom;
   text-indent: 50px;
}
```

The links now stack up nicely, with a single black line appearing between each one. However, the top black line on the first link is no longer showing. To put this back you need to reset the height of the first anchor to 40 pixels—the full height of the image. You can do this by applying a class of first to the first list item:

```
li.first a {
   height: 40px;
   line-height: 40px;
}
```

The list now looks like a stylish vertical navigation bar. To complete the effect, the last thing you need to do is apply the hover and selected states. To do this, you simply shift the background image on the anchor links to the right, uncovering the hover state graphic. This style is applied to the anchor links when the user hovers over them. It is also applied to any anchors that have a class of selected applied to their parent list item.

```
a:hover, .selected a {
   background-position: right bottom;
   color: #fff;
}
```

This technique should now work in all the major browsers except IE for Windows. Unfortunately, IE inexplicably adds extra space above and below the list items. To fix this bug, you need to set the display property on the list items to inline:

```
li {
   display: inline: /* :KLUDGE: Removes large gaps in IE/Win */
}
```

And there you have it: a styled vertical nav bar, complete with rollovers.

Highlighting the current page in a nav bar

In the previous vertical nav bar example, I used a class to indicate the current page. For small sites with the navigation embedded in the page, you can simply add the class on a page-by-page basis. For large sites, there is a good chance that the navigation is being built dynamically, in which case the class can be added on the back end. However, for medium-sized sites, where the main navigation doesn't change, it is common to include the navigation as an external file. In these situations, wouldn't it be good if there were a way to highlight the page you are on, without having to dynamically add a class to the menu? Well, with CSS there is.

This concept works by adding an ID or a class name to the body element of each page, denoting which page or section the user is in. You then add a corresponding ID or class name to each item in your navigation list. The unique combination of body ID and list ID/class can be used to highlight your current section or page in the site nav.

Take this HTML fragment as an example. The current page is the home page, as indicated by an ID of home on the body. Each list item in the main navigation is given a class name based on the name of the page the list item relates to:

```html
<body id="home">
<ul id="mainNav">
<li class="home"><a href="#">Home</a></li>
<li class="about"><a href="#">About</a></li>
<li class="news"><a href="#">News</a></li>
<li class="products"><a href="#">Products</a></li>
<li class="services"><a href="#">Services</a></li>
</ul>
</body>
```

To highlight the current page you simply target the following combination of IDs and class names:

```css
#home #mainNav .home a,
#about #mainNav .about a ,
#news #mainNav .news a,
#products #mainNav .products a,
#services #mainNav .services a {
  background-position: right bottom;
  color: #fff;
  cursor: default;
}
```

When the user is on the home page, the nav item with a class of home will display the selected state, whereas on the news page, the nav item with the class of news will show the selected state. For added effect, I have changed to cursor style to show the default arrow cursor. That way, if you mouse over the selected link, your cursor will not change state and you won't be tempted to click a link to a page you are already on.

Creating a horizontal nav bar

As well as using lists to create vertical nav bars, they can also be used to create horizontal ones. In this example, I am going to demonstrate how to create a horizontal navigation bar like the one in Figure 5-4.

| HOME | ABOUT | NEWS | PRODUCTS | SERVICES | CLIENTS | CASE STUDIES |

Figure 5-4. Horizontal nav bar

As in the previous example, you start with a simple, unordered list:

```
<ul>
<li><a href="#">Home</a></li>
<li><a href="#">About</a></li>
<li><a href="#">News</a></li>
<li><a href="#">Products</a></li>
<li><a href="#">Services</a></li>
<li><a href="#">Clients</a></li>
<li><a href="#">Case Studies</a></li>
</ul>
```

You then zero down the padding and margins, as well as remove the default bullets. For this example I want my horizontal nav bar to be 720 pixels wide, and to have a repeating orange gradient as a background:

```
ul {
    margin: 0;
    padding: 0;
    list-style: none;
    width: 720px;
    background: #FAA819 url(images/mainNavBg.gif) repeat-x;
}
```

The list is currently displayed vertically. To make it display horizontally, you can use one of two methods. You can either set the list items to display inline, or you can float them all left. Displaying the list items as inline is probably the simpler method. However, from personal experience I have found that it can produce buggy results; therefore, I tend to favor the floating method:

```
ul li {
    float: left;
}
```

Remember that when an element is floated, it no longer takes up any space in the flow of the document. As such, the parent list effectively has no content and collapses down, hiding the list background. As you learned in Chapter 2, there are two ways to make parent elements contain floated children. One method is to add a clearing element. Unfortunately this adds unnecessary markup to the page so should be avoided if possible.

91

The other method is to float the parent element as well, and clear it further down the line, say, using the site footer. This is the method I normally use:

```
ul {
    margin: 0;
    padding: 0;
    list-style: none;
    width: 720px;
    float: left;
    background: #FAA819 url(images/mainNavBg.gif) repeat-x;
}
```

As in the vertical navigation bar example, the links in the horizontal nav bar are made to behave like buttons by setting their display property to block. If you wanted each button to be a fixed size, you could explicitly set its height and width. In this example, I want the width of each button to be based on the size of the anchor text. To do this, rather than setting a width, I have applied 2ems of padding to the left and right sides of each anchor link. As in the previous example, the link text is being vertically centered using line height. Lastly, the link underlines are turned off and the link color is changed to white:

```
ul a {
    display: block;
    padding: 0 2em;
    line-height: 2.1em;
    text-decoration: none;
    color: #fff;
}
```

I want to create dividers between each link in the nav bar. This can be done by applying a divider graphic as a background image to the left of each anchor link:

```
ul a {
    display: block;
    padding: 0 2em;
    line-height: 2.1em;
    background: url(images/divider.gif) repeat-y left top;
    text-decoration: none;
    color: #fff;
}
```

However, the first link in the nav bar will have an unwanted divider. Adding a class to the first list item and setting the background image to none can remove this:

```
ul .first a {
    background: none;
}
```

Lastly, the rollover state in this example is simply a change in link color:

```
ul a:hover {
  color: #333;
}
```

This nav bar works well on most modern browsers, but it doesn't work as expected in IE 5.2 on the Mac. This is because IE 5.2 on the Mac doesn't shrink-wrap the floated list items because the enclosed anchors have been set to display as block-level elements. To avoid this problem, we simply need to float the anchors as well:

```
ul a {
  display: block;
  float: left;
  padding: 0 2em;
  line-height: 2.1em;
  background: url(images/divider.gif) repeat-y left top;
  text-decoration: none;
  color: #fff;
}
```

And there you have it: a well-styled horizontal nav bar with good, cross-browser support.

Simplified "sliding doors" tabbed navigation

In Chapter 3 you learned about Douglas Bowman's sliding doors technique, and how it could be used to create flexible, rounded-corner boxes. This technique can also be used to create flexible, expandable tabbed navigation. Using this method, tabs are created from one large image and one side image. As the text in the tabs expands, more of the large image is uncovered. The smaller image stays flush to the left, covering up the hard edge of the larger image and completing the effect (see Figure 5-5).

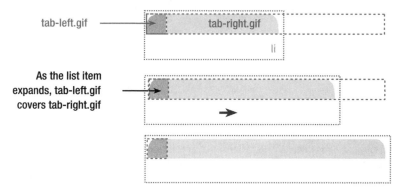

Figure 5-5. Example of the "sliding doors" technique

The images used to create the tabs in the following example can be seen in Figure 5-6. Both of these images are very large. This is to allow the font size to be increased by several hundred percent without the tabs appearing to break.

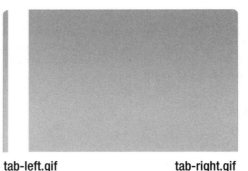

tab-left.gif **tab-right.gif**

Figure 5-6. The two images that make up the tabs

The HTML for this example is exactly the same as in the previous, horizontal nav bar example:

```
<ul>
<li><a href="#">Home</a></li>
<li><a href="#">About</a></li>
<li><a href="#">News</a></li>
<li><a href="#">Products</a></li>
<li><a href="#">Services</a></li>
<li><a href="#">Clients</a></li>
<li><a href="#">Case Studies</a></li>
</ul>
```

As in the previous example, the margin and padding are zeroed, the list bullets are removed, and a width is set for the navigation bar. The tabbed navigation bar is also floated left in order to contain any enclosed floats:

```
ul {
  margin: 0;
  padding: 0;
  list-style: none;
  width: 720px;
  float: left;
}
```

Like the previous example, the list elements are floated left to make them display horizontally rather than vertically. However, this time, the larger of the two images that make up the tab is applied as a background image to the list item. As this image forms the right side of the tab, it is positioned to the right:

```
ul li {
  float: left;
  background: url(images/tab-right.gif) no-repeat top right;
}
```

As in the previous example, the anchors are set to display as block-level elements to make the whole area clickable. The width of each tab is again controlled by the width of the contents, and setting the line height similarly controls the height. To complete the tab effect, the left part of the tab is applied as a background on the anchor and aligned left. As the tab changes size, this image will always be aligned left, sitting over the top of the larger image and covering the hard left edge. Lastly, to make sure this technique works in IE 5.2 on the Mac, the anchors are floated as well.

```
li a {
  display: block;
  padding: 0 2em;
  line-height: 2.5em;
  background: url(images/tab-left.gif) no-repeat top left;
  text-decoration: none;
  color: #fff;
  float: left;
}
```

To create the rollover effect, you can simply change the link color:

```
ul a:hover {
  color: #333;
}
```

The resulting tabbed navigation should look like Figure 5-7.

Figure 5-7. "Sliding doors" tabbed navigation at normal size

If you increase the text size in your browser, you should see that the tabs scale nicely, as demonstrated in Figure 5-8.

Figure 5-8. "Sliding doors" tabbed navigation after the text size has been scaled several times

This method provides an easy and hassle-free way to make attractive and accessible tabbed navigation bars.

CSS image maps

Image maps allow web developers to specify regions of an image to act as hotspots. Image maps were very popular several years ago, but they are much less common these days. This is partly due to the popularity of Flash, and partly due to the move toward simpler and less presentational markup. While image maps are still a perfectly valid part of HTML, they do mix presentation with content. However, it is possible to create simple image maps with a combination of lists, anchors, and some advanced CSS.

For this example I am using a photograph of the Clearleft gang posing for pictures on the Brighton seafront (see Figure 5-9). When I hover over each person, I want a rectangular box to appear. Clicking on this box will take me to that person's website.

Figure 5-9. Rich, Jeremy, and me posing for pictures on the Brighton seafront

The first thing you need to do is add your image to the page, inside a named div:

```
<div id="pic">
<img src="images/group-photo.jpg" width="640" height="425"➥
alt="Richard, Andy and Jeremy" />
</div>
```

Then, add a list of links to each person's website after the image. Each list item needs to be given a class to identify the person in that list item. You can also give each link a title attribute containing the name of the person. That way, when the link is hovered over, a tooltip showing who the person is will be displayed on most browsers.

```
<div id="pic">
<img src="images/group-photo.jpg" width="640" height="425"➥
alt="Richard, Andy and Jeremy" />
<ul>
```

```
      <li class="rich">
        <a href="http://www.clagnut.com/" title="Richard Rutter">
        Richard Rutter
        </a>
      </li>
      <li class="andy">
        <a href="http://www.andybudd.com/" title="Andy Budd">
        Andy Budd
        </a>
      </li>
      <li class="jeremy">
        <a href="http://www.adactio.com/" title="Jeremy Keith">
        Jeremy Keith
        </a>
      </li>
    </ul>
  </div>
```

Set the width and height of the div so that it matches the dimensions of the image. Then set the position property of the div to relative. This last step is the key to this technique as it allows the enclosed links to be positioned absolutely, in relation to the edges of the div, and hence the image.

```
#pic {
  width: 640px;
  height: 425px;
  position: relative; /* The key to this technique */
}
```

You won't want the list bullets to display, so remove them by setting the list-style property to none. For completeness you may as well zero down the list's margin and padding as well:

```
#pic ul {
  margin: 0;
  padding: 0;
  list-style: none;
}
```

The next thing to do is style the links. By positioning the anchor links absolutely, they will all be moved to the top-left corner of the containing div. They can then be positioned individually over the correct people, forming the hotspots. However, first you will need to set their widths and heights to create your desired hit area. The link text is still displayed; therefore, it is necessary to hide it off the screen by using a large, negative text indent:

```
#pic a {
  position: absolute;
  width: 100px;
  height: 120px;
  text-indent: -1000em;
}
```

The individual links can now be positioned over the relevant people:

```css
#pic .rich a {
  top: 15px;
  left: 95px;
}

#pic .andy a {
  top: 115px;
  left: 280px;
}

#pic .jeremy a {
  top: 250px;
  left: 425px;
}
```

Lastly, to create the rollover effect, a solid white border is applied to the links when they are hovered over:

```css
#pic a:hover {
  border: 1px solid #fff;
}
```

And that is the basic technique finished. If you try rolling over one of the pictures, you should see something similar to Figure 5-10.

Figure 5-10. The CSS image map being rolled over

flickr-style image maps

If you have used the photo sharing service flickr, you may have come across a similar technique used to annotate images (see Figure 5-11). When you roll over an annotated image, a double-bordered box will appear over the area containing each note. When you hover over one of these boxes, it will highlight and display the note. With a spot of tweaking, we can achieve the same thing using the previous technique.

Figure 5-11. Image notes on flickr

To create the double-border box you need to add a couple of extra spans inside each anchor link. The note will also need the addition of an extra span. Once the extra spans have been added, the amended list should look like this:

```
<ul>
  <li class="rich">
    <a href="http://www.clagnut.com/">
    <span class="outer">
    <span class="inner">
    <span class="note">Richard Rutter</span>
    </span>
    </span>
    </a>
  </li>
...
</ul>
```

The CSS starts off identical to the previous example, setting the dimensions of the wrapper div to those of the image, and the position property to relative. The list padding and margin are again zeroed down and the bullets removed:

```css
#pic {
  width: 640px;
  height: 425px;
  position: relative;
}

#pic ul {
  margin: 0;
  padding: 0;
  list-style: none;
}
```

As before, the enclosed anchor links are positioned absolutely and given dimensions to form the hotspots. However, this time you don't want to hide the content of the link—you want to display it. As such, rather than hiding it off screen, give the anchor text a color and remove its default underline. The highlight effect on rollover is going to be created by adding a yellow border when the anchor is hovered over. To avoid the anchor from shifting position slightly when hovered over, it is necessary to give the link a 1-pixel transparent border:

```css
#pic a {
  position: absolute;
  width: 100px;
  height: 120px;
  color: #000;
  text-decoration: none;
  border: 1px solid transparent;
}
```

As before, you will need to position the anchors over each person:

```css
#pic .rich a {
  top: 15px;
  left: 95px;
}

#pic .andy a {
  top: 115px;
  left: 280px;
}

#pic .jeremy a {
  top: 250px;
  left: 425px;
}
```

To create the double-border effect, the outer and inner spans need to have their display properties set to block. They can then be given dimensions and colored borders. In this case, the outer span is being given a black border while the inner span is given a white border:

```
#pic a .outer {
  display: block;
  width: 98px;
  height: 118px;
  border: 1px solid #000;
}

#pic a .inner {
  display: block;
  width: 96px;
  height: 116px;
  border: 1px solid #fff;
}
```

You can then apply the rollover effect to the anchor link. This is done by changing the anchor's border color from transparent to yellow on hover:

```
#pic a:hover {
  border-color: #d4d82d;
}
```

To display the note when the hotspot is rolled over, you first need to position the contents of the note span beneath the hotspot. To do this, set the position of the note span to absolute, and give it a negative bottom position. To pretty up the notes, set a width, some padding, and a background color, then center the text:

```
#pic a .note {
  position: absolute;
  bottom: -3em;
  width: 9em;
  padding: 0.2em 0.5em;
  background-color:#ffc;
  text-align: center;
}
```

If you check the page in the browser, it should look something like Figure 5-12.

Figure 5-12. The flickr style rollovers are starting to take shape.

As you can see, the effect is starting to take shape. The notes look OK, but it would be nice if they were centered horizontally below the hotspot, rather than flush to the left. You can do this by positioning the left edge of the note span at the midpoint of the hotspot. Next, move the note span left, half the width of the note, using negative margins. The hotspot in this example is 100 pixels wide, so I have set the left position of the note to be 50 pixels. The notes are 10ems wide, including the padding, so setting a negative left margin of 5ems will horizontally center the note beneath the hotspot.

```
#pic a .note {
  position: absolute;
  bottom: -3em;
  width: 9em;
  padding: 0.2em 0.5em;
  background-color:#ffc;
  text-align: center;
  left: 50px;
  margin-left: -5em;
}
```

With the notes now centered, it's time to work on their interactivity. The notes should be hidden by default and only displayed when the hotspot is hovered over. To do this you could set the display property to none and then change it to block when the anchor link is hovered over. However, this would prevent some screenreaders from accessing the contents of the note. Instead, I am going to hide the text off the left side of the screen, and reposition it on hover:

```
#pic a .note {
   position: absolute;
   bottom: -3em;
   width: 9em;
   padding: 0.2em 0.5em;
   background-color:#ffc;
   text-align: center;
   left: -30000px;
   margin-left: -5em;
}

#pic a:hover .note {
   left: 50px;
}
```

We are almost there now. Just one more tweak is required to finish the technique. Rather than continuously display the hotspots' double borders, it would be nice if the borders only displayed when the image was rolled over. That way, people can enjoy the image normally, unfettered by the hotspots. However when the image is hovered, the hotspots appear, letting the visitor know more information is available to be discovered. You can do this by removing the borders from the outer and inner spans and putting them back when the image is hovered over:

```
#pic:hover a .outer {
 border: 1px solid #000;
}

#pic:hover a .inner {
 border: 1px solid #fff;
}
```

Unfortunately, as you have already learned, IE 6 only supports hovering on anchor links. To get around this problem, it is also a good idea to display the borders when the hotspots are hovered over directly:

```
#pic:hover a .outer, #pic a:hover .outer {
 border: 1px solid #000;
}

#pic:hover a .inner, #pic a:hover .inner {
 border: 1px solid #fff;
}
```

And there you have it: a flickr-style, advanced CSS image map (see Figure 5-13).

Figure 5-13. The finished product

Remote rollovers

A remote rollover is a hover event that triggers a display change somewhere else on the page. This is accomplished by nesting one or more elements inside an anchor link. Then, using absolute positioning, you can position the nested elements individually. Despite being displayed in different places, they are both contained within the same parent anchor, so will both react to the same hover event. As such, when you hover over one element, it can affect the style of another element.

In this example, you are going to build on the basic CSS image map technique by placing a list of links below the image. When the links are hovered over, the image hotspots will be outlined. Conversely, when you hover over the hot areas on the picture, the text links will highlight.

The HTML for this example is similar to that of the basic CSS image map example. However, you will need two additional spans: one wrapped around the link text, and one empty span to act as the hotspot. This will allow you to position the link text beneath the image and the hotspots over the respective people.

```
<div id="pic">
<img src="images/group-photo.jpg" width="640" height="425"➥
alt="Richard, Andy and Jeremy" />
<ul>
<li class="rich">
```

```
<a href="http://www.clagnut.com/" title="Richard Rutter">
<span class="hotspot"></span>
<span class="link">&raquo; Richard Rutter</span>
</a>
</li>
<li class="andy">
<a href="http://www.andybudd.com/" title="Andy Budd">
<span class="hotspot"></span>
<span class="link">&raquo; Andy Budd</span>
</a>
</li>
<li class="jeremy">
<a href="http://www.adactio.com/" title="Jeremy Keith">
<span class="hotspot"></span>
<span class="link">&raquo; Jeremy Keith</span>
</a></li>
</ul>
</div>
```

The basic list styling is the same as the image map example:

```
#pic {
  width: 640px;
  height: 425px;
  position: relative;
}

#pic ul {
  margin: 0;
  padding: 0;
  list-style: none;
}
```

The first thing you need to do is set the position property of the hotspots to absolute, and then specify their dimensions. In this example each hotspot is the same size, but you could set different sizes on each one if you wanted. Just as in the previous technique, this will position all of the anchors at the top-left corner of the image. You can then position each hotspot over the relevant person in the image, using the top and left positioning properties.

```
#pic a .hotspot {
  width: 100px;
  height: 120px;
  position: absolute;
}

#pic .rich a .hotspot {
  top: 15px;
  left: 95px;
}
```

```
#pic .andy a .hotspot {
  top: 115px;
  left: 280px;
}

#pic .jeremy a .hotspot {
  top: 250px;
  left: 425px;
}
```

Similarly, the spans containing the link text are also positioned absolutely and are given a width of 15ems. They too are positioned in relation to the enclosing list, in this case visually below the list using negative bottom positions:

```
#pic a .link {
  position: absolute;
  width: 15em;
}

#pic .rich a .link {
  bottom: -2em;
  left: 0;
}

#pic .andy a .link {
  bottom: -3.2em;
  left: 0;
}

#pic .jeremy a .link {
  bottom: -4.4em;
  left: 0;
}
```

The hotspots should now be in the correct place, as should the text links.

To create the rollover effect on the hotspot when either the hotspot or the text is hovered, you need to apply a border to the hotspot span, when the parent anchor is hovered over:

```
#pic a:hover .hotspot {
  border: 1px solid #fff;
}
```

Similarly, to change the color of the text when either the text or the hotspot span is hovered over, you need to change the style on the span when the parent anchor is hovered over:

```
#pic a:hover .link {
  color: #0066FF;
}
```

If you test this example, it works perfectly in Safari and Firefox (see Figure 5-14). If you hover over a person's name, the link text changes color, and a box appears over that person in the picture. The same happens if you hover over the person in the image.

Figure 5-14. Remote rollover demonstration. When the link text at the bottom of the image is rolled over, an outline appears over the associated person in the image.

Unfortunately, this example doesn't quite work on IE on Windows. It would seem that IE/Win has problems targeting nested elements inside an anchor link, using the :hover dynamic pseudo-class. However, there is a simple, if somewhat odd, workaround. Adding the following rule on the anchors hover state seems to fix the confusion in IE and allow it to honor nested hover state rules:

```
#pic a:hover {
  border: none;
}
```

While the styling of this example is quite simple, you are really only limited by your imagination. One of the best examples of this technique in the wild can be seen at http://dbowman.com/photos, the personal photo gallery of the technique's creator, Douglas Bowman (see Figure 5-15).

Figure 5-15. When you roll over the slide graphics on Douglas Bowman's photo gallery site, a translucent "next photo" graphic appears over the image.

A short note about definition lists

Throughout this chapter I have discussed how unordered lists (and by extension, ordered lists) can be used to create a variety of effects. However, there is a third, often overlooked list type that has been gaining more attention of late: the definition list. A definition list consists of two core components: a definition term <dt> and one or more definition descriptions <dd>.

```
<dl>
<dt>Apple</dt>
<dd>Red, yellow or green fruit</dd>
<dd>Computer company</dd>
<dt>Bananna</dt>
<dd>Curved yellow fruit</dd>
</dl>
```

As the name suggests, the primary purpose of a definition list is to mark up definitions. However, the (X)HTML specification is rather vague and suggests definition lists could be used for other applications like product properties or conversations. This stretches the concept of definitions somewhat, but still makes a certain amount of sense in the context of (X)HTML's history as a simple text formatting language.

Many web standards pioneers seized on the fact that definition lists could be used to structurally group a series of related elements and started to use them to create everything from product listing and image galleries, to form and even page layouts. While these techniques are undoubtedly clever, I personally believe they stretch the implied meaning of definition lists beyond their natural breaking point.

One of the arguments for using definition lists in this fashion is that no other (X)HTML element allows for this type of association. However, this isn't strictly true as the purpose of the div element is to group a document up into logical sections. More worryingly, this is exactly the same type of argument used when justifying tables for layout. This raises concerns that definition lists are starting to be used inappropriately.

Because of this I am not going to cover any of these advanced techniques in this book. If you would like to learn more about definition list styling, check out some of these resources:

- Max Design on definition lists: http://tinyurl.com/8e9fn
- E-commerce definition lists: http://tinyurl.com/9sn54
- Form layout with definition lists: http://tinyurl.com/7ef7q
- Manipulating definition lists for fun and profit: http://tinyurl.com/8g3ll

Summary

In this chapter you have learned how flexible lists can be. You learned how to create vertical and horizontal navigation bars, including accessible tabbed navigation. Finally, you learned how to use positioning to create pure CSS image maps and remote rollovers.

In the next chapter you will learn how to create accessible form layouts and data tables, and how to style them with CSS.

6 STYLING FORMS AND DATA TABLES

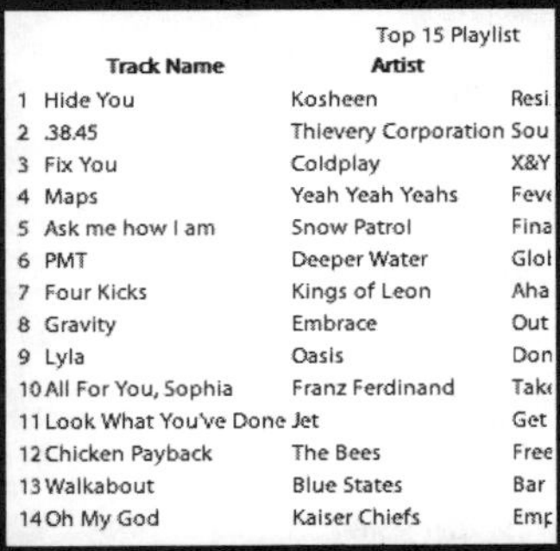

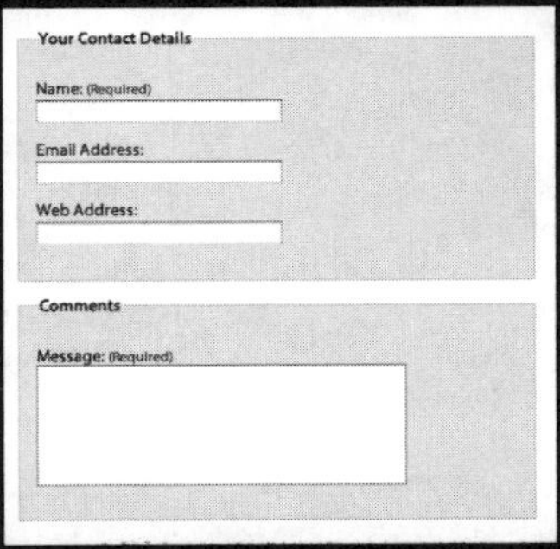

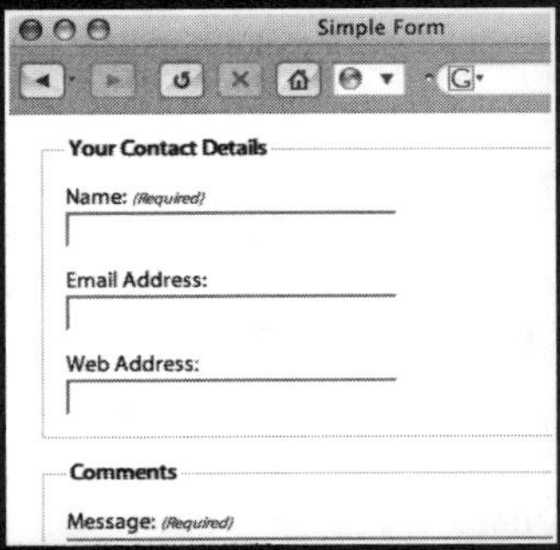

As more and more interactivity is called for on the Web, forms are becoming an increasingly important part of modern web applications. Forms allow users to interact with systems, enabling them to do everything from registering feedback to booking complicated travel itineraries. As such, forms can be as simple as an email address and a message field, or they can be hugely complex, spanning multiple pages. Form layout has traditionally been done using tables; however, in this chapter you will learn that even complicated forms can be laid out using CSS.

Tables are slowly regaining their rightful position purely as a way of displaying tabular data, rather than a means of page layout. As well as needing to capture user data, web applications increasingly need to display this data in a usable and an easy-to-understand format. Form and data table design have been relatively neglected in favor of higher-profile areas of design. However, good information and interaction design can make or break a modern web application.

In this chapter you will learn about

- Creating attractive and accessible data tables
- Creating simple and complicated form layouts
- Styling various form elements
- Providing accessible form feedback

Styling data tables

Even relatively simple data tables can be hard to read if they contain more than a few rows and columns. With little separation between data cells, information blurs together, resulting in a jumbled and confusing layout. For instance, in Figure 6-1 the track name and artist name for track 11 blur into one long sentence. The same is true for the artist and album names on track 2. You can read this information if you concentrate, but it does slow down how quickly you can read and process the information on the table.

Top 15 Playlist		
Track Name	**Artist**	**Album**
1 Hide You	Kosheen	Resist
2 .38.45	Thievery Corporation	Sounds From the Thievery Hi-Fi
3 Fix You	Coldplay	X&Y
4 Maps	Yeah Yeah Yeahs	Fever To Tell
5 Ask me how I am	Snow Patrol	Final Straw
6 PMT	Deeper Water	Global Underground Moscow
7 Four Kicks	Kings of Leon	Aha Shake Heartbreak
8 Gravity	Embrace	Out of Nothing
9 Lyla	Oasis	Don't Believe the Truth
10 All For You, Sophia	Franz Ferdinand	Take me Out
11 Look What You've Done	Jet	Get Born
12 Chicken Payback	The Bees	Free the Bees
13 Walkabout	Blue States	Bar Lounge Classics
14 Oh My God	Kaiser Chiefs	Employment
15 Rock Scene	Athlete	Tourist

Figure 6-1. Compact data tables can be very confusing at first glance.

Conversely, tables with a lot of whitespace can also be very difficult to read as columns and cells start to lose their visual association with each other. This is particularly problematic when you're trying to follow rows of information on tables with very large column spacing, such as the one in Figure 6-2. If you are not careful, it is easy to accidentally stray into the wrong row when moving between columns. This is most noticeable in the middle of the table where the hard edge of the top and bottom of the table provide less of a visual anchor.

	Top 15 Playlist		
	Track Name	Artist	Album
1	Hide You	Kosheen	Resist
2	.38.45	Thievery Corporation	Sounds From the Thievery Hi-Fi
3	Fix You	Coldplay	X&Y
4	Maps	Yeah Yeah Yeahs	Fever To Tell
5	Ask me how I am	Snow Patrol	Final Straw
6	PMT	Deeper Water	Global Underground Moscow
7	Four Kicks	Kings of Leon	Aha Shake Heartbreak
8	Gravity	Embrace	Out of Nothing
9	Lyla	Oasis	Don't Believe the Truth
10	All For You, Sophia	Franz Ferdinand	Take me Out
11	Look What You've Done	Jet	Get Born
12	Chicken Payback	The Bees	Free the Bees
13	Walkabout	Blue States	Bar Lounge Classics
14	Oh My God	Kaiser Chiefs	Employment
15	Rock Scene	Athlete	Tourist

Figure 6-2. Widely spaced tables can also be difficult to immediately comprehend.

By contrast, a few minutes spent designing your data tables can greatly improve their comprehension and the speed at which information can be retrieved.

For instance, the contents of the table in Figure 6-3 have been given visual space with a small amount of vertical and horizontal padding. The main column headings have been distinguished from the data with a subtle repeating background image. The alternating colored rows help guide the eye horizontally between each cell of information, while not overloading the reader with too much visual clutter. To further aid the reader, a hover effect has been applied on each row to act like a ruler and highlight the row that is currently being read.

Top 15 Playlist			
	Track Name	Artist	Album
1	Hide You	Kosheen	Resist
2	.38.45	Thievery Corporation	Sounds From the Thievery Hi-Fi
3	Fix You	Coldplay	X&Y
4	Maps	Yeah Yeah Yeahs	Fever To Tell
5	Ask me how I am	Snow Patrol	Final Straw
6	PMT	Deeper Water	Global Underground Moscow
7	Four Kicks	Kings of Leon	Aha Shake Heartbreak
8	Gravity	Embrace	Out of Nothing
9	Lyla	Oasis	Don't Believe the Truth
10	All For You, Sophia	Franz Ferdinand	Take me Out
11	Look What You've Done	Jet	Get Born
12	Chicken Payback	The Bees	Free the Bees
13	Walkabout	Blue States	Bar Lounge Classics
14	Oh My God	Kaiser Chiefs	Employment
15	Rock Scene	Athlete	Tourist

Figure 6-3. Stylized data table

6

Table-specific elements

If data tables can be difficult for sighted users, imagine how complicated and frustrating they must be for people using assistive technologies such as screenreaders. Fortunately, the (X)HTML specification includes a number of elements and attributes intended to increase the accessibility of data tables for these devices. Not all of these elements are currently supported by screenreaders, but it is definitely good practice to use them where possible.

summary and caption

The first of these elements is a table caption, which basically acts as a heading for the table. Although this is not a required element, it is always a good idea to use a caption wherever possible. Another useful addition is a table summary. The summary attribute can be applied to the table tag, and is used to describe the content of the table. Much like an image's alt text, the summary should effectively summarize the data in the table, and a well-written summary may alleviate the need to read the contents of the table.

```
<table id="playlistTable" summary="Top 15 songs played. Top artist➥
  include Coldplay, Yeah Yeah Yeahs, Snow Patrol, Deeper Water, Kings➥
  of Leon, Embrace, Oasis, Franz Ferdinand, Jet, The Bees, Blue States,➥
  Kaiser Cheifs and Athlete.">
<caption>Top 15 Playlist</caption>
</table>
```

thead, tbody, and tfoot

Using thead, tbody, and tfoot allows the developer to break tables up into logical sections. For instance, you can place all of your column headings inside the thead element, providing you with a means of separately styling that particular area. If you choose to use a thead or tfoot element, you must use at least one tbody element. You can only use one thead and tfoot element in a table, but you can use multiple tbody elements to help break complicated tables into more managable chunks.

Row and column headings should be marked up as th rather than td, although if something is both a heading and data it should be left as a td. Table headings can be given a scope attribute of row or col to define whether they are row or column headings. They can also be given a value of rowgroup or colgroup if they relate to more than one row or column.

```
<thead>
  <tr>
  <th id="playlistPosHead" scope="col">Playlist Position</th>
  <th scope="col">Track Name</th>
  <th scope="col">Artist</th>
  <th scope="col">Album</th>
  </tr>
</thead>
```

col and colgroups

While the `tr` element allows developers to apply styles to whole rows, it is much more difficult to apply a style to an entire column. To get around this problem, the W3C introduced the colgroup and `col` elements. Colgroups are a way of defining and grouping one or more columns using the `col` element. Unfortunately, not many browsers support the styling of col and colgroup elements.

```
<colgroup>
  <col id="PlaylistCol" />
  <col id="trackCol" />
  <col id="artistCol" />
  <col id="albumCol" />
</colgroup>
```

Data table markup

Putting all of these (X)HTML elements and attributes together, you can create the basic outline for the styled table seen in Figure 6-3.

```
<table cellspacing="0" id="playlistTable" summary="Top 15 songs
played.
Top artists include Cold Play, Yeah Yeah Yeahs, Snow Patrol, Deeper ➥
Water, Kings of Leon, Embrace, Oasis, Franz Ferdinand, Jet, The Bees,➥
Blue States, Kaiser Chiefs and Athlete.">
  <caption>Top 15 Playlist</caption>
  <colgroup>
    <col id="PlaylistCol" />
    <col id="trackCol" />
    <col id="artistCol" />
    <col id="albumCol" />
  </colgroup>
  <thead>
    <tr>
      <th id="playlistPosHead" scope="col">Playlist Position</th>
      <th scope="col">Track Name</th>
      <th scope="col">Artist</th>
      <th scope="col">Album</th>
    </tr>
  </thead>
  <tbody>
    <tr class="odd">
      <td>1</td>
      <td>Hide You</td>
      <td>Kosheen</td>
      <td>Resist</td>
```

```
    </tr>
    <tr>
      <td>2</td>
      <td>.38.45</td>
      <td>Thievery Corporation</td>
      <td>Sounds From the Thievery Hi-Fi</td>
    </tr>
    <tr class="odd">
      <td>3</td>
      <td>Fix You</td>
      <td>Cold Play</td>
      <td>X&amp;Y</td>
    </tr>
    ...
  </tbody>
</table>
```

Styling the table

The CSS specification has two table border models: separate and collapsed. In the separate model, borders are placed around individual cells, whereas in the collapsed model cells share borders. Most browsers default to the separate model, but I personally find the collapsed model to be of more use. As such, one of the first things you will want to do is set the border-collapse property of your table to collapse. To stop the table from being too wide you will want to limit its width, and to help define the table area, adding a border is a good idea. It is also a good idea to give the table cells a little breathing room by applying a small amount of vertical and horizontal padding.

```
table {
  border-collapse: collapse;
  width: 50em;
  border: 1px solid #666;
}

th, td {
  padding: 0.1em 1em;
}
```

CSS has a border-spacing property that allows you to control the spacing between cells. Unfortunately, this property is not understood by IE 6 and below for Windows, rendering its use fairly limited. Instead, to remove the default padding between cells you will have to fall back on the old but reliable cellspacing property. This property is, strictly speaking, presentational in nature. However, it is still valid (X)HTML and is currently the only means of controlling cell spacing in IE 6/Win.

```
<table cellspacing="0" id="playlistTable" summary="Top 15 songs…">
```

Adding the visual style

The groundwork has been set, so it is now time to start adding the visual interest. To make the table caption look a little more like a regular heading, you can increase the font size and make it bold. You can also give the caption some breathing room by applying a top and bottom margin.

```
caption {
  font-size: 1.2em;
  font-weight: bold;
  margin: 1em 0;
}
```

It would be nice to give the columns some definition by applying a light border to them. This can be done by applying a right border to all of the col elements and then removing this border from the last element:

```
col {
  border-right: 1px solid #ccc;
}

col#albumCol {
  border: none;
}
```

Unfortunately, as mentioned earlier, not many browsers support this method. Therefore, if column borders are important to your design, you will probably need to apply them on individual cells instead. The problem with this approach is that you will then need to add a class to the last cell in each row, in order to turn the last border off. This is annoying but necessary if your design calls for it.

To distinguish the initial row of table headings, you can apply a small tiling image as a background to the thead element. A slightly darker top and bottom border is added to this element as well. Table headings are usually centered and emboldened by default. If you want, you can override this style.

```
thead {
  background: #ccc url(images/bar.gif) repeat-x left center;
  border-top: 1px solid #a5a5a5;
  border-bottom: 1px solid #a5a5a5;
}

th {
  font-weight: normal;
  text-align: left;
}
```

From a visual point of view, you may not want to display the "track number" heading, but you will want it to be available for screenreader users. To hide this heading, you can simply give the particular table heading a large negative text indent:

```
#playlistPosHead {
  text-indent: -1000em;
}
```

Added extras

The table should really be taking shape by now. To provide the alternating blue and white lines, a class of odd has been applied to each odd-numbered row. Those rows are then styled with a blue background:

```
.odd {
  background-color: #edf5ff;
}
```

When CSS 3 selectors finally arrive, you will be able to create alternating styles without needing to add markup, using the :nth-child selector:

```
tr:nth-child(odd) {
  background-color: #edf5ff;
}
```

Unfortunately at the time of writing, no major browser supports this selector. Instead, if you don't want to manually add a class to each alternating row in your (X)HTML, you could apply the class using the DOM. For more information on this and many other DOM scripting techniques, check out *Dom Scripting: Web Design with JavaScript and the Document Object Model*, by Jeremy Keith (friends of ED, 2005; www.domscripting.com).

Finally, you can create some extra visual feedback by allowing the rows to change color when they are hovered over. However, you do not want the row containing the table headings to change color, so this needs to be overridden:

```
tr:hover {
  background-color:#3d80df;
  color: #fff;
}

thead tr:hover {
  background-color: transparent;
  color: inherit;
}
```

Unfortunately, IE 6 and below does not support the :hover dynamic pseudo-class on any elements other than the anchor element. However, as this is an embellishment rather than an important feature, it is not much of a problem. Users of more modern browsers will appreciate the added usability benefits, while those using IE 6 and below will be unaware that they are missing anything.

You now have a beautifully styled data table that is easy for both sighted users and those using assistive devices to use and understand.

Simple form layout

Short and relatively simple forms are easiest to fill in when the form labels appear vertically above their associated form elements. Users can simply move down the form step by step, reading each label and completing the following form element. This method works best on short forms collecting relatively simple and predictable information such as contact details (see Figure 6-4).

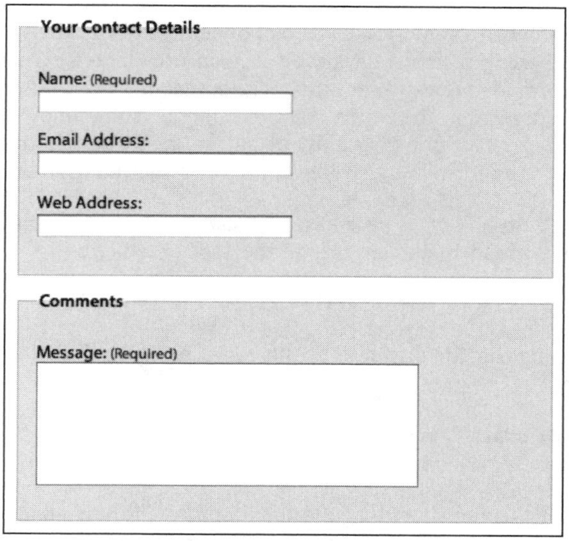

Figure 6-4. Simple form layout

Useful form elements

HTML provides a number of useful elements that can help add structure and meaning to a form. The first one of these is the fieldset element. Fieldsets are used for grouping related blocks of information. In Figure 6-4, two fieldsets are being used: one for the contact details and one for the comments. Most user agents apply a thin border around fieldsets, which can be turned off by setting the border property to none. Unfortunately, Opera 7 and below has somewhat buggy fieldset behavior and the only way to turn borders off is to set them to be transparent:

```
fieldset {
   border: solid 0 transparent;
}
```

To identify the purpose of each fieldset, you can use a legend element. Legends act a little like a fieldset's heading, usually appearing vertically centered with the top of the fieldset and indented a little to the right. Unfortunately, legends are notoriously difficult to style because of the inconsistent way browsers place them. Some browsers, like Firefox and Safari, use padding to create a small indent. However, other browsers, such as Opera and IE, have large default indents that are not controllable using padding, margins, or even positioning. As such, if you choose to use legends you will have to accept a certain amount of variation between browsers.

Form labels

Lastly, the label element can help add structure and increase the accessibility of your forms. As the name suggests, this element is used to add a meaningful and descriptive label to each form element. In many browsers, clicking on the label element will cause the associated form element to gain focus. The real benefit of using labels is to increase form usability for people using assistive devices. If a form uses labels, screenreaders will correctly associate a form element with its label. Without labels, the screenreader will have to "guess" which text relates to which form element, sometimes getting it wrong. Screenreader users can also bring up a list of all the labels in a form, allowing them to audibly scan through the form in much the same way a sighted user would.

Associating a label with a form is very easy and can be done in one of two ways: either implicitly, by nesting the form element inside the label element:

```
<label>email <input name="email" type="text"/><label>
```

or explicitly by setting the for attribute of the label equal to the id name of the associated form element:

```
<label for="email">email<label>
<input name="email" id="email" type="text"/>
```

You will notice that this input, and all the form controls in this chapter, contain both a name and an id attribute. The id attribute is required to create the association between the form input and the label, while the name is required so that the form data can be sent back to the server.

Labels associated with form controls using the for attribute don't need to be near those controls in the source code; they could be in a completely different part of the document. However, from a structural point of view this isn't wise, and should be avoided unless there is a compelling reason to do so.

The basic layout

Using these three structural elements you can start laying out your form by marking up the contents of the first fieldset. The unstyled form can be seen in Figure 6-5.

```
<fieldset>
  <legend>Your Contact Details</legend>
  <p>
    <label for="author">Name:</label>
```

```
      <input name="author" id="author" type="text" />
    </p>
    <p>
      <label for="email">Email Address:</label>
      <input name="email" id="email" type="text" />
    </p>
    <p>
      <label for="url">Web Address:</label>
      <input name="url" id="url" type="text" />
    </p>
  </fieldset>
```

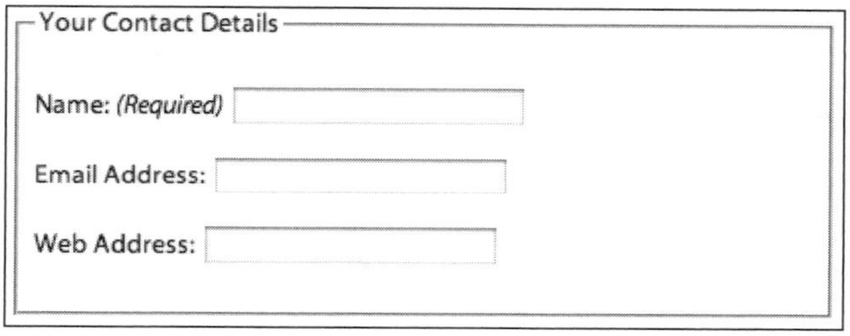

Figure 6-5. Unstyled form

This example sees form labels and elements nested inside paragraph elements. With CSS turned off, the form is still legible as each row is visually separated by whitespace. However, there is some discussion as to whether paragraphs should be used in form layouts, as they are not paragraphs of text. If in doubt, you can always use div *elements instead.*

First, you will need to set the general styles for the fieldset and legend elements. The fieldsets must be vertically separated using margins, and the contents can be given breathing space using padding. To highlight the fieldsets, you can give them a light background with a slightly darker, 1-pixel border. Try not to make the background too dark, though, as this can add too much visual weight to the form, making it more difficult to comprehend. Making the legends bold can also help break up the information and make it easier to digest.

```
fieldset {
  margin: 1em 0;
  padding: 1em;
  border : 1px solid #ccc;
  background: #f8f8f8;
}

legend {
  font-weight: bold;
}
```

121

Positioning the labels so they appear vertically above the form elements is actually very simple. Labels are inline elements by default. However, setting their display property to block will cause them to generate their own block box, forcing the input elements onto the line below. The width of text input boxes varies from browser to browser, so for consistency you should explicitly set the width of your text input boxes. In this example pixels are used, but you could of course use ems to create a more scalable form layout.

```
label {
  display: block;
}

input {
  width: 200px;
}
```

Other elements

This layout works equally well for other form elements such as text areas:

```
<fieldset>
  <legend>Comments</legend>
  <p>
    <label for="text">Message: </label>
    <textarea name="text" id="text" cols="20" rows="10">
    </textarea>
  </p>
</fieldset>
```

The dimensions of text areas also vary across browsers, so it is a good idea to set their widths and heights for consistency also:

```
textarea {
  width: 300px;
  height: 100px;
}
```

Unlike text areas and text inputs, radio buttons and check boxes need to be handled differently. Rather than having their labels above them, these elements usually have their labels to the right of them. When stacked vertically all the elements are left aligned, creating a nice solid vertical and making them easier to select (see Figure 6-6).

Figure 6-6. Radio button layout

Earlier in this example, the width of the text boxes was defined by applying a width to the input element. However, the input element covers other form widgets such as check boxes, radio buttons, and submit buttons, as well as the more common text input box. As such, by setting the input element to be 200 pixels wide, all of the input elements will be 200 pixels.

One way around this problem is to use the attribute selector to target particular types of form element. So instead of setting all the inputs to 200 pixels, you could specifically target text inputs:

```
input[type="text"] {
  width: 200px;
}
```

Unfortunately, the attribute selector is only supported on more modern browsers and does not work in IE 6 and below. Until the attribute selector is more widely supported; the best way to distinguish between input elements is to give them a class.

So for instance, in this example you could give radio buttons a class name of radio:

```
<fieldset>
  <legend>Remember Me</legend>
  <p>
    <input id="remember-yes" class="radio" name="remember" type="radio"➥
                      value="yes" />
    <label for="remember-yes">Yes</label>
  </p>
  <p>
    <input id="remember-no" class="radio" name="remember" type="radio"➥
                      value="no" checked="checked" />
    <label for="remember-no">No</label>
  </p>
</fieldset>
```

You could then override the previously set input width by setting the width of radio buttons to auto. The same can be done for check boxes and submit buttons:

```
input.radio, input.checkbox, input.submit {
  width: auto;
}
```

Floating the radio buttons left will bring them back on the same level as their labels, and a small amount of right margin will provide the desired spacing between the two elements:

```
input.radio {
  float: left;
  margin-right: 1em;
}
```

6

Embellishments

The layout is now complete, but you can incorporate a few nice additions for more advanced browsers. For instance, you could help users easily anchor themselves to the form field they are filling in by changing the element's background color when it receives focus:

```
input:focus, textarea:focus {
  background: #ffc;
}
```

You can also harmonize the look of the text field and text area elements by giving them custom borders. This is particularly useful for Firefox, which renders the bottom and right borders on these elements as white, causing them to lose definition when on a white background (see Figure 6-7).

Figure 6-7. The bottom and left borders of text inputs and text areas in Firefox are white, causing them to lose definition on white backgrounds.

In this example an attribute selector is used to target the text inputs as this style is mostly for the benefit of Firefox, which understands this selector.

```
input[type="text"], textarea {
  border-top: 2px solid #999;
  border-left: 2px solid #999;
  border-bottom: 1px solid #ccc;
  border-right: 1px solid #ccc;
}
```

Required fields

Many forms contain fields that must be filled in. You can indicate these required fields by placing styled text, or an asterisk, next to them. Because this information is emphasizing the field's required status, the most appropriate element for this information is an em or strong element:

```
<p>
<label for="author">Name:<em class="required">(required)</em>/label>
<input name="author" id="author" type="text" />
</p>
```

You can then style this information however you want. In this example I'm reducing the font size and making the text red:

```
.required {
  font-size: 0.75em;
  color:#760000;
}
```

And there you have it: a simple yet attractive-looking form layout using pure CSS.

Complicated form layout

For longer and more complicated forms, vertical space starts to become an issue, as does the ease of scanning. To improve scanning and reduce the amount of vertical space used, it makes sense to position the labels and form elements horizontally, rather than vertically above one another. Creating a form such as the one in Figure 6-8 is actually very simple and uses almost exactly the same code as the previous example.

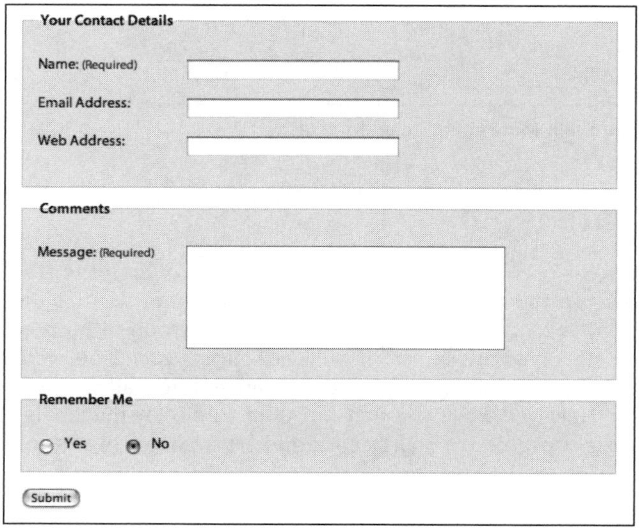

Figure 6-8. Horizontal form alignment

The only difference between this and the previous example is that, instead of setting the label to be a block-level element, you float the labels left instead. You also need to give the label a width so that all of the form elements line up nicely:

```
label {
    float: left;
    width: 10em;
}
```

This width causes a large gap between the radio buttons, so to tighten this up you will need to set the width on these labels explicitly. In this example all of the input elements in the "remember me" fieldset are radio buttons. As such, this fieldset can be given an ID and the width on all the enclosed labels is simply overridden. However, if this was not the case, you could simply add a class to the labels or their parent paragraphs instead:

```
#remember-me label {
    width: 4em;
}
```

Forms are rarely as simple as the one in Figure 6-8, and you will often need to create exceptions to your basic form styling rules to handle things such as multiple form widgets on a single line, or columns of check boxes or radio buttons (see Figure 6-9). The next couple of sections will explain how to handle these types of exceptions.

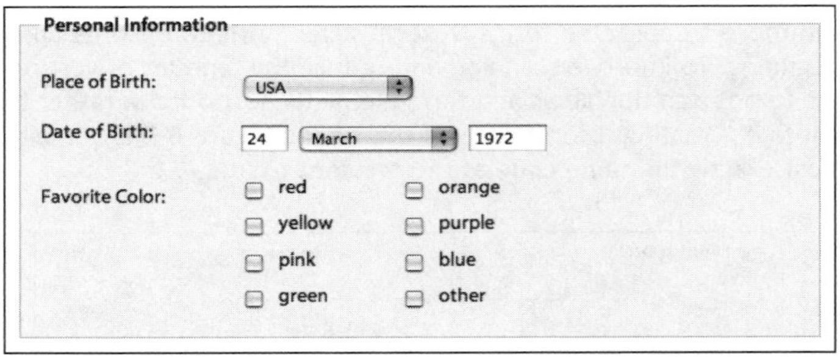

Figure 6-9. More complicated form layouts

Accessible date input

As you learned in the previous examples, form labels are important for the accessibility of your forms. However, there are situations when you may not want to display a label for every element. For instance, in Figure 6-9 you can see a group of form elements for collecting date information. In this situation visually displaying each label would be overkill, as it would split the date of birth up into three separate entities rather than being perceived as a single entity. However, while you may not want to display the labels, it is still important that the labels appear in the source code and are available to screenreaders.

```
<p>
  <label for="dateOfBirth">Date of Birth:</label>
  <input name="dateOfBirth" id="dateOfBirth" type="text" />
  <label id="monthOfBirthLabel" for="monthOfBirth">➥
  Month of Birth:</label>
  <select name="monthOfBirth" id="monthOfBirth">
    <option value="1">January</option>
    <option value="2">February</option>
    <option value="3">March</option>
  </select>
  <label id="yearOfBirthLabel" for="yearOfBirth">Year of Birth:</label>
  <input name="yearOfBirth" id="yearOfBirth" type="text" />
</p>
```

To create this layout you first need to hide the "month of birth" and "year of birth" labels. Setting the labels' display property to none would stop the labels from displaying, but it would also prevent many screenreaders from accessing them. Instead, you can position the labels off screen using a large negative text indent. In the generic form style we created earlier, labels have been given a set width. To prevent the labels from affecting the layout, the width needs to be zeroed down for these labels as well:

```
#monthOfBirthLabel, #yearOfBirthLabel {
  text-indent: -1000em;
  width: 0;
}
```

The various form controls can then be sized individually and given margins to control their horizontal spacing:

```
input#dateOfBirth {
  width: 3em;
  margin-right: 0.5em;
}

select#monthOfBirth {
  width: 10em;
  margin-right: 0.5em;
}

input#yearOfBirth {
  width: 5em;
}
```

6

Multicolumn check boxes

Creating a two-column layout for large groups of check boxes or radio buttons is a little more involved. Labels only work for individual elements, not groups of elements. Ideally we would wrap the whole group in a fieldset and use the legend to act like a label for the group. Unfortunately, due to the inconsistent way browsers handle the positioning of legends, this is not currently a practical solution. So until the browsers offer more consistent support, the best option is to use a heading element instead.

To create the column effect, the check boxes are split into two sets, and each set is wrapped in a div. These elements are then grouped together by wrapping them in a fieldset with a descriptive ID:

```
<fieldset id="favoriteColor">
  <h2>Favorite Color:</h2>
  <div>
    <p>
      <input class="checkbox" id="red" name="red" type="checkbox"➥
                  value="red" />
      <label>red</label>
      ...
    </p>
  </div>
  <div>
    <p>
      <input class="checkbox" id="orange" name="orange"
type="checkbox"~CCC
                  value="orange" />
      <label>orange</label>
    </p>
    ...
  </div>
  <br class="clear" />
</fieldset>
```

Because a generic fieldset style has already been created, the first thing you need to do is override those styles, zeroing down the padding and margin, removing the borders and setting the background color to be transparent:

```
fieldset#favoriteColor {
  margin: 0;
  padding: 0;
  border: none;
  background: transparent;
}
```

The heading is going to act like a label so it needs to be floated left and given a width of 10ems like the other labels. The headline also needs to look like a label, so the font weight needs to be set to normal and the font size needs to be reduced. The two-column layout can then be created by giving the divs a width and floating them left:

```
#favoriteColor h2 {
  width: 10em;
  float: left;
  font-size: 1em;
  font-weight: normal;
}

#favoriteColor div {
  width: 8em;
  float: left;
}
```

Because the divs are being floated, they no longer take up any space and appear to spill out of the fieldset (see Figure 6-10).

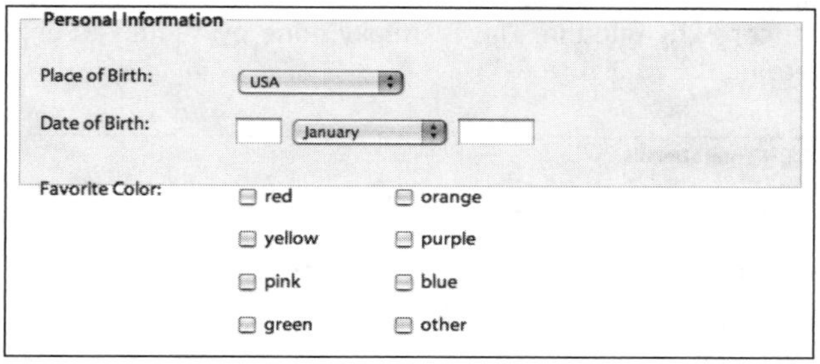

Figure 6-10. The floated divs spill out of the parent fieldset.

To force the fieldset to enclose these floats, a clearing element has been inserted after the second div. In this case a <br /> element is used with a class of clear:

```
.clear {
  clear: both;
}
```

All the labels in this form have been floated left and set to be 10ems wide. However, the labels for the check boxes do not need to be floated and require a much smaller width. As such, you will want to reduce the width of the labels and prevent them from floating. Firefox seems to treat the unfloated labels as block-level elements, forcing the check boxes onto the next line. To avoid this problem you need to explicitly set the display property to inline:

```
#favoriteColor label {
  width: 3em;
  float: none;
  display: inline;
}
```

The labels and check boxes are now all nicely aligned. However, the default margin on each paragraph is causing too much vertical space. To tighten up the spacing, you can reduce the top and bottom margins of the paragraphs:

```
#favoriteColor p {
    margin: 0.3em 0;
}
```

And there you have a relatively complex form layout. The basic form style takes care of the general layout, and then exceptions can be handled on an individual basis by overriding these styles.

Form feedback

Forms will usually require some type of feedback message to highlight fields that have been missed or incorrectly filled in. This is usually done by adding an error message next to the appropriate field (see Figure 6-11).

Figure 6-11. Example of form feedback

To produce this effect you could wrap your feedback text in a span and place it after the text input in the source code. However, for everything to line up correctly, both the span and the preceding input would need to be floated. This will have an effect on the behavior of the enclosing paragraph, which in turn will have an effect on the whole layout. Furthermore, many screenreaders will ignore text between form elements, unless they are enclosed in a label. To avoid these problems, the best approach is to include the error message text inside the form label, and then position it using CSS:

```
<p>
    <label for="email">Email Address:
    <span class="feedback">Incorrect email address. Please try again.➥
    </span>
    </label>
    <input name="email" id="email" type="text" />
</p>
```

To position the feedback span, you first need to set the position of all of the paragraphs in the form to relative, thereby setting up a new positioning context. You can then position the feedback span absolutely, so it appears to the right of the text input:

```
form p {
  position: relative;
}

.feedback {
  position: absolute;
  margin-left: 11em;
  left: 200px;
  right :0;
}
```

Rather annoyingly, IE 6 and below incorrectly set the width of the feedback span to be the minimum width possible. To get around this problem, you need to set an explicit width for this browser. One way to do this is using the star HTML hack as detailed in Chapter 8:

```
* html .feedback{
  width: 10em;
}
```

You can then apply whatever styling you want to your feedback messages. In this case I have made the text bold red, and have applied a warning image to the left side of the message:

```
form p {
  position: relative;
}

.feedback {
  position: absolute;
  margin-left: 11em;
  left: 200px;
  font-weight: bold;
  color: #760000;
  padding-left: 18px;
  background: url(images/error.png) no-repeat left top;
}
```

You could also use this technique to provide positive feedback or advice on how to fill out particular parts of the form.

6

Summary

In this chapter you have learned how different form layouts can work in different situations. You can now lay out complicated forms using CSS, without harming a single table in the process. You have learned how tables should be used, for data rather than layout, and have learned that data table design can be fun.

In the next chapter you will use everything you have learned so far to start building CSS-based layouts.

7 LAYOUT

One of the major benefits of CSS is the ability to control page layout without needing to use presentational markup. However, CSS layout has gained a rather undeserved reputation of being difficult, particularly among those new to the language. This is partly due to browser inconsistencies, but mostly due to a proliferation of different layout techniques available on the Web. It seems that every CSS author has their own technique for creating multicolumn layouts, and new CSS developers will often use a technique without really understanding how it works. This "black box" approach to CSS layout may get quick results, but ultimately stunts the developer's understanding of the language.

All these CSS layout techniques rely on three basic concepts: positioning, floating, and margin manipulation. The different techniques really aren't that different, and if you understand the core concepts, it is relatively easy to create your own layouts with little or no hassle.

In this chapter you will learn about

- Horizontally centering a design on a page
- Creating two- and three-column float-based layouts
- Creating fixed-width, liquid, and elastic layouts
- Making columns stretch to the full height of the available space

Centering a design

Long lines of text can be difficult and unpleasant to read. As modern monitors continue to grow in size, the issue of screen readability is becoming increasingly important. One way designers have attempted to tackle this problem is by centering their designs. Rather than spanning the full width of the screen, centered designs span only a portion of the screen, creating shorter and easier-to-read line lengths.

Centered designs are very fashionable at the moment, so learning how to center a design in CSS is one of the first things most developers want to learn. There are two basic methods for centering a design: one uses auto margins and the other uses positioning and negative margins.

Centering a design using auto margins

Say you have a typical layout where you wish to center a wrapper div horizontally on the screen:

```
<body>
  <div id="wrapper">
  </div>
</body>
```

To do this you simply define the width of your wrapper div and then set the horizontal margins to auto:

```
#wrapper {
  width: 720px;
  margin: 0 auto;
}
```

In this example I have decided to fix the width of my wrapper div in pixels, so that it fits nicely on an 800×600 resolution screen. However, you could just as easily set the width as a percentage of the body or relative to the size of the text using ems.

This works on all modern browsers. However, IE 5.x and IE 6 in quirks mode doesn't honor auto margins. Luckily, IE misunderstands text-align: center, centering everything instead of just the text. You can use this to your advantage by centering everything in the body tag, including the wrapper div, and then realigning the contents of the wrapper back to the left:

```
body {
  text-align: center;
}

#wrapper {
  width: 720px;
  margin: 0 auto;
  text-align: left;
}
```

Using the text-align property in this way is a hack—but a fairly innocuous hack that has no adverse effect on your code. The wrapper now appears centered in IE as well as more standards-compliant browsers (see Figure 7-1).

Figure 7-1. Centering a design using auto margins

There is one final thing that needs to be done in order for this method to work smoothly in all browsers. In Netscape 6, when the width of the browser window is reduced below the width of the wrapper, the left side of the wrapper spills off the side of the page and cannot be accessed. To keep this from happening, you need to give the body element a minimum width equal to or slightly wider than the width of the wrapper element:

```
body {
    text-align: center;
    min-width: 760px;
}

#wrapper {
    width: 720px;
    margin: 0 auto;
    text-align: left;
}
```

Now if you try to reduce the width of the window below the width of the wrapper div, scroll bars will appear, allowing you to access all of the content.

Centering a design using positioning and negative margins

The auto margin method of centering is by far the most common approach, but it does involve using a hack to satisfy IE 5.x. It also requires you to style two elements rather than just the one. Because of this, some people prefer to use positioning and negative margins instead.

You start as you did before, by defining the width of the wrapper. You then set the position property of the wrapper to relative and set the left property to 50%. This will position the left edge of the wrapper in the middle of the page.

```
#wrapper {
    width: 720px;
    position: relative;
    left: 50%;
}
```

However, you don't want the left edge of the wrapper centered—you want the middle of the wrapper centered. You can do this by applying a negative margin to the left side of the wrapper, equal to half the width of the wrapper. This will move the wrapper half its width to the left, centering it on screen:

```
#wrapper {
    width: 720px;
    position: relative;
    left: 50%;
    margin-left: -360px;
}
```

Your choice of centering technique comes down to personal taste. However, it is always useful to have several techniques up your sleeve, as you never know when one may come in handy.

Float-based layouts

There are a few different ways of doing CSS-based layout, including absolute positioning and using negative margins. I find float-based layouts the easiest method to use. As the name suggests, in a float-based layout you simply set the width of the elements you want to position, and then float them left or right.

Because floated elements no longer take up any space in the flow of the document, they no longer appear to exert any influence on the surrounding block boxes. To get around this, you will need to clear the floats at various points throughout the layout. Rather than continuously floating and clearing elements, it is quite common to float nearly everything, and then clear once or twice at strategic points throughout the document, such as the page footer.

Two-column floated layout

To create a simple two-column layout using floats, you need to start off with a basic (X)HTML framework. In this example the (X)HTML consists of a branding area, a content area, an area for the main navigation, and finally a page footer. The whole design is enclosed in a wrapper div, which will be horizontally centered using one of the preceding methods:

```
<div id="wrapper">
<div id="branding">
  ...
</div>
<div id="content">
  ...
</div>
<div id="mainNav">
  ...
</div>
<div id="footer">
  ...
</div>
</div>
```

The main navigation for this design will be on the left side of the page and the content will be on the right. However, I have chosen to put the content area above the navigation in the source order for usability and accessibility reasons. First, the main content is the most important thing on the page and so should come first in the document. Second, there is no point forcing screenreader users to trawl through a potentially long list of links before they get to the content if they don't have to.

Normally when people create float-based layouts, they float both columns left, and then create a gutter between the columns using margin or padding. When using this approach, the columns are packed tightly into the available space with no room to breathe. Although this wouldn't be a problem if browsers behaved themselves, buggy browsers can cause tightly packed layouts to break, forcing columns to drop below each other.

This can happen on IE because IE/Win honors the size of an element's content, rather than the size of the element itself. In standards-compliant browsers, if the content of an element gets too large, it will simply flow out of the box. However, on IE/Win, if the content of an element becomes too big, the whole element expands. If this happens in very tightly packed layouts, there is no longer enough room for the elements to sit next to each other, and one of the floats will drop. Other IE bugs, such as the 3-pixel text jog bug and the double-margin float bug (see Chapter 9), can also cause float dropping.

To prevent this from happening, you need to avoid cramming floated layouts into their containing elements. Rather than using horizontal margin or padding to create gutters, you can create a virtual gutter by floating one element left and one element right (see Figure 7-2). If one element inadvertently increases in size by a few pixels, rather than immediately running out of horizontal space and dropping down, it will simply grow into the virtual gutter.

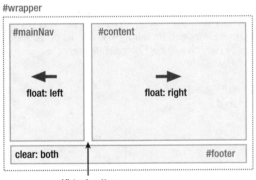

Figure 7-2. Creating a two-column layout using floats

The CSS for achieving this layout is very straightforward. You simply set the desired width of each column, then float the navigation left and the content right:

```
#content {
  width: 520px;
  float: right;
}

#mainNav {
  width: 180px;
  float: left;
}
```

Then, to ensure that the footer is positioned correctly below the two floats, the footer needs to be cleared:

```
#footer {
  clear: both;
}
```

The basic layout is now complete. Just a few small tweaks are required to tidy things up. First, the content in the navigation area is flush to the edges of the container and needs some breathing room. You could add horizontal padding directly to the navigation element, but this will invoke IE 5.x's proprietary box model. To avoid this, add the horizontal padding to the navigation area's content instead:

```
#mainNav {
  padding-top: 20px;
  padding-bottom: 20px;
}

#mainNav li {
  padding-left: 20px;
  padding-right: 20px;
}
```

The right side of the content area is also flush to the right edge of its container and needs some breathing room. Again, rather than apply padding directly to the element, you can apply padding to the content and avoid having to deal with IE's box model problems:

```
#content h1, #content h2, #content p {
  padding-right: 20px;
}
```

And there you have it: a simple, two-column CSS layout (see Figure 7-3).

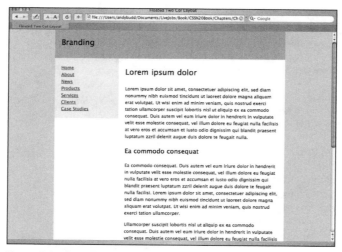

Figure 7-3. Floated two-column layout

Three-column floated layout

The HTML needed to create a three-column layout is very similar to that used by the two-column layout, the only difference being the addition of two new divs inside the content div: one for the main content and one for the secondary content.

```
<div id="content">
<div id="mainContent">
…
</div>
<div id="secondaryContent">
…
</div>
</div>
```

Using the same CSS as the two-column technique, you can float the main content left and the secondary content right, inside the already floated content div (see Figure 7-4). This essentially divides the second content column in two, creating your three-column effect.

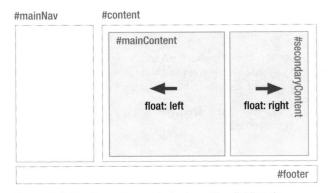

Figure 7-4. Creating a three-column layout by dividing the content column into two columns

As before, the CSS for this is very simple. You just set your desired widths and then float the main content left and the secondary content right:

```
#mainContent {
  width: 320px;
  float: left;
}


#secondaryContent {
  width: 180px;
  float: right;
}
```

You can tidy up the layout slightly by removing the padding from the content element and applying it to the content of the secondary content instead:

```css
#secondaryContent h1, #secondaryContent h2,
  #secondaryContent p {
  padding-left: 20px;
  padding-right: 20px;
}
```

This leaves you with a nice and solid three-column layout (see Figure 7-5).

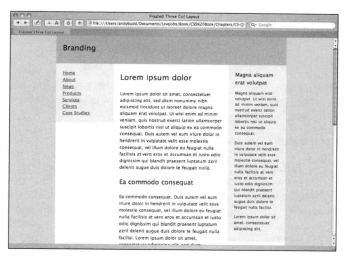

Figure 7-5. Three-column layout using floats

Fixed-width, liquid, and elastic layout

So far, all the examples have used widths defined in pixels. This type of layout is known as fixed-width layout, or sometimes "ice layout" due to its rigid nature. Fixed-width layouts are very common as they give the developer more control over layout and positioning. If you set the width of your design to be 720 pixels wide, it will always be 720 pixels. If you then want a branding image spanning the top of your design, you know it needs to be 720 pixels wide to fit. Knowing the exact width of each element allows you to lay them out precisely and know where everything will be. This predictability makes fixed-width layout by far the most common layout method around.

However, fixed-width designs have their downsides. First, because they are fixed, they are always the same size no matter what your window size. As such, they don't make good use of the available space. On large screen resolutions, designs created for 800×600 can appear tiny and lost in the middle of the screen. Conversely, a design created for a 1024×760 screen will cause horizontal scrolling on smaller screen resolutions. With an increasingly diverse range of screen sizes to contend with, fixed-width design is starting to feel like a poor compromise.

Another issue with fixed-width design revolves around line lengths and text legibility. Fixed-width layouts usually work well with the browser default text size. However, you only have to increase the text size a couple of steps before sidebars start running out of space and the line lengths get too short to comfortably read.

To work around these issues, you could choose to use liquid or elastic layout instead of fixed-width layout.

Liquid layouts

With liquid layouts, dimensions are set using percentages instead of pixels. This allows liquid layouts to scale in relation to the browser window. As the browser window gets bigger, the columns get wider. Conversely, as the window gets smaller, the columns will reduce in width. Liquid layouts make for very efficient use of space, and the best liquid layouts aren't even noticeable.

However, liquid layouts are not without their own problems. At small window widths, line lengths can get incredibly narrow and difficult to read. This is especially true in multicolumn layouts. As such, it may be worth adding a min-width in pixels or ems to prevent the layout from becoming too narrow.

Conversely, if the design spans the entire width of the browser window, line lengths can become long and difficult to read. There are a couple of things you can do to help avoid this problem. First, rather than spanning the whole width, you could make the wrapper span just a percentage—say, 85 percent. You could also consider setting the padding and margin as percentages as well. That way, the padding and margin will increase in width in relation to the window size, stopping the columns from getting too wide, too quickly. Lastly, for very severe cases, you could also choose to set the maximum width of the wrapper in pixels to prevent the content from getting ridiculously wide on oversized monitors.

> Be aware that IE 5.x on Windows incorrectly calculates padding in relation to the width of the element rather than the width of the parent element. Because of this, setting padding as a percentage can produce inconsistent results in those browsers.

You can use these techniques to turn the previous fixed-width, three-column layout into a fluid, three-column layout. Start by setting the width of the wrapper as a percentage of the overall width of the window. In this example I have chosen 85 percent as it produces good results on a range of screen sizes. Next, set the width of the navigation and content areas as a percentage of the wrapper width. After a bit of trial and error, setting the navigation area to be 23 percent and the content area to 75 percent produced nice results. This leaves a 2-percent virtual gutter between the navigation and the wrapper to deal with any rounding errors and width irregularities that may occur:

```
#wrapper {
  width: 85%;
}

#mainNav {
  width: 23%;
```

```
    float: left;
}

#content {
  width: 75%;
  float: right;
}
```

You then need to set the widths of the columns in the content area. This gets a bit trickier as the widths of the content divs are based on the width of the content element and not the overall wrapper. If you want the secondaryContent to be the same width as the main navigation, you need to work out what 23 percent of the wrapper is in terms of the width of the content area. This is 23 (width of the nav) divided by 75 (width of the content area), multiplied by 100—which works out at around 31 percent. You will want the gutter between the content columns to be the same width as the gutter between the navigation and content areas. Using the same method, this works out to be around 3 percent, meaning that the width of the main content area should be 66 percent:

```
#mainContent {
  width: 66%;
  float: left;
}

#secondaryContent {
  width: 31%;
  float: right;
}
```

This produces a liquid layout that is optimal at 1024×780 but is comfortable to read at both larger and smaller screen resolutions (see Figure 7-6).

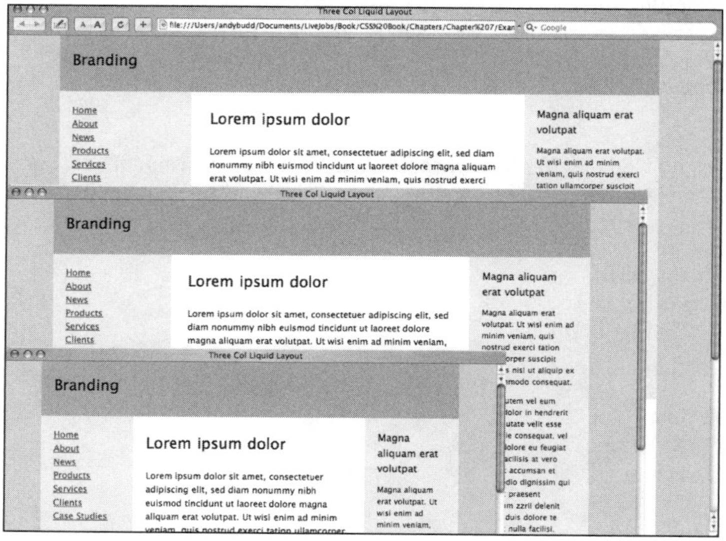

Figure 7-6. Three-column liquid layout at 800×600, 1024×768, and 1152×900

Because this layout scales so nicely, there isn't any need to add a `max-width` property. However, the content does start to get squashed at smaller sizes, so you could set a minimum width of 720px on the wrapper element if you liked.

Elastic layouts

While liquid layouts are useful for making the most of the available space, line lengths can still get uncomfortably long on large resolution monitors. Conversely, lines can become very short and fragmented in narrow windows or when the text size is increased a couple of steps. If this is a concern, then elastic layouts may be a possible solution.

Elastic layouts work by setting the width of elements relative to the font size instead of the browser width. By setting widths in ems, you ensure that when the font size is increased the whole layout scales. This allows you to keep line lengths to a readable size and is particularly useful for people with reduced vision or cognitive disorders.

Like other layout techniques, elastic layouts are not without their problems. Elastic layouts share some of their problems with fixed-width layouts, such as not making the most use of the available space. Also, because the whole layout increases when the text size is increased, elastic layouts can become much wider than the browser window, forcing the appearance of horizontal scroll bars. To combat this, it may be worth adding a `max-width` of 100% to the body tag. `max-width` isn't currently supported by IE 6 and below, but it is supported by standards-compliant browsers such as Safari and Firefox.

Elastic layouts are much easier to create than liquid layouts as all of the HTML elements essentially stay in the same place relative to each other; they just all increase in size. Turning a fixed-width layout into an elastic layout is a relatively simple task. The trick is to set the base font size so that 1em roughly equals 10 pixels.

The default font size on most browsers is 16 pixels. Ten pixels works out at 62.5 percent of 16 pixels, so setting the font size on the body to `62.5%` does the trick:

```
body {
   font-size: 62.5%;
}
```

Because 1em now equals 10 pixels at the default font size, we can convert our fixed-width layout into an elastic layout by converting all the pixel widths to em widths:

```
#wrapper {
  width: 72em;
  margin: 0 auto;
  text-align: left;
}

#mainNav {
  width: 18em;
  float: left;
}
```

```
#content {
  width: 52em;
  float: right;
}

#mainContent {
  width: 32em;
  float: left;
}

#secondaryContent {
  width: 18em;
  float: right;
}
```

This produces a layout that looks identical to the fixed-width layout at regular text sizes (see Figure 7-7), but scales beautifully as the text size is increased (see Figure 7-8).

Figure 7-7. Elastic layout at the default text size

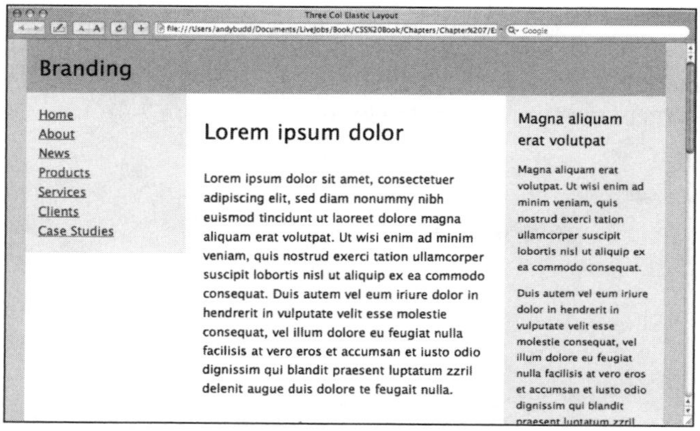

Figure 7-8. Elastic layout after the text size has been increased a few times

Elastic-liquid hybrid

Lastly, you could choose to create a hybrid layout that combines both elastic and liquid techniques. This hybrid approach works by setting the widths in ems, then setting the maximum widths as percentages:

```
#wrapper {
  width: 72em;
  max-width: 100%;
  margin: 0 auto;
  text-align: left;
}

#mainNav {
  width: 18em;
  max-width: 23%;
  float: left;
}

#content {
  width: 52em;
  max-width: 75%;
  float: right;
}

#mainContent {
  width: 32em;
  max-width: 66%;
  float: left;
}

#secondaryContent {
  width: 18em;
  max-width: 31%;
  float: right;
}
```

On browsers that support max-width, this layout will scale relative to the font size but will never get any larger than the width of the window (see Figure 7-9).

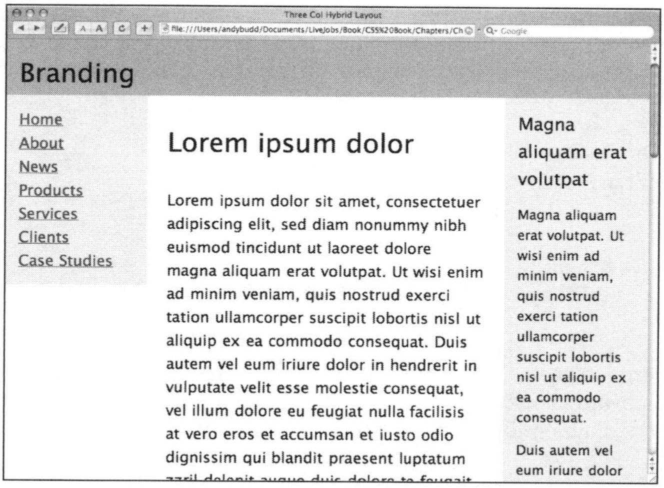

Figure 7-9. The elastic-liquid hybrid layout never scales larger than the browser window.

Liquid and elastic images

If you choose to use a liquid or an elastic layout, fixed-width images can have a drastic effect on your design. When the width of the layout is reduced, images will shift and may interact negatively with each other. Images will create natural minimum widths, preventing some elements from reducing in size. Other images will break out of their containing elements, wreaking havoc on finely tuned designs. Increasing the width of the layout can also have dramatic consequences, creating unwanted gaps and unbalancing designs. But never fear—there are a few ways to avoid such problems.

For images that need to span a wide area, such as those found in the site header or branding areas, consider using a background image rather than an image element. As the branding element scales, more or less of the background image will be revealed:

```
#branding {
  height: 171px;
  background: url(images/branding.png) no-repeat left top;
}

<div id="branding"></div>
```

If the image needs to be on the page as an image element, try setting the width of the container element to 100% and the overflow property to hidden. The image will be truncated so that it fits inside the branding element but will scale as the layout scales:

```css
#branding {
  width: 100%;
  overflow: hidden;
}
```

```html
<div id="branding">
  <img src="images/branding.png" width="1600" height="171" />
</div>
```

For regular content images, you will probably want them to scale vertically as well as horizontally to avoid clipping. You can do this by adding an image element to the page without any stated dimensions. You then set the percentage width of the image, and add a max-width the same size as the image to prevent pixelization.

> Remember that max-width only works in more modern browsers such as Safari and Firefox. If you are concerned about the image pixelating in older browsers, make the image as large as you will ever need it to be.

For example, say you wanted to create a news story style with a narrow image column on the left and a larger text column on the right. The image needs to be roughly a quarter of the width of the containing box, with the text taking up the rest of the space. You can do this by simply setting the width of the image to 25% and then setting the max-width to be the size of the image—in this case 200 pixels wide:

```css
.news img {
  width: 25%;
  max-width: 200px;
  float: left;
  padding: 2%;
}

.news p {
  width: 68%;
  float: right;
  padding: 2% 2% 2% 0;
}
```

As the news element expands or contracts, the image and paragraphs will also expand or contract, maintaining their visual balance (see Figure 7-10). However, on standards-compliant browsers, the image will never get larger than its actual size.

Lorem ipsum dolor sit amet, consectetuer adipiscing elit, sed diam nonummy nibh euismod tincidunt ut laoreet dolore magna aliquam erat volutpat. Ut wisi enim ad minim veniam, quis nostrud exerci tation ullamcorper suscipit lobortis nisl ut aliquip ex ea commodo consequat. Duis autem vel eum iriure dolor in hendrerit in vulputate velit esse molestie consequat, vel illum dolore eu feugiat nulla facilisis at vero eros et accumsan et iusto odio dignissim.

Lorem ipsum dolor sit amet, consectetuer adipiscing elit, sed diam nonummy nibh euismod tincidunt ut laoreet dolore magna aliquam erat volutpat. Ut wisi enim ad minim veniam, quis nostrud exerci tation ullamcorper suscipit lobortis nisl ut aliquip ex ea commodo consequat. Duis autem vel eum iriure dolor in hendrerit in vulputate velit esse molestie consequat, vel illum dolore eu feugiat nulla facilisis at vero eros et accumsan et iusto odio dignissim.

Lorem ipsum dolor sit amet, consectetuer adipiscing elit, sed diam nonummy nibh euismod tincidunt ut laoreet dolore magna aliquam erat volutpat. Ut wisi enim ad minim veniam, quis nostrud exerci tation ullamcorper suscipit lobortis nisl ut aliquip ex ea commodo consequat. Duis autem vel eum iriure dolor in hendrerit in vulputate velit esse molestie consequat, vel illum dolore eu feugiat nulla facilisis at vero eros et accumsan et iusto odio dignissim.

Figure 7-10. Giving images a percentage width allows them to scale nicely in relation to their surroundings.

Faux columns

You may have noticed that the navigation and secondary content areas on all these layouts have been given a light gray background. Ideally the background would stretch the full height of the layout, creating a column effect. However, because the navigation and secondary content areas don't span the full height, neither do their backgrounds.

To create the column effect, you need to create fake columns by applying a repeating background image to an element that does span the full height of the layout, such as a wrapper div. Dan Cederholm coined the term "faux column" to describe this technique.

Starting with the fixed-width, two-column layout, you can simply apply a vertically repeating background image, the same width as the navigation area, to the wrapper element (see Figure 7-11):

```
#wrapper {
  background: #fff url(images/nav-bg-fixed.gif) repeat-y left top;
}
```

Figure 7-11. Faux fixed-width column

For the three-column fixed width layout, you can use a similar approach. This time, however, your repeating background image needs to span the whole width of the wrapper and include both columns (see Figure 7-12). Applying this image in the same way as before creates a lovely faux two-column effect (see Figure 7-13).

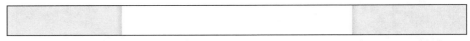

Figure 7-12. Background image used to create the faux three-column effect

Figure 7-13. Faux three-column effect

Creating faux columns for fixed-width designs is relatively easy, as you always know the size of the columns and their position. Creating faux columns for fluid layouts is a little more complicated; the columns change shape and position as the browser window is scaled. The trick to fluid faux columns lies in the use of percentages to position the background image.

If you set a background position using pixels, the top-left corner of the image is positioned from the top-left corner of the element by the specified number of pixels. With percentage positioning, it is the corresponding point on the image that gets positioned. So if you set a vertical and horizontal position of 20 percent, you are actually positioning a point 20 percent from the top left of the image, 20 percent from the top left of the parent element (see Figure 7-14).

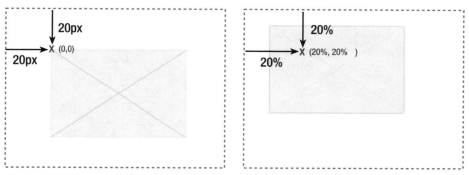

Figure 7-14. When positioning using percentages, the corresponding position on the image is used.

This is very useful as it allows you to create background images with the same horizontal proportions as your layout, and then position them where you want the columns to appear.

To create a faux column for the navigation area, you start by creating a very wide background image. In this example, I have created an image that is 2000 pixels wide and 5 pixels high. Next you need to create an area on the background image to act as the faux column. The navigation element has been set to be 23 percent of the width of the wrapper, so you need to create a corresponding area on the background image that is 23 percent wide. For a background image that is 2000 pixels wide, the faux column part of the image needs to be 460 pixels wide. Output this image as a GIF, making sure that the area not covered by the faux column is transparent.

The right edge of the faux column is now 23 percent from the left side of the image. The right edge of the navigation element is 23 percent from the left edge of the wrapper element. That means if you apply the image as a background to the wrapper element, and set the horizontal position to be 23 percent, the right edge of the faux column will line up perfectly with the right edge of the navigation element.

```
#wrapper {
    background: #fff url(images/nav-faux-column.gif) repeat-y 23% 0;
}
```

You can create the background for the secondary content area using a similar method. The left edge of this faux column should start 77 percent from the left edge of the image, matching the position of the secondaryContent element relative to the wrapper. Because the wrapper element already has a background image applied to it, you will need to add a second wrapper element inside the first. You can then apply your second faux column background image to this new wrapper element.

```
#wrapper2 {
  background: url(images/secondary-faux-column.gif) repeat-y 77% 0;
}
```

If you have worked out your proportions correctly, you should be left with a beautiful three-column liquid layout with columns that stretch the height of the wrapper (see Figure 7-15).

Figure 7-15. Faux three-column layout

Summary

In this chapter you learned how to create simple two- and three-column fixed-width layouts using floats. You then learned how these layouts could be converted into liquid and elastic layouts with relative ease. You learned about some of the problems associated with liquid and elastic layouts and how liquid images and hybrid layouts can help solve some of these problems. Lastly, you saw how to create full height column effects on both fixed-width and liquid layouts, using vertically repeating background images. This chapter touched on some of the techniques used to create CSS-based layouts. However, there are a lot of techniques out there, enough to fill a whole book of their own.

One of the big problems developers face with CSS layouts is that of browser inconsistency. To get around browser rendering issues, various hacks and filters have been created. In the next chapter, you will learn about some of the better-known hacks and how to use them responsibly.

8 HACKS AND FILTERS

In an ideal world, properly coded CSS would work in every browser with CSS support. Unfortunately, we do not live in an ideal world, and browsers are littered with bugs and inconsistencies. To create pages that displayed the same across a variety of browsers, CSS developers had to get creative. By using bugs and unimplemented CSS, developers were able to selectively apply different rules to different browsers. Hacks and filters are a powerful weapon in a CSS developer's arsenal. However, with great power comes great responsibility. It is important to know about the various common hacks and how they work, but it is equally important to know when and when not to use them.

In this chapter you will learn about

- The difference between hacks and filters
- Good versus bad filters and how to use them responsibly
- IE conditional comments
- The star HTML filter
- The commented backslash filter and the Holly hack
- The backslash filter and the modified simplified box model hack (MSBMH)
- The !important and underscore filters
- The child and attribute filters

An introduction to hacks and filters

A CSS filter is a way of displaying or hiding rules or declarations from a particular browser or group of browsers. Filters rely on weaknesses in a browser such as parsing bugs and unimplemented or incorrectly implemented CSS to show or hide rules from that browser.

A CSS hack is simply an ugly and inelegant way of getting a browser to behave the way you want it to. CSS hacks are typically used to get around specific browser bugs such as IE's proprietary box model. Unfortunately, the term *hack* has rather negative connotations and implies that there is a better way of doing something when often there isn't. Therefore, some people favor the term *patch* to indicate that it is actually incorrect browser behavior that is being dealt with.

CSS hacks can use filters to apply one rule to one browser and a different rule to another. Alternatively, hacks can use incorrect CSS implementation to "trick" browsers into behaving the way you want them to. In essence, a CSS filter is a specific type of hack used for filtering different browsers. Unfortunately, most people tend to use the generic term *hack* to describe filters. As such, when people talk about CSS hacks, they are usually talking specifically about filters.

A warning about hacks and filters

As a language, CSS was designed to be very forward compatible. If a browser doesn't understand a particular selector, it will ignore the whole rule. Likewise, if it doesn't understand a particular property or value, it will ignore the whole declaration. This feature means that the addition of new selectors, properties, and values should have no adverse effect on older browsers.

You can use this feature to supply rules and declarations to more advanced browsers, safe in the knowledge that older browsers will degrade gracefully. When a new version of the browser is launched, if it now supports the CSS you were using as a filter, it should work as expected. If you are using the more advanced CSS to circumvent a problem in the older browsers, hopefully this problem will have been solved in the newer version. Because of this behavior, the use of unsupported CSS as a filtering mechanism is a relatively safe option. I say *relatively* because there is always a chance that the browser will support your new CSS but still exhibit the bug you were trying to fix.

Using filters that rely on parsing bugs is a slightly more dangerous route. This is because you are relying on a bug, not a feature. Similar to the previous method, if the parsing bug gets fixed but the bug you are trying to fix hasn't been addressed, you could end up with problems. However, more of a concern is that parsing bugs could find their way into newer versions of browsers. Say, for instance, a new version of Firefox has a particular parsing bug. If that bug is being used as a filter to supply IE with different width values to account for its proprietary box model, all of a sudden Firefox would inherit that width, potentially breaking a lot of sites.

It is also worth bearing in mind that some hacks and filters will invalidate your code. For instance, using a CSS 3 selector will fail the validator as it currently only validates against the CSS 2 spec. However, if several browsers support the selector, there is a good chance it will make it into the final specification. In situations like these, as long as you know that you are using valid CSS 3, the fact that your CSS fails to validate to CSS 2 probably is not a big deal. More worrisome are hacks that use illegal characters as they have the potential for causing all kinds of parsing errors in future, yet-to-be-developed browsers.

As a general rule, it is probably safer to use filters that rely on unsupported CSS, rather than ones that use some kind of browser bug.

Using hacks sensibly

There is a rather unfortunate overreliance on hacks and filters, especially among those new to CSS. When something does not work in a particular browser, many CSS developers will immediately employ a hack, seeing it as some kind of magic bullet. In fact, some developers seem to measure their expertise by the number of obscure hacks and filters they know.

However, not all CSS problems are the result of browser bugs. As you will see in Chapter 9, many problems arise from errors in your code or an incomplete understanding of the CSS specification. Even if a problem is the result of a browser bug, you may not need to resort to a hack. Unlike the printed page, the way a design is displayed on the Web has as much to do with the user and their setup as it has with the designer. If your design is off by 3 pixels in IE 5.0, as long as it doesn't seriously affect the rest of your site and the page is usable, the bug probably isn't worth fixing. If you do employ a hack to fix a minor display bug in an older browser, as well as making a lot of extra work for yourself, you could be building in problems for future browsers. Remember, it is the browser implementation of CSS that is the culprit here, not your site.

8

In CSS there are many ways to skin a template, so if something is causing a problem, try achieving the same effect another way. Many CSS errors are caused by overcomplicated code and markup. If you keep your code simple and clear, most hacks can be avoided.

If you have done your homework and realize that the only option is to employ some form of hack or filter, you need to do so in a sensible and controlled manner. If your CSS files are small and simple, and you only need to employ a couple of hacks, it is probably safe to place these hacks in your main CSS files. However, hacks are usually fairly complicated and can make your code more difficult to read. If your CSS files are long, or you need to use more than a couple of hacks, you may be best separating them into their own stylesheets. As well as making your code easier to read, if a hack starts causing problems in a future browser, you will know exactly where it is. Similarly, if you decide to drop support for a particular browser, removing the associated hacks is as simple as removing the CSS file.

To help you choose the correct filter for the job, several sites have published tables outlining which filters work in which browsers (see Figure 8-1). The best known and most up-to-date of these support charts can be found at Centricle (http://centricle.com/ref/css/filters/) and Dithered (www.dithered.com/css_filters/).

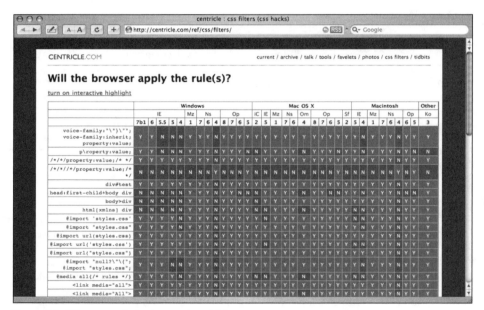

Figure 8-1. Filter support chart over at centricle.com

Filtering separate stylesheets

Putting your hacks into browser-specific CSS files and then using filters to send them to the required browsers can greatly simplify hack management. There are currently two main ways of achieving this. One way is to use parsing bugs to send particular CSS files to the desired browsers using the @import rule. The other way is to use IE conditional comments.

Internet Explorer conditional comments

Conditional comments are a proprietary, and thus nonstandard, Microsoft extension of regular (X)HTML comments. As the name suggests, conditional comments allow you to show blocks of code depending on a condition, such as a browser version. Despite being nonstandard, conditional comments appear to all other browsers as regular comments, and so are essentially harmless. Conditional comments first appeared in IE 5 on Windows and are supported by all subsequent versions of the Windows browser.

To deliver a specific stylesheet to all versions of IE 5 and above, you could place the following code in the head of your (X)HTML document:

```
<!-- [if IE]
<style type="text/css">
@import ("ie.css");
</style>
-->
```

Versions of IE 5 and above on Windows would receive the stylesheet ie.css while all other browsers would simply see some commented-out text. With conditional comments you could target a particular browser such as IE 5.0:

```
<!-- [if IE 5]
<style type="text/css">
@import ("ie50.css");
</style>
-->
```

You could also target sets of browsers such as IE 5.5 and greater:

```
<!-- [if gte IE 5.5000]
<style type="text/css">
@import ("ie55up.css");
</style>
-->
```

Or IE 5 and IE 5.5:

```
<!-- [if lt IE 6]
<style type="text/css">
@import ("ie.css");
</style>
-->
```

This technique works extremely well and is relatively simple to remember. The main downside is that these comments need to live in your HTML, not your CSS. If at some stage you wish to stop supporting a particular browser, you will need to remove the comments from every page. If this is a concern, you may want to look at Tantek Çelik's selection of filters, which we'll look at next.

8

Band pass filters

Tantek Çelik created a series of filters (http://tantek.com/CSS/Examples/) based on browser parsing errors that allow you to supply stylesheets to selected browsers using the @import rule. Because this is a CSS rule, all of these filters can live in a single CSS file, allowing all your filtered files to be controlled from one place. Separating your hacks into browser-specific CSS files can greatly simplify your hack management. If you decide to remove support for a specific browser, such as IE 5.0, you can simply remove the associated stylesheet, rather than having to trawl through lines of code.

To pass a CSS file to IE 5 and 5.5 on Windows, you can use Tantek's mid-pass filter:

```
@media tty {
 i{content:"\";/*" "*/}} @import 'ie5x.css'; /*";}
}/* */
```

This filter looks like a jumble of meaningless rules, and to many browsers that is exactly what it is. Browsers only capable of understanding CSS 1 will not recognize the @media rule and completely ignore it. More capable browsers will see a single declaration inside the @media rule, targeting the <i> element. Due to the existence of an escape character present before the second quote mark, the value of the content property is treated as a single string of meaningless characters. Essentially, modern browsers will see a rule that looks like this:

```
@media tty {
  i {
    content:"Blah, blah blah";
  }
}
```

> An escape character is a reserved character—usually a backslash—that causes the following reserved character to be ignored by the parser. So if you wanted to auto-generate a quote mark using the CSS content property, you would have to escape it, or it would prematurely close the open quote:
>
> blockquote:before {content: "\""}

The tty media type refers to terminals and teletype machines. Fortunately, no devices currently support this media type, so the whole rule is effectively ignored by compliant browsers.

However, IE 5.x/Win doesn't honor the escape character, and closes the content declaration prematurely. The following characters close both the <i> and @media rules, causing the @import rule to be applied. Any superfluous characters are commented out, and the whole rule looks like this to IE 5.x/Win:

```
@media tty {
  i{
```

```
    content:"blah";
    /* blah */
    }
}
@import 'ie5x.css';
/* blah */
```

This is all quite complicated, so luckily you don't need to know how these filters work; you just need to know how to use them.

In order to target a particular version of IE 5.x/Win, two variations of the mid-pass filter were created that exploited various bugs in those particular browsers. These were called the IE 5/Windows band pass filter:

```
@media tty {
  i{content:"\";/*" "*/}}; @import 'ie50win.css'; {;}/*";}
}/* */
```

and the IE 5.5/Windows band pass filter:

```
@media tty {
  i{content:"\";/*" "*/}}@m; @import 'ie55win.css'; /*";}
}/* */
```

The other browser you may want to explicitly target is IE 5.2 on the Mac. You can do this using Tantek's IE 5/Mac band pass filter, which exploits a different escaping bug, this time within comments:

```
/*\*//*/
@import "ie5mac.css";
/**/
```

IE 5/Mac incorrectly escapes the second asterisk, causing the @import rule to be applied. As such, IE 5/Mac sees something like this:

```
/* blah */
@import "ie5mac.css";
/**/
```

All other browsers correctly ignore the escaping element, as it is enclosed within a comment, and the @import rule is commented out. Essentially, all other browsers see a rule that looks like this:

```
/* blah *//*
  blah
*/
```

As with the other band pass filters, it is not necessary to understand how this filter works in order to use it. The beauty of these filters is they specifically target bugs in older, out-of-date browsers. Therefore, you should be able to use these filters safe in the knowledge that they shouldn't cause problems in newer browsers.

8

Filtering individual rules and declarations

If your CSS files are small and you only need to employ a few hacks, you can choose to add the associated filters into your main stylesheets. However, remember that all these rules and declaration-specific filters do add extra weight and complexity to your code.

The child selector hack

The safest filters rely on unimplemented CSS rather than browser bugs. As these filters use valid CSS selectors to apply valid declarations, they are not, strictly speaking, filters at all. They are simply valid CSS rules that certain browsers fail to understand. The first of these filters is known as the child selector hack. IE 6 and below on Windows does not support the child selector, so you can use it to hide rules from those browsers. For this filter to work, you must make sure that there is no whitespace before or after the child selector.

In this example, the child selector hack is being used to hide a transparent background PNG image from IE 5-6/Win:

```
html>body {
  background-image: url(bg.png);
}
```

IE 7 is expected to support the child selector. It is also expected to support native PNG transparency. By using the child selector filter in this way, you are building in forward compatibility by allowing newer versions of IE to view the transparent background without needing to revisit the code.

Attribute selector hack

Another interesting way to filter rules is by using the attribute selector. Many modern browsers such as Safari and Firefox support the attribute selector, but it is not supported by IE 6 and below. As such, you can use the attribute selector as a way of styling classes and IDs for more advanced browsers. In this example, the attribute selector is being used to apply a background PNG to the content div on more compliant browsers:

```
div[id="content"] {
  background-image: url(bg.png);
}
```

Again, both the attribute selector and PNG alpha transparency support are scheduled for IE 7, which means this method should work seamlessly when IE 7 launches.

This method can be used in some very creative ways. For instance, Andy Clarke used this technique to create two completely different themes for his personal site, www.allthatmalarkey.co.uk. More advanced browsers get a nice, high-definition color theme (see Figure 8-2), while less capable browsers get a retro two-tone theme (see Figure 8-3).

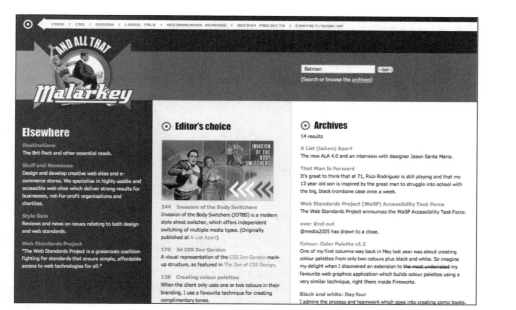

Figure 8-2. Using the attribute selector, Andy Clarke's personal site provides more advanced browsers with a colorful theme.

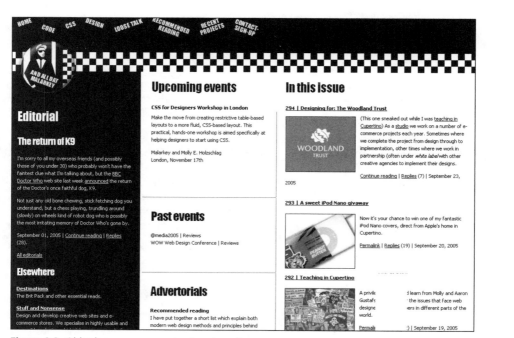

Figure 8-3. Older browsers see a retro two-tone theme.

The star HTML hack

One of the best-known and possibly most useful CSS filters is known as the star HTML hack. This filter is incredibly easy to remember and targets IE 6 and below. As you are aware, the HTML element is supposed to be the first, or root, element on a web page. However, all current versions of IE have an anonymous root element wrapping around the HTML element. By using the universal selector, you can target an HTML element enclosed inside another element. Because this only happens in IE 6 and below, you can apply specific rules to these browsers:

```
* html {
    font-size: small;
}
```

Adding a universal selector followed by an html type selector to the start of any regular CSS rule will hide that rule from everything other than IE. The most common way to use this filter is to set a rule that you want all browsers other than IE to apply, and then override that rule in IE using the star HTML hack. For example, IE renders 1-pixel dotted lines as ugly dashed lines by mistake. To avoid these ugly dashed lines, you could set the hover border style on your anchors to dotted but override this in IE, making them solid instead:

```
a:hover {
    border: 1px dotted black;
}

* html a:hover {
    border-style: solid;
}
```

It is very unlikely that this bug will appear other browsers, and it is expected to be fixed in IE 7. Therefore, the star HTML hack provides a relatively safe way of targeting IE 6 and below.

IE/Mac commented backslash hack

Another useful filter is known as the commented backslash hack. IE 5 on the Mac incorrectly allows escaping inside comments, so this filter works by adding a backslash in front of the closing comment identifier. All other browsers will ignore this escape and apply the following rules. However, IE 5/Mac will think that the comment is still open, ignoring everything until the next close comment string.

```
/* Hiding from IE5/Mac  \*/
#nav a {
    width: 5em;
}
/* End Hack */
```

This bug forms the basis of the IE 5/Mac band pass filter you saw earlier.

If you combine the star HTML and commented backslash filters, you get the Holly hack, named after its inventor, Holly Bergevin. By combining these two rules, it is possible to apply rules to IE 6 and below on Windows:

```
/* Hiding from IE5/Mac  \*/
* html {
  height: 1px;
}
/* End Hack */
```

This can be very useful for attacking and fixing all kinds of Windows-specific IE bugs, and is possibly one of the most used filters around.

> "Big John" and Holly Bergevin run www.positioniseverything.net, *the definitive resource on browser bugs and workarounds. Together they discovered or documented many of the hacks and bugs seen in this and the following chapter.*

The escaped property hack

IE 5.*x* on Windows ignores escape characters. This bug forms the basis of the mid-pass filter you learned about earlier. It also forms the basis of the much easier escaped property filter. As the name suggests, this filter works by adding an escape character within a property. All modern browsers should ignore this escape character, but IE 5.*x*/Win thinks this is part of the property name and, not recognizing the property, ignores the declaration.

```
#content {
  w\idth: 100px
}
```

As such, the escaped property filter provides a simple way of hiding styles from IE 5.*x*/Win. However, you need to be careful when using this filter as the backslash character cannot come before the numbers 0 to 9 or the letters a to f (or A to F). This is because these values are used in hex notation and may therefore get escaped.

Tantek's box model hack

Tantek's box model hack was one of the first CSS filters ever invented. Tantek Çelik created this filter at the behest of Jeffrey Zeldman to allow him to work around IE's proprietary box model (see Chapter 9). This filter works by passing one width to IE 5 on Windows and another width to all other browsers. It does this using the same escape character bug used in the band pass filters:

```
div.content {
  width:400px;
  voice-family: "\"}\"";
  voice-family:inherit;
  width:300px;
}
```

8

Unfortunately, Opera 5 has the same parsing bug as IE 5.*x*/Win. As such, a second rule is required to give Opera the correct width:

```
html>body .content {
   width:300px;
}
```

If it weren't for this filter, pure CSS layout may never have been possible. However, these days it is seen as an ugly and complicated filter, best avoided. I have included it in here purely for its historical significance and because you will still see it being used in older stylesheets. These days, it is much more common to use the modified simplified box model hack.

> *For more on the history of this, and several other filters, see Tantek Çelik's excellent article, "Pandora's Box (Model) of CSS Hacks and Other Good Intentions," at* http://tantek.com/log/2005/11.html.

The modified simplified box model hack

The escaped property hack can be combined with the star HTML hack to create the modified simplified box model hack, or MSBMH for short. This hack is used for working around IE's proprietary box model by providing one length value to IE 5.*x*/Win and then the correct length value to IE 6/Win and all other browsers:

```
#content {
   width: 80px;
   padding: 10px;
}

* html #content {
   width: 100px;
   w\idth: 80px;
}
```

The modified simplified box model hack is easier to remember and much cleaner than Tantek's box model hack, and so is currently the preferred box model hack. This filter can be used for more than just box model hacks, so don't let the name limit you.

The !important and underscore hacks

There may be some instances where you wish to apply one declaration to IE 6 and below on Windows and another to all other browsers, within the same rule. To do this, you could use the commented property hack, or you could use the !important or the underscore hack.

The !important hack works because IE 6 and below on Windows has problems dealing with multiple properties in a single rule:

```
#nav {
  position: fixed !important;
  position: static;
}
```

IE 4-6/Win will ignore the first declaration and apply the second. All other browsers will apply the first declaration because it is using the !important keyword, which increases the rule's priority within the cascade (see Chapter 1).

Similar to the !important hack is the underscore hack. By placing an underscore in front of a property, compliant browsers will no longer recognize that property and the declaration will be ignored. However, IE 6 and below on Windows ignores the underscore and thus applies the rule. So in this example, all modern browsers will apply a position of fixed, skipping the unknown second rule. IE 4-6/Win will ignore the underscore and will override the first rule, setting the position to static.

```
#nav {
  position: fixed;
  _position: static;
}
```

The Owen hack

All of the filters so far have been aimed at various versions of IE. This is partly because IE has more bugs than most current browsers. However, it is also because IE is by far the most prevalent browser, so more bugs get found and documented. But there are other buggy browsers out there, including Opera 6 and below.

The Owen hack allows authors to hide styles from Opera 6 and below, as well as from IE 6 and below on Windows. This filter works because these browsers do not implement the first-child selector. Because there can only ever be one head element, it is always a first-child. The body tag always comes after the head tag, and so can be targeted using an adjacent sibling selector. The resulting selector is understood by more compliant browsers, while being ignored by version 6 and below of Opera and IE on Windows.

In the following example, the Owen hack is being used to add a background PNG image on the body tag for more compliant browsers, hiding it from IE/Win and Opera, versions 6 and below:

```
head:first-child+body {
  background-image: url("bg.png");
}
```

8

If you only want to target Opera 6 and below, you need to combine the Owen hack with the child selector hack. Say you wanted to display an upgrade notice to Opera 6 users. You would first use the child selector hack to show your upgrade message to every browser except IE 6 and below on Windows. You could then use the Owen hack to hide the message from more modern browsers:

```
html>body #getFirefox {
  display: static;
}

head:first-child+body  #getFirefox {
  display: none;
}
```

Summary

In this chapter you have learned that hacks and filters can be an important weapon in any CSS developer's arsenal. However, hacks need to be used sparingly, and preferably as a last resort. If you do need to use hacks or filters, do so with forward compatibility and ease of maintenance in mind.

In the next chapter, you will learn about different ways to attack and fix CSS bugs. You will be introduced to some of the most common and perplexing browsers bugs around, and you will learn how to fix them using your newfound arsenal of techniques.

9 BUGS AND BUG FIXING

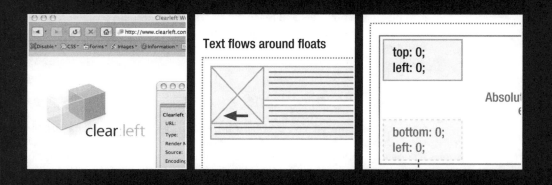

Compared to many programming languages, CSS is a relatively simple language to learn. The syntax is straightforward, and due to its presentational nature, there is no complicated logic to grapple with. The difficulties start when it comes time to test your code on different browsers. Browser bugs and inconsistent rendering are a major stumbling block for most CSS developers. Your designs look fine on one browser, but your layout inexplicably breaks on another.

The misconception that CSS is difficult comes not from the language itself, but the hoops you need to jump through to get your sites working in all the major browsers. Bugs are difficult to find information on, poorly documented, and often misunderstood. Hacks are seen by many as magic bullets—arcane sigils with exotic names that, when applied to your code, will magically fix your broken layouts. Hacks are definitely potent tools in your armory, but they need to be applied with care and generally as a last resort. A much more important skill is the ability to track, isolate, and identify bugs. Only once you know what a bug is can you look for ways to squash it.

In this chapter you will learn about

- How to track down CSS bugs
- The mysterious hasLayout property
- The most common browser bugs and their fixes

Bug hunting

We all know that browsers are buggy, some of them more than others. When a CSS developer comes across a problem with their code, there is the immediate temptation to mark it as a browser bug and apply the appropriate hack. However, browser bugs aren't as common as everybody likes to think. The most common CSS problems arise not from the browser bugs, but from an incomplete understanding of the CSS specification.

Many developers are self-taught, and build up a mental model of how they believe things should behave. When something doesn't work the way they expect, the natural temptation is to blame the browsers and reach for a hack. To avoid these problems, it is always best to approach a CSS bug assuming that you have done something wrong. Only once you are sure that there are no errors on your part should you consider the problem to be the result of a browser bug.

Common CSS problems

Some of the simplest CSS problems are caused by typos and syntactical errors in your code. One of the best ways to prevent these types of bugs is to run your code through the CSS validator (http://jigsaw.w3.org/css-validator/). This should pick up any grammatical errors, showing you the lines the errors are on and a brief description of each error (see Figure 9-1).

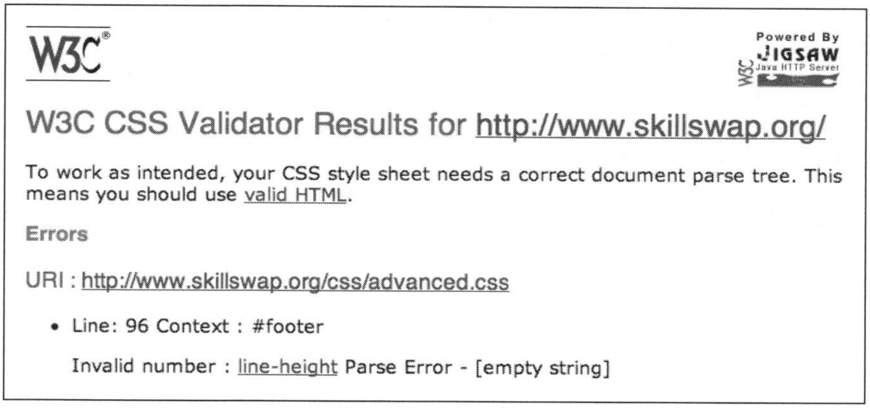

Figure 9-1. Result from the W3C CSS validator

When validating your (X)HTML and CSS, you may be greeted with a page full of errors. This can be quite intimidating at first, but don't worry. Most of these errors will be the result of one or two actual errors. If you fix the first error mentioned and revalidate, you will see that many of the original errors will have disappeared. Do this a couple of times and your code should quickly become error free.

Remember that the validator is only an automated tool and is not infallible. There are a growing number of reported bugs with the validator, so if you think something is right but the validator is saying something different, always check against the latest CSS specification. I always check my code against CSS 2.1 as this is the version of CSS that best matches current browser implementation.

Problems with specificity and sort order

As well as syntactic errors, one of the more common problems revolves around specificity and sort order. Specificity problems usually manifest themselves when you apply a rule to an element, only to find it not having any effect. You can apply other rules and they work fine, but certain rules just don't seem to work. In these situations the problem is usually that you have already defined rules for this element elsewhere in your document using a more specific selector.

In this example, a CSS developer has set the background color of all the paragraphs in the content area to be transparent. However, they want the intro paragraph to be orange and so have applied that rule directly to the intro paragraph:

```
#content p {
  background-color: transparent;
}

.intro {
 background-color: #FEECA9;
}
```

9

If you test this code in a browser, you will see that the intro paragraph is still transparent. This is because the selector targeting all the paragraphs in the content area is more specific than the selector targeting the intro paragraph. To achieve the desired result, you need to make the selector targeting the intro paragraph more specific. In this case, the best way to achieve this is to add the id for the content element to the start of the intro paragraph selector:

```css
#content p {
  background-color: transparent;
}

#content .intro {
  background-color: #FEECA9;
}
```

Problems with margin collapsing

Margin collapsing (see Chapter 2) is another CSS feature that, if misunderstood, can cause a lot of gray hairs. Take the simple example of a paragraph nested inside a div element:

```html
<div id="box">
  <p>This paragraph has a 20px margin.</p>
</div>
```

The box div is given a 10-pixel margin and the paragraph is given a 20-pixel margin:

```css
#box {
  margin: 10px;
  background-color:#d5d5d5;
}

p {
  margin: 20px;
  background-color:#6699FF;
}
```

You would naturally expect the resulting style to look like Figure 9-2, with a 20-pixel margin between the paragraph and the div, and a 10-pixel margin around the outside of the div.

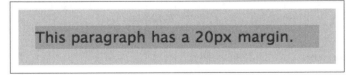

Figure 9-2. How you would expect the preceding style to look

However, the resulting style actually looks like Figure 9-3.

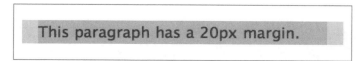

Figure 9-3. How the style actually looks

Two things are going on here. First, the paragraph's 20-pixel top and bottom margins collapse with the 10-pixel margin on the div, forming a single 20-pixel vertical margin. Second, rather than being enclosed by the div, the margins appear to protrude from the top and bottom of the div. This happens because of the way elements with block-level children have their height calculated.

If an element has no vertical border or padding, its height is calculated as the distance between the top and bottom border edges of its contained children. Because of this, the top and bottom margins of the contained children appear to protrude from the containing element. However, there is a simple fix. By adding a vertical border or padding, the margins no longer collapse and the height of the element is calculated as the distance between the top and bottom margin edges of its contained children instead.

To get the preceding example looking like Figure 9-2, you simply need to add padding or a border around the div:

```
#box {
  margin: 10px;
  padding: 1px;
  background-color:#d5d5d5;
}

p {
  margin: 20px;
  background-color:#6699FF;
}
```

Most problems with margin collapsing can be fixed with the addition of a transparent border or 1 pixel of padding.

Bug hunting basics

The first step in tracking down a bug is to validate your (X)HTML and CSS to check for typos or syntactic errors. Some display errors are caused by browsers rendering pages in quirks mode. As such, it is a good idea to check that you are using the correct DOCTYPE for your markup language in order for your pages to render in standards mode (see Chapter 1). You can tell the mode your page is rendering in by installing the Firefox developer's toolbar (http://tinyurl.com/cmh38). If your page is rendering in quirks mode, the checkmark at the top right of the toolbar will be gray. If your page is rendering in standards mode, the checkmark will turn blue. Clicking on this checkmark will provide more information about the page, as well as explicitly define the rendering mode (see Figure 9-4).

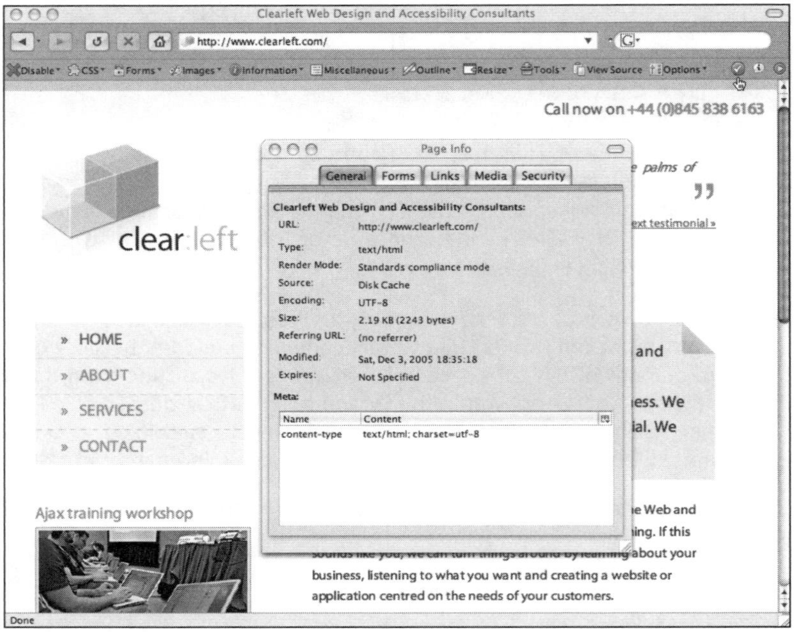

Figure 9-4. The Firefox web developer's toolbar shows your page is displaying in standards or quirks mode.

Many developers will develop their pages primarily using Internet Explorer, so each time they make a change, they will preview the page in IE to see if it is working correctly. Once the pages are almost ready, they will then test in a variety of browsers and try to fix any "bugs" that appear. However, this is a dangerous approach that can cause many long-term problems.

IE 5.*x*/Win is a notoriously buggy browser with several important CSS flaws, including the way it handles floats and its incorrect implementation of the box model. IE 6 is slightly less buggy, but still has numerous bugs and inconsistencies. By using IE as their primary development browser, many developers mistakenly interpret IE's behavior as the correct behavior, and wonder why more modern browsers "break" their carefully crafted CSS layouts. In reality the pages are actually "broken" in IE and are displaying correctly in the more modern browsers.

A much safer approach is to use more standards-compliant browsers such as Firefox or Safari as your primary development browser. If your layout works in one of these browsers, in all likelihood you are doing things in the correct way. You can then test your pages on less capable browsers and find workarounds for any display problems you find.

Isolate the problem

Next, you need to try to isolate the problem. By isolating the problem and identifying the symptoms, you can hopefully figure out what is causing the problem and fix it. One way to do this is by applying borders or outlines to the relevant elements to see how they interact:

```
#promo1 {
  float: left;
  margin-right: 5px;
  border: 1px solid red;
}

#promo2 {
  float: left;
  border: 1px solid green;
}
```

I tend to add borders directly to my code. You could use the outline option in the developer's toolbar plug-in for Firefox, or one of many bookmarklets for outlining different elements. Sometimes just the act of adding borders will fix the problem, usually indicating a margin collapsing issue.

Try changing a few properties to see if they affect the bug, and if so, in what way. It may be useful to attempt to exaggerate a bug. For instance, if the gap between these two boxes is bigger than you expected in IE, try upping the margin to see what happens. If the space between the boxes in IE has doubled, you have probably fallen foul of IE's double-margin float bug.

```
#promo1 {
  float: left;
  margin-right: 40px;
  border: 1px solid red;
}

#promo2 {
  float: left;
  border: 1px solid green;
}
```

Try some common fixes. For instance, many IE bugs are fixed by setting the position property to relative, by setting the display property to inline (on floated elements), or by setting a dimension such as width or height. You will learn more about these common fixes and why they work later in the chapter.

Many CSS problems can be found and fixed quickly, with a minimum of effort. If the problem starts to drag on, you should consider creating a minimal test case.

9

Creating a minimal test case

A minimal test case is simply the smallest amount of (X)HTML and CSS required to replicate the bug. By creating a minimal test case, you help cut out some of the variables and make the problem as simple as possible.

To create a minimal test case, you should first duplicate the problem files. Start by removing extraneous (X)HTML until you are left with just the basics. Then start commenting out stylesheets to work out which stylesheets are causing the problem. Go into those stylesheets and start deleting or commenting out blocks of code. If the bug suddenly stops, you know that the last block of code you commented out is contributing to the problem. Keep going until you are left only with the code that is causing the problems.

From here you can start investigating the bug in more detail. Delete or comment out declarations and see what happens. How does that change the bug? Change property values and see if the problem goes away. Add common fixes to see if they have any effect. Edit the (X)HTML to see if that has any effect. Use different combinations of (X)HTML elements. Some browsers have strange whitespace bugs, so try removing whitespace from your (X)HTML.

Fix the problem, not the symptoms

Once you know the root of the problem, you are in a much better position to implement the correct solution. Because there are many ways to skin a CSS site, the easiest solution is simply to avoid the problem in the first place. If margins are causing you problems, think about using padding instead. If one combination of (X)HTML elements is causing problems, try changing the combination.

Many CSS bugs have very descriptive names. This makes searching for answers on the Web fairly easy. So if you have noticed that IE is doubling the margins on all floated elements, do a search for "Internet Explorer Double Margin Float Bug" and you are bound to find a solution.

If you find that you cannot avoid the bug, then you may have to simply treat the symptoms. This usually revolves around finding a filter that affects the problem browser and parsing a separate rule to that browser.

Ask for help

If you have created a minimal test case, tried common solutions, searched for possible fixes, and still cannot find a solution, then ask for help. You'll find lots of active CSS communities out there, such as CSS-Discuss (www.css-discuss.org/), the Web Standards Group (http://webstandardsgroup.org/), and the Webmaster World CSS forums (http://tinyurl.com/duh2n). These communities are full of people who have been developing CSS sites for many years, so there is a good chance somebody will have experienced your bug before and know how to fix it. If you have a new or particularly intriguing bug, people may be willing to pitch in with suggestions and even help you work out a fix.

The thing to remember when asking for help is that most web developers are extremely busy people. If you haven't validated your code or have simply posted a link to your full site expecting them to trawl through hundreds of line of code, don't expect a flood of help. The best way to ask for help on a mailing list or forum is to use a title that accurately describes the problem, write a succinct summary of the problem, and then either paste in your minimal test case or, if it is more than a few lines of code, link to the test case on your site.

Having "layout"

We all know that browsers can be buggy, and IE on Windows seems buggier than most. One of the reasons IE/Win behaves differently from other browsers is because the rendering engine uses an internal concept called "layout." Because layout is a concept particular to the internal working of the rendering engine, it is not something you would normally need to know about. However, layout problems are the root of many IE/Win rendering bugs, so it is useful to understand the concept and how it affects your CSS.

What is "layout"?

Internet Explorer on Windows uses the layout concept to control the size and positioning of elements. Elements that are said to "have layout" are responsible for sizing and positioning themselves and their children. If an element does not "have layout," its size and position are controlled by the nearest ancestor with layout.

The layout concept is a hack used by IE's rendering engine to reduce its processing overhead. Ideally all elements would be in control of their own size and positioning. However, this causes huge performance problems in IE. As such, the IE/Win development team decided that by applying layout only to those elements that actually needed it, they could reduce the performance overhead substantially.

Elements that have layout by default include

- body
- html in standards mode
- table
- tr, td
- img
- hr
- input, select, textarea, button
- iframe, embed, object, applet
- marquee

9

The concept of layout is specific to IE on Windows, and is not a CSS property. Layout cannot be explicitly set in the CSS, although setting certain CSS properties will give an element layout. It is possible to see if an element has layout by using the JavaScript function, hasLayout. This will return true if the element has layout and false if it doesn't. hasLayout is a read-only property and so cannot be set using JavaScript.

Setting the following CSS properties will automatically give that element layout:

- position: absolute
- float: left or right
- display: inline-block
- width: any value
- height: any value
- zoom: any value (Microsoft property—doesn't validate)
- writing-mode: tb-rl (Microsoft property—doesn't validate)

What effect does layout have?

Layout is the cause of many IE/Win rendering bugs. For instance, if you have a paragraph of text next to a floated element, the text is supposed to flow around the element. However, in IE 6 and below on Windows, if the paragraph has layout—by setting the height, for example—it is constrained to a rectangular shape, stopping the text from flowing around the float (see Figure 9-5).

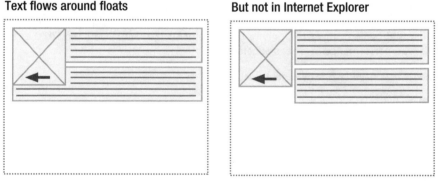

Figure 9-5. Text is supposed to flow around adjacent floated elements. However, on IE/Win, if the text element has layout, this doesn't happen.

This can cause all kinds of problems with floated layouts. Worse still, many people who use IE as their main browser mistakenly assume this is the correct behavior and get confused when other browsers treat floats differently.

Another problem revolves around how elements with layout size themselves. If the content of an element becomes larger than the element itself, the content is supposed to flow out of the element. However, in IE 6 and below on Windows, elements with layout incorrectly grow to fit the size of their contents (see Figure 9-6).

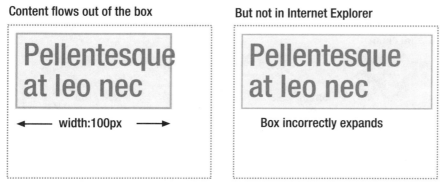

Content flows out of the box

Pellentesque at leo nec

◄─── width:100px ───►

But not in Internet Explorer

Pellentesque at leo nec

Box incorrectly expands

Figure 9-6. Elements with layout incorrectly grow to fit their contents.

This means that width in IE/Win actually acts more like a min-width. This behavior is also the cause of many broken floated layouts in IE/Win. When the content of a floated box incorrectly forces the width of the box to grow, the box becomes too big for the available space and drops below the other floated elements.

Other problems include

- Elements with layout not shrinking to fit
- Floats being auto-cleared by layout elements
- Relatively positioned elements not gaining layout
- Margins not collapsing between elements with layout
- The hit area of block-level links without layout only covering the text

In the next section, we are going to cover some of the most common browser bugs, and you will notice that many of the fixes for IE on Windows involve setting properties that force the element to have layout. In fact, if you come across an IE/Win bug, one of the first things you can do is try applying rules that force layout to see if that fixes the problem.

If you would like to learn more about IE's internal hasLayout property, I recommend reading "On Having Layout" at http://tinyurl.com/acg78.

Common bugs and their fixes

One of the greatest skills any CSS developer can have is the ability to spot common browsers bugs. By knowing the various elements that conspire to cause these bugs, you can spot and fix them before they ever become a problem.

9

Double-margin float bug

One of the most common and easy-to-spot bugs is the double-margin float bug in IE 6 and below. As the name suggests, this Windows bug doubles the margins on any floated elements (see Figure 9-7).

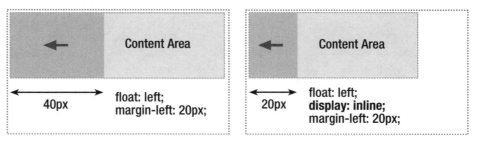

Figure 9-7. Demonstration of IE/Win's double-margin float bug

This bug is easily fixed by setting the `display` property of the element to `inline`. As the element is floated, setting the `display` property to `inline` won't actually affect the display characteristics. However, it does seem to stop IE 6 and below on Windows from doubling all of the margins. This is such a simple bug to spot and fix: every time you float an element with horizontal margins, you should automatically set the `display` property to `inline`.

Three-pixel text jog bug

Another very common IE 5-6/Win bug is the 3-pixel text jog bug. This bug manifests itself when you have text adjacent to a floated element. For instance, say you had an element floated left and you don't want the text in the adjacent paragraph to wrap around the float. You would do this by applying a left margin to the paragraph, the same width as the image:

```
.myFloat {
  float: left;
  width: 200px;
}

p {
  margin-left: 200px;
}
```

When you do this, a mysterious 3-pixel gap appears between the text and the floated element. As soon as the floated element stops, the 3-pixel gap disappears (see Figure 9-8).

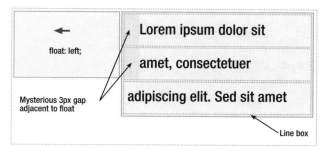

Figure 9-8. Demonstration of the IE 5-6/Win's 3-pixel text jog bug

Fixing this bug requires a two-pronged attack. First, the element containing the text is given an arbitrary height. This forces the element to have layout, which seemingly removes the text jog. Because IE 6 and below on Windows treats height like min-height, setting a tiny height has no effect on the actual dimensions of the element in that browser. However, it will affect other browsers, so the Holly hack is used to hide this rule from everything other than IE 6 and below on Windows:

```
/* Hide from IE5-Mac. Only IE-Win sees this. \*/

* html p {
  height: 1%;
}
/* End hide from IE5/Mac */
```

Unfotunately, doing this causes another problem. As you learned earlier, elements with layout are constrained to a rectangular shape and appear next to floated elements rather than underneath them. The addition of 200 pixels of padding actually creates a 200-pixel gap between the floated element and the paragraph in IE 5-6/Win. To avoid this gap, you need to reset the margin on IE 5-6/Win back to zero:

```
/* Hide from IE5-Mac. Only IE-Win sees this. \*/

* html p {
  height: 1%;
  margin-left: 0;
}
/* End hide from IE5/Mac */
```

9

179

The text jog is fixed, but another 3-pixel gap has now appeared, this time on the floated image. To remove this gap, you need to set a negative 3-pixel right margin on the float:

```
/* Hide from IE5-Mac. Only IE-Win sees this. \*/

* html p {
  height: 1%;
  margin-left: 0;
}

* html .myFloat {
  margin-right: -3px;
}
/* End hide from IE5/Mac */
```

This will fix the problem if the floated element is anything other than an image. However, if the floated element is an image, there is one last problem to solve. IE 5.x/Win adds a 3-pixel gap to both the left and the right of the image, whereas IE 6 leaves the image's margins untouched. As such, another hack is required to remove the 3-pixel gap from IE 5.x/Win only:

```
/* Hide from IE5-Mac. Only IE-Win sees this. \*/

* html p {
  height: 1%;
  margin-left: 0;
}

* html img.myFloat {
  margin: 0 -3px;
  ma\rgin: 0;
}
/* End hide from IE5/Mac */
```

This solves the problem, but in a really nasty and complicated way. As such, if possible you would be better off splitting these rules up into separate, browser-specific stylesheets. If you did this, you could have one stylesheet for IE 5.x on Windows:

```
p {
  height: 1%;
  margin-left: 0;
}

img.myFloat {
  margin: 0 -3px;
}
```

And another for IE 6:

```
p {
  height: 1%;
```

```
    margin-left: 0;
  }

  img.myFloat {
    margin: 0;
  }
```

IE 6 duplicate character bug

Another curious bug involving floats is IE 6's duplicate character bug. Under certain conditions, the last few characters in the last of a series of floats will be duplicated beneath the float, as shown in Figure 9-9.

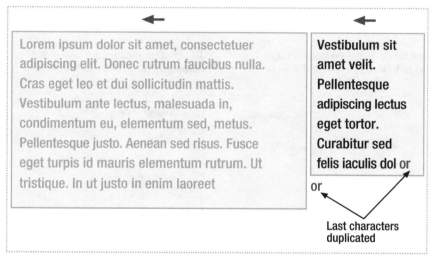

Figure 9-9. Demonstration of IE 6's duplicate character bug

This bug manifests itself when you have multiple comments in between the first and last of a series of floated elements. The first two comments have no effect, but each subsequent comment causes two characters to be duplicated. So three comments would result in two duplicate characters, four comments would result in four duplicate characters, and five comments would result in six duplicate characters.

```
<div id="content">
<!-- mainContent -->
<div id="mainContent">
…
</div><!-- end mainContent -->
<!-- secondaryContent -->
<div id="secondaryContent">
…
</div>
```

Strangely, this bug seems related to the 3-pixel text jog bug you saw previously. To fix the bug you can remove 3 pixels from the final float by setting a negative right margin, or make the container 3 pixels wider. However, both these methods are likely to cause problems in IE 7, which isn't expected to exhibit this bug. Because of this, the easiest and safest way to avoid this bug is to remove the comments from your HTML code.

IE 6 peek-a-boo bug

Another strange and infuriating bug is IE 6's peek-a-boo bug, so called because under certain conditions text will seem to disappear, only to reappear when the page is reloaded. This happens when there is a floated element followed by some nonfloated elements and then a clearing element, all contained within a parent element that has a background color or image set. If the clearing element touches the floated element, the nonfloated elements in-between seem to disappear behind the parent element's background color or image, only to reappear when the page is refreshed (see Figure 9-10).

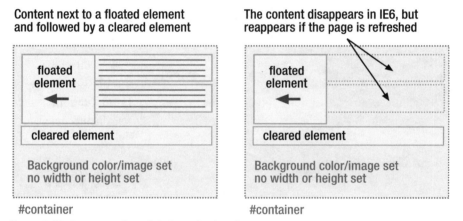

Figure 9-10. Demonstration of IE 6's peek-a-boo bug

Luckily, there are a number of ways you can combat this bug. The easiest way is probably to remove the background color or image on the parent element. However, this is often not practical. Another way is to stop the clearing element from touching the floated element. The bug doesn't seem to manifest itself if the container element has specific dimensions applied. The bug also doesn't manifest itself if the container is given a line height. Lastly, setting the position property of the float and the container to relative also seems to alleviate the problem.

Absolute positioning in a relative container

The last major browser bug I am going to cover involves absolutely positioned elements within a relatively positioned container. You learned in earlier chapters how useful nesting an absolutely positioned element in a relative container can be. However, IE 6 and below has a number of bugs when you use this technique.

These bugs arise from the fact that relatively positioned elements don't gain IE/Win's internal hasLayout property. As such, they don't create a new positioning context and all of the positioned elements get positioned relative to the viewport instead (see Figure 9-11).

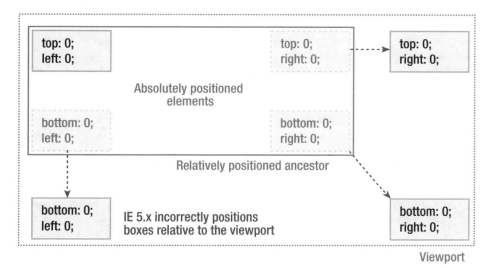

Figure 9-11. Demonstration showing how IE 5.x incorrectly positions absolutely positioned elements within a relative container

To get IE 6 and below on Windows to behave correctly, you need to force the relatively positioned container to have layout. One way to do this is to explicitly set a width and height on the container. However, you will often want to use this technique when you don't know the width and height of the container, or when you want one or both of these properties to be flexible.

Instead, you can use the Holly hack to supply an arbitrary height to the container. This will give the container layout, but because elements in IE 6 and below incorrectly expand to fit their contents, the actual height won't be affected.

```
/* Hides from IE-Mac \*/
* html .container {
  height: 1%;
}
/* End hide from IE-Mac */
```

Stop picking on Internet Explorer

Internet Explorer isn't the only buggy browser around, so you may wonder why I have been focusing my attentions on IE bugs. Don't worry, it's not another case of Microsoft bashing; there are good reasons for this focus.

9

First, IE has by far the biggest browser market share. With so many copies in circulation, IE bugs tend to get found and documented pretty quickly. When a major CSS bug gets discovered in IE, scores of developers will be on the case trying to find a fix or a workaround. Because of this popularity, there are more well-documented bugs and fixes for IE than any other browser.

The other major issue is the pace of development. Browsers such as Firefox, Safari, and Opera are constantly being updated, with new builds appearing with remarkable frequency. Almost as soon as a bug is discovered, it is fixed and a new version of the browser released. Because of this, any Firefox or Safari bug I talk about now will probably have been fixed by the next revision.

This pace of development is excellent, but it does have its own problems. Rather than having two or three versions of a browser to deal with, you may have 20 or 30. You can never be sure if your users have the latest version, and this makes testing extremely difficult. IE, on the other hand, didn't see a major revision for about 5 years. As such, there has been much more time for bugs to surface and much more impetus to find a fix.

Luckily, IE 7 promises to be a much more compliant browser. Many of the better known IE bugs have been addressed, along with increased support for advanced CSS 2.1 selectors such as the child and attribute selectors. As with all browsers, new bugs will surface, and IE 7 will be far from perfect. However, the faster people can be convinced to upgrade to modern browsers such as IE 7 and Firefox, the quicker older browsers such as IE 5.0 can be retired.

In the interim, it is worth exploring Dean Edwards' excellent IE 7 patch. This series of JavaScript files aims to bring IE 5-6/Win up to speed with IE 7. This includes improved selector implementation and numerous bug fixes. For more information about this patch, visit http://dean.edwards.name/IE7/.

Summary

In this chapter, you have learned some important techniques for tracking down and squashing CSS bugs. You have learned about IE on Windows internal hasLayout property and how this is the root of many IE/Win browser bugs. Finally, you have learned about some of the most common browser bugs and how to fix them.

Next you will see how all of this information can be put together, through two stunning case studies created by two of the best CSS designers and developers of our time.

CASE STUDY 1
MORE THAN DOODLES

by Simon Collison

Throughout this book, Andy has detailed some Holy Grail CSS methods, be they difficult to implement, or merely misunderstood or misused. It is clear that as designers we have a very rich palette from which to paint, but it is also clear that in some cases the obvious approach is not necessarily the best approach. It is with this in mind that Cameron and I have sought to pull a number of these methods into two fresh experimental designs, to explore the pluses and minuses for each approach, and to illustrate their use in two functional, accessible, standards-compliant websites.

Most of us want our jobs to be easier. We want complete control over our layouts, and maximum impact from minimal markup. It is absolutely true that this power comes with patience and practice, but by adding a few pivotal hooks to your XHTML, you leave yourself free to work solely with your CSS to transform all those XHTML elements into jaw-dropping eye candy.

In this case study you will learn about

- Controlling the content area with descendant selectors
- Floating the columns
- Highlighting the current page based on the body class
- Creating drop-in boxes for columns
- Using transparent custom corners and borders
- Combining classes for targeted actions
- Using image classes and exceptions
- Dealing with links
- Creating floated drop shadows

About this case study

This case study will show you how to take a chunk of simple semantic markup and apply a neat and tidy CSS technique to it as efficiently and effectively as possible. Your markup will, for the most part, not be littered with div hooks and limiting extraneous bloat, for as Andy has already pointed out throughout this book, CSS is smarter than all that. These examples will rely on juicy stuff such as descendant selectors, attribute selectors, inheritance, and so on to do all the hard work, leaving the XHTML lean, mean, and spotlessly clean—for the most part.

You will be given the keys to *More Than Doodles* (Figure 1), an entirely fictitious production featuring nonfictitious illustrators on its pages. The idea of a news site focused on illustration and digital art seems appropriate, for no adventurous designer would seek to produce such a site without the liberal use of images, complementary design features, and a little pizzazz. Thus, the site becomes a challenge where it is tempting to overload the page and suffer horrendously swollen markup as a result. The need is for many images and maximum control, but minimal bandwidth-busting bloat. It's time to liberate some of the techniques Andy has been discussing and put them into practice.

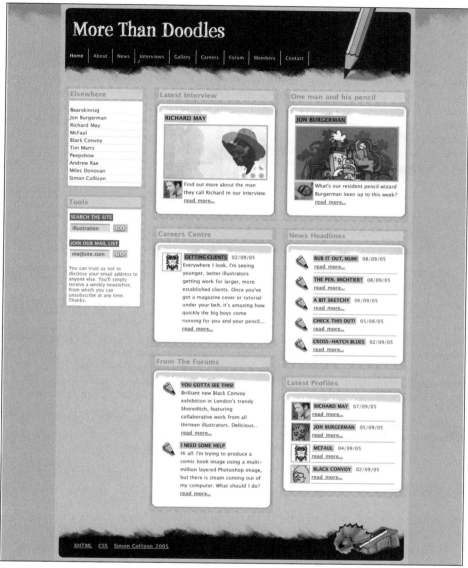

Figure 1. More Than Doodles homepage

The design stops short of being truly adventurous, in the interests of keeping the case study on track and easy to understand. Armed with the techniques in this book, however, you should soon see how simple it would be to take the design to the next level, and I hope you will want to experiment with the design to these ends.

CS1

Controlling content area with descendant selectors

Let's start by defining "content area" as the area of the page coming under the horizontal main navigation in the header, and the footer at the base of the page (Figure 2). In other words, it's the area where the page-specific action happens. Your content area can be arranged in three ways: one-column (full width of the content area), two-column (thin sidebar and wider main column to the right), and finally three-column (thin sidebar, with two equal-width columns to the right). Depending on what you want each page to do, you have the option of dynamically controlling the column display using the joy of the *descendant selector*.

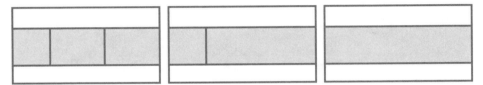

Figure 2. Content area (shaded) and column layouts

Descendant selectors give you ultimate control of your designs. To recap, a selector such as h3 {color: #000} would typically render all level 3 headings in a document black. That's easy. So let's say you have an h3 in your sidebar, and you'd prefer it to render in red. Simply create an h3 selector that is descendant of your sidebar, for example #sidebar h3 {color: #FF0000}. Thus you have two selectors separated by a combinator—in this case a single whitespace character, tailored to target a particular instance of an element in your XHTML document. That's a descendant selector, and *More Than Doodles* uses plenty of those.

So why not use this method for the opening body tag of each page? After all, assigning IDs and classes to the body is the easiest way to control a number of selectors in your CSS, for everything in your body section will be open to its influence if you so desire.

The XHTML

For this section, you are concerned with the following XHTML in any of the templates, where "content" represents any display items contained within the columns:

```
<div id="primaryContent">
  content
</div>

<div id="secondaryContent">
  content
</div>

<div id="sideContent">
  content
</div>
```

Ideally, if you didn't want a secondary or side column on a particular page, you should remove those elements from your XHTML to reduce page weight and avoid confusing some search engines. However, for the purposes of this case study, you'll keep them all in as constants, and show or hide them depending on the attribute you specify in the opening body tag.

A note about naming conventions

For the purposes of this case study, I'm using especially descriptive names for the columns. Who is to say that #primaryContent won't end up holding secondary content at some point in the future, and vice versa? To clarify the following methods, let's assume that we have a static hierarchy in place, as it's easier to visualize the layout if we think in these terms. As #primaryContent remains in use at all times, it perhaps makes sense to name it so for now.

Three-column layout

Let's jump straight to the three-column layout used on the homepage. Including the following element selector in the body tag will produce a thin sidebar, plus the two equal-width columns to the right of it:

```
<body id="threeColLayout">
```

The properties of the middle, primary column are defined with the following CSS:

```
#threeColLayout #primaryContent {
    float:left;
    width:270px;
    margin: 0 0 20px 195px;
}
```

The id selector threeColLayout in the body tag provides a vital hook with which to call in the appropriate #primaryContent value. This is where the descendant selector comes in. Notice that #primaryContent is proceded by #threeColLayout. Therefore, this version of #primaryContent only comes into play when it is a descendant of #threeColLayout.

Also, the right, secondary column is defined as follows (this column is only used on a three-column layout):

```
#secondaryContent{
    float:left;
    width:270px;
    margin: 0 0 20px 15px;
}
```

CS1

189

Finally, there is the thinner, left column, or sidebar:

```
#sideContent{
  float:left;
  width:180px;
  margin: 0 0 20px -750px;
}
```

You'll learn how these columns are floated later, but first notice that each main column has a set width of 270px. These, combined with the side column, will produce the three-column layout shown in Figure 3.

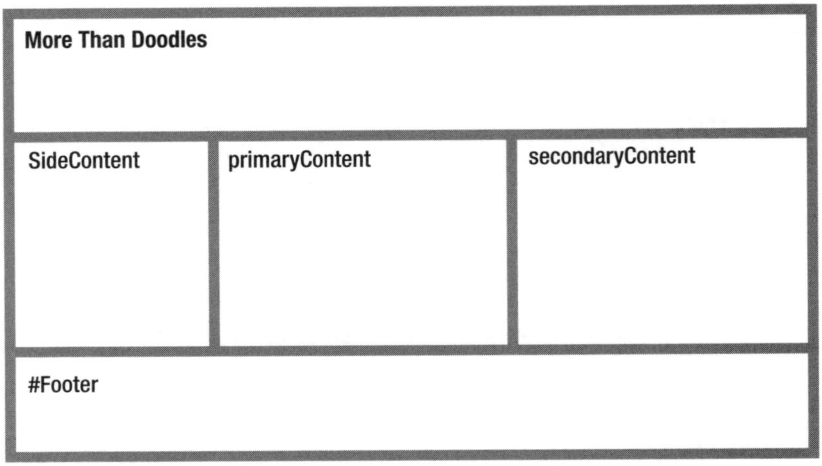

More Than Doodles

SideContent   primaryContent   secondaryContent

#Footer

Figure 3. Three-column layout

Two-column layout

The two-column layout is used on the gallery page. Replace the three-column body element with the following one (note the adjustment of the id attribute):

```
<body id="twoColLayout">
```

Look at this CSS, which is added just after the original threeColLayout #primaryContent, #secondaryContent, and #sideContent declarations:

```
#twoColLayout #primaryContent {
  width:555px;
  float:left;
  margin: 0 0 20px 195px;
}
```

Again, the descendant selector is used. The #threeColLayout version is ignored in this instance, in favor of the #twoColLayout version, and as a result the primary column stretches from 270px width to 555px width, without any adjustments to the content area markup (see Figure 4).

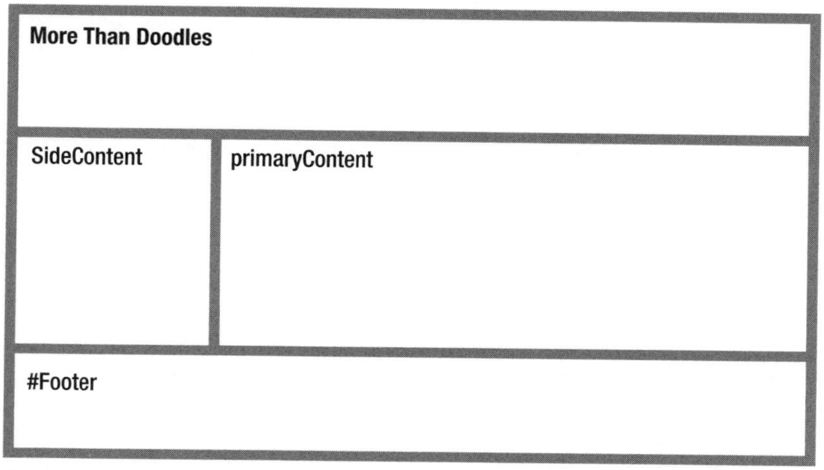

Figure 4. Two-column layout

One-column layout

The one-column layout is used on the contact page. Simply assign the one-column id attribute to the body tag as follows:

```
<body id="oneColLayout">
```

By specifying oneColLayout, the default CSS for primaryContent will be called:

```
#primaryContent {
  width:750px;
  margin: 0 0 20px 0;
  background: #FFF;
}
```

CS1

That's a full-width column stretched to fit the containing wrapper, as shown in Figure 5.

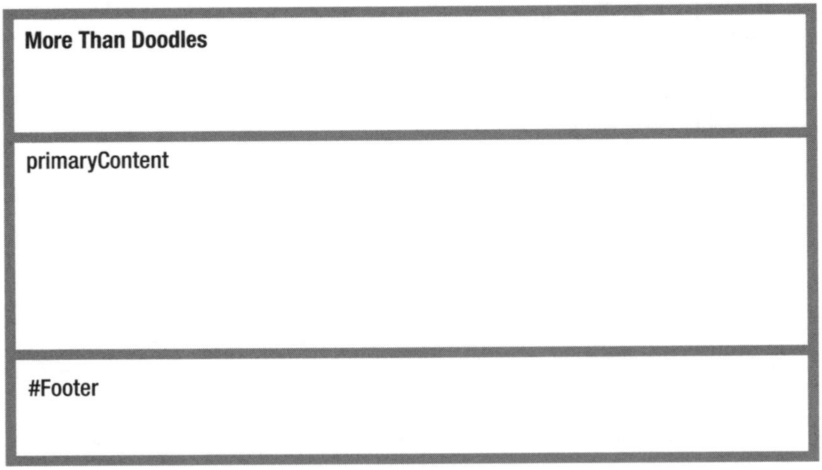

```
More Than Doodles



primaryContent





#Footer


```

Figure 5. One-column layout

Removing unwanted columns

Great, you want a two-column layout, but #secondaryContent is left in the XHTML? This causes the potential problem of that column being displaced under the other columns. Ideally, the secondaryContent element should be removed entirely to reduce page weight, but if it isn't (perhaps you are dynamically changing the id attribute based on a user choice) and for the purposes of this example, it needs to be made invisible. Again this is controlled using a descendant selector:

```
#twoColLayout #secondaryContent {
  display: none;
}
```

Therefore, any instance of #secondaryContent used on a two-column layout page will be hidden completely.

Finally, this approach can be further utilized for one-column layouts. Here, we are *grouping* two descendant selectors to ensure they have the same value; thus any instances of the second or side columns are removed using display:none (see Figure 6):

```
#oneColLayout #secondaryContent, #oneColLayout #sideContent {
  display: none;
}
```

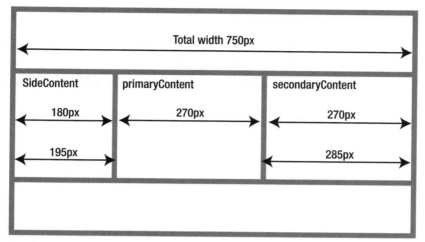

Figure 6. Calculating widths

Remember, use display: none wisely. Leaving unwanted markup in a page only serves to up the bloat quota. There is also a school of thought that suggests it's a search engine optimization no-no. Google may wonder why you are hiding content from the user, and may assume you're up to no good. Spare a thought also for anyone using a screenreader, for hidden content still exists and will therefore be read by such devices.

Floating the columns

Earlier, I mentioned that our three columns are *floated*. There are several reasons why the columns are floated inside the content area.

First, using negative margins in the CSS allows you to determine where the columns appear (left, center, right) without compromising the semantic layout of the actual XHTML. In the previous section, you will have noted that the primary column appears in the center of our layout, visually to the right of the less important side column. Turn the CSS off, and the primary column content will appear above the side column content in the linear layout, owing to its placement in the XHTML.

Good stuff, but isn't all of this negative margin positioning a little bit mathematical? Well, yes it is, but with the initial calculations worked out, everything else just falls into place. When it came to redefining #primaryContent for each rule in the previous section, only the specified widths of the columns needed attention; the margins remained unaffected.

CS1

The calculations

Now then, power up the calculator. Thankfully, this layout does not suffer from the woes of box model variants or border widths, owing to the use of box modules that will later be contained inside the columns. Those boxes have their own margins, so there is no padding inside our columns. Therefore, the key figures here are the width of our containing wrapper and the widths and margins of the columns as specified in the CSS.

First, look at the CSS for the wrapper:

```
#wrapper {
  width:750px;
  margin:0 auto;
  padding: 0 10px 10px 10px;
  background-color: #D7D493;
}
```

This gives a page width of 750 pixels. Padding of 10 pixels is added left and right, but the working content area remains 750 pixels regardless. Now look again at the CSS for the three-column layout:

```
#threeColLayout #primaryContent {
  float:left;
  width:270px;
  margin: 0 0 20px 195px;
}
#secondaryContent{
  float:left;
  width:270px;
  margin: 0 0 20px 15px;
}
#sideContent{
  float:left;
  width:180px;
  margin: 0 0 20px -750px;
}
```

What do we have here? Well, first the column widths. Taking the width value from each, we get 270 + 270 + 180, which gives a total column width of 720 pixels. That leaves the remaining 30 pixels to be made up from the two 15-pixel margins, and so the total column width does equal the wrapper width of 750 pixels.

But wait: only one 15-pixel left margin is specified, in #secondaryContent. Where's the other? Well, note that #primaryContent has a left margin of 195 pixels. This results from #primaryContent allowing space on its left for the 180-pixel #sideContent and a 15-pixel margin between the two. And 180 pixels + 15 pixels = 195 pixels. Figure 6 shows this in detail.

Floating the columns in the right place

So, the widths make sense, and the columns will fit together in any order. But they need to be in a specific order. In the XHTML they appear as primary, secondary, side. On the styled page, they need to be side, primary, secondary.

By specifying the float in each column, you ensure that the columns align left to right. Without the float, they would of course appear on top of each other, and a little uneven due to the various margin properties that would push them away from the side of the wrapper.

Even if you didn't include the #sideContent id attribute in your XHTML, or you hid it, the primary column would still hold its ground 195 pixels from the left side due to its 195-pixel left margin, and your secondary column would still sit directly to the right of it (see Figure 7). Remove that left margin, and the two columns would sit flush with the left side of the wrapper.

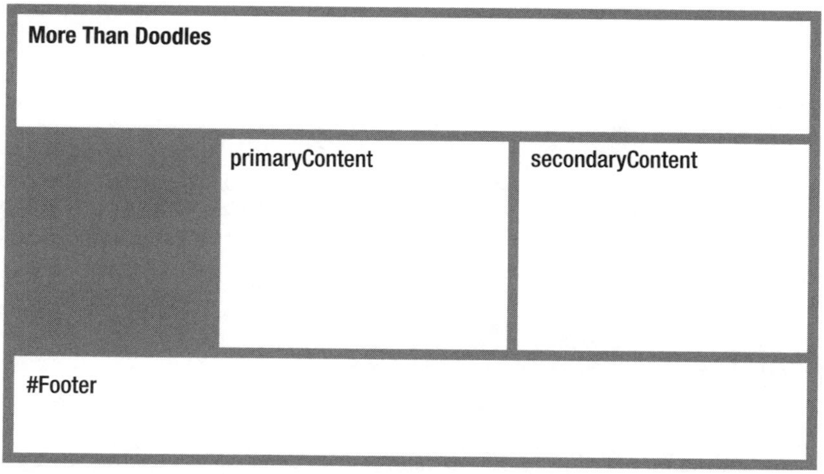

Figure 7. Three-column layout with #sideContent removed

CS1

But the side column comes last in the XHTML, so what makes it sit to the left of the two other columns? Well, that's where its –750-pixel left margin works wonders. The total width of the two main columns, plus their left margins, is 270 + 270 + 15 + 195, totaling 750 pixels. Simply calling in #sideContent after those wouldn't work, because the wrapper isn't wide enough, and anyway you want it to appear first. Therefore use a left margin of –750 pixels to pull #sideContent into the 195-pixel gap to the left of the main column, basically layering #sideContent over the dead space (Figure 8).

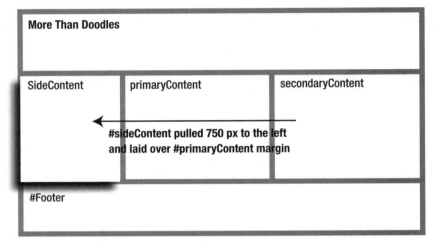

Figure 8. Floating #sideContent with a negative margin

Because any #primaryContent selector, be it a descendant or not, has the same negative margin, this approach will of course work for both three- and two-column layouts.

With this in mind, it should be obvious that by carefully adjusting each column's left and/or right margin properties, it is perfectly possible to order the columns in any way you wish, regardless of their position in the XHTML, just as long as the total widths of columns and margins do not exceed the wrapper width.

Highlighting the current page based on the body class

You've learned the merits of using id attributes in the body element, where an id attribute is specified to control layout. Now it's time to add a further attribute to the body element with the intention of highlighting the current page in the main menu (Figure 9).

There are numerous ways of highlighting the page you are on, and many designers might use some clever PHP scripting to trigger the CSS, perhaps highlighting the Home link on the menu if on the homepage. That's cool, but it's just as easy with a smart bit of CSS application reliant on a simple class attribute.

Figure 9. Highlighting the current page

Previously, you added an id to the body element to determine column layout. That leaves you unable to use another id (you can combine classes, but not ids). Therefore for this example, a class must be used to identify the nature of the selected page:

```
<body id="threeColLayout" class="home">
```

So the page is identified as the homepage. The next step is to identify each navigation link with matching id names, as follows:

```
<ul id="mainNav">
  <li><a href="#" id="home">Home</a></li>
  <li><a href="#" id="about">About</a></li>
  <li><a href="#" id="news">News</a></li>
  <li><a href="#" id="interviews">Interviews</a></li>
  <li><a href="#" id="gallery">Gallery</a></li>
  <li><a href="#" id="careers">Careers</a></li>
  <li><a href="#" id="forum">Forum</a></li>
  <li><a href="#" id="members">Members</a></li>
  <li><a href="#" id="contact">Contact</a></li>
</ul>
```

Finally, in the CSS the relationship between the element selector in the body and the id attached to each link is cemented. The first part, body.home, targets the action to instances where the element selector is home. The second part, #mainNav a#home, looks inside the #mainNav unordered list for a link identified as home. If a match is found, the action is performed.

```
body.home #mainNav a#home {
  color: #fff;
}
body.home #mainNav a:hover#home {
  color: #000;
}
```

CS1

197

Thus, whenever the user views the homepage, the link color will be set to white (Figure 9), but will still be black on rollover. The only remaining job is to replicate the CSS for every unique link id, grouping the targets into a neat all-encompassing definition. Note that only three links are shown here to save space:

```
body.home #mainNav a#home, body.gallery #mainNav a#gallery,
    body.contact #mainNav a#contact {
  color: #fff;
}
body.home #mainNav a:hover#home, body.gallery #mainNav a:hover#gallery,
    body.contact #mainNav a:hover#contact {
  color: #000;
}
```

Sure, that looks a bit unwieldy, but it'll look worse when there are nine sections to account for! It's considerably less code than a PHP equivalent, and would be much worse if we didn't group the definitions.

Drop-in boxes for columns

The concept of the columns (#primaryContent, #secondaryContent, etc.) should be clear by now, but what about their contents? Well, it's pretty apparent that there is no point having flexible columns that stretch dependent on selectors if their contents are fixed width. Therefore, it is vital that you have at your disposal a containing box that can stretch and contract based on the column it sits within. This is where the drop-in boxes come in.

On the design you'll see that the white rounded corner areas sit just inside a slightly larger shaded container. That's a box. You can have as many boxes as you like inside a column, as shown in Figure 10.

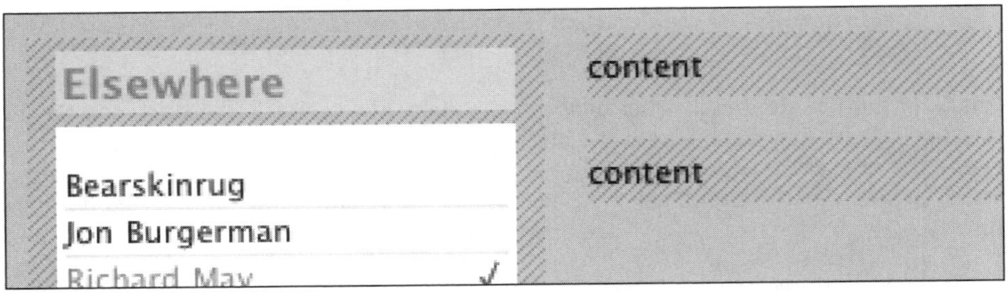

Figure 10. Two box containers inside the #primaryContent column

The markup for the two boxes is as follows:

```
<div id="primaryContent">
  <div class="box">
    content
  </div>
  <div class="box">
    content
  </div>
</div>
```

The CSS for the box is very simple, and is not restricted by height, width, percentage, position, float, or anything else. It consists merely of a tiled background image, a top margin to separate each box, and left and right padding to contain the rounded corner area (which we'll look at in the next section):

```
.box {
  margin: 15px 0 0 0;
  padding: 5px 0 5px 0;
  background:url(diags.gif);
}
```

With no physical restrictions in the CSS, .box is free to expand and contract dependent on the column it lives in, and as a result it is used in all three columns.

Right-angled or rounded corners—you decide

Inside each box, you have two options. You can either use a flat white box with right-angled corners, or you can opt for a juicily joyous white box with rounded corners.

Flat, right-angled corners

CS1

If you want the flat white box in the sidebar, simply call it in with the .cbside class:

```
<div class="box">
  <h2>Latest Interview</h2>
  <div class="cbside">
    content
  </div>
</div>
```

The CSS is as follows:

```
.cbside {
  width:160px;
  margin: 5px 0 0 10px;
  padding: 10px 0 5px 0;
  background: #FFF;
}
```

Fine. That looks OK, for a box. It sits nicely inside the .box shaded container in the sidebar. However, this site needs a bit more oomph, and you have the option of using the amazing flexible transparent custom corners and borders.

So, let's prepare for something special

Instead of .cbside, use .cbb, as follows:

```
<div class="box">
  <h2>Latest Interview</h2>
  <div class="cbb">
    content
  </div>
</div>
```

Now, .cbb does two things here. First, it acts as an alternative display style for any users not fortunate enough to have JavaScript enabled on their browser, and as it stands will produce a flat white box exactly like the one created by the .cbside class. Here's the CSS:

```
.cbb {
  margin: 0 10px 0 10px;
  background: #FFF;
  padding: 5px 0 5px 0;
  line-height: 170%;
}
```

This is nothing particularly special as it stands, but this class also acts as a hook for the JavaScript. What? JavaScript? Yes, and there are a hundred reasons why.

Transparent custom corners and borders

Credit for this superb technique must go to talented Swedish designer Roger Johansson (www.456bereastreet.com/archive/200505/transparent_custom_corners_and_border), who has honed this method to near perfection. Essentially, the goal is to create beautiful, stretchy custom corners and borders without adding a barrage of meaningless divs for each and every instance.

Another bonus is that this method allows the use of transparent background images to achieve the effect. Thus, the custom corners will expand to fit the content they contain, and can sit on any background color or pattern.

Note also that if the user does not have JavaScript enabled on their browser, a default, corner-less box will replace the rounded corners, ensuring content is still housed appropriately (Figure 11).

Last but not least, the CSS can be used to exploit a filter to ensure browsers unable to display PNG images receive transparent GIFs as an alternative. For my money, this technique is just about flawless.

Figure 11. With JavaScript enabled (left), and without (right)

The JavaScript searches for any classes named cbb and replaces them with all the appropriate divs required to achieve the effect. Your source code will still show class="cbb" and none of the divs inserted by the JavaScript. It's super neat.

Be sure to copy the JavaScript file and upload it to your server, and include the following statement in the head section of your pages:

```
<script type="text/javascript" src="cb.js"></script>
```

CS1

201

The images

Next, you need to create two images to be positioned around the content by the CSS. The technique uses just two images rather than lots of individual corner images to reduce server requests and make things easier to rework if need be. I suggest grabbing either my images or Roger's original images and manipulating them to your own needs. For *More Than Doodles* the main image emulates the sketchy header graphic while still showing a thin rounded white border (Figure 12).

Figure 12. The box image (shown at reduced width)

Notice the image is big—a width of 1600 pixels. This is mainly so that it is large enough to cope with very wide liquid layouts on any screen resolution. If, like me, you are limiting your design to something under 800 pixels, there is no need to make such a long image. The CSS will be throwing this image all over the place and chopping pieces out of it to create the right-sized box and horizontal borders as dictated by its container (Figure 13).

Figure 13. The border image

The border image fulfills several roles. Both the left and right borders are shown in the tiny tile, and we'll use the CSS to pull this image left or right and tile it vertically as required.

Remember, until IE 7 is widely used, it's important to assume that the user's version of IE has no support for alpha transparency PNGs. So, if you care about IE users, you'll need to make two GIF versions of these images.

The CSS

The next step is to grab the following CSS and adjust it to your needs. The default CSS created by Roger is available with his tutorial, but here we'll look at the version I have tweaked. Let's look at each chunk of the CSS separately. First, we specify .cb (custom border), the class used by the JavaScript to replace .cbb (the non-JS version):

```
.cb {
  float:left;
  width:100%;
  margin: 0.5em 0;
  line-height: 170%;
}
```

Next we need to define the classes that will place the top custom corners and horizontal borders. The first thing to note is the use of the !important declaration. We need this where we specify the transparent PNG image for good browsers that support PNGs. Directly below that we specify the GIF image for IE/Win and other platforms with no PNG support:

```
.bt {
  background:url(box.png) no-repeat 100% 0 !important;
  background:url(box.gif) no-repeat 100% 0;
  margin:0 0 0 18px;
  height:27px;
}
.bt div {
  height:27px;
  width:18px;
  position:relative;
  left:-18px;
  background:url(box.png) no-repeat 0 0 !important;
  background:url(box.gif) no-repeat 0 0;
}
```

This double background declaration appears throughout the CSS, as you'll see. Note also the various positioning rules for our main corner image. Next we define similar rules for the bottom corners and vertical borders:

```
.bb {
  background:url(box.png) no-repeat 100% 100% !important;
  background:url(box.gif) no-repeat 100% 100%;
  margin:0 0 0 12px;
  height:14px;
}
.bb div {
  height:14px;
  width:12px;
  position:relative;
  left:-12px;
  background:url(box.png) no-repeat 0 100% !important;
  background:url(box.gif) no-repeat 0 100%;
}
```

Then add the CSS for the borders—first left, and then right:

```
.i1 {
margin-left: 0;
padding: 0 0 0 7px;
}
.i2 {
  padding: 0 12px 0 0;
  background:url(borders.png) repeat-y 100% 0 !important;
  background:url(borders.gif) repeat-y 100% 0;
}
```

CS1

Finally, the appearance of the main content inside the borders needs controlling. Use this to set the background color (ensure it matches your corner and border images!) and insert some padding between the borders and the content:

```
.i3 {
  background:#FFF;
  border: 1px solid #FFF;
  border-width:1px 0;
  padding:0 5px;
}
```

A word of caution is needed here. The use of the !important declaration should be restricted to very special case scenarios only, as it exists not to filter for browsers but to create a balance of power between author and user stylesheets—a critical concept in accessibility.

For more detail about the various positioning properties in the CSS, be sure to visit Roger's detailed tutorial "Customising custom borders and corners" (www.456bereastreet.com/archive/200506/customising_custom_corners_and_borders/), which uses a simple diagram to explain the way the images are broken up and how this correlates exactly with the CSS.

Combining classes for targeted actions

Now, I mentioned in the section about highlighting the current page that it is possible to combine classes. This functionality provides real power when it comes to reusing elements. For example, you can use .box as often as you want, but you may not always want the elements it contains to be equal. So, you could make several versions of .box and set the unique properties for each, but why would you want to repeat the margin, padding, and background styles for each and end up with more class names to worry about? This is where combined classes come in.

Now, if you wanted every h3 inside every box to have a green background, you might create the following styles:

```
h3 {
  text-transform: uppercase;
  display: inline;
  font-size: 92%;
  margin: 10px 5px 0 5px;
  padding: 2px;
}
.custom_background {
  background: #F762E0;
}
```

You might then call that as follows:

```
<div class="box">
  <h2>Latest Interview</h2>
   <div class="cbb">
    <h3 class="custom_background">My Green Header</h3>
    content
   </div>
</div>
```

Argh! You're getting the extra markup blues—forced to always have that attribute plugged into the heading. No, no, no. Instead, create unique background headers for each section, keeping the existing h3 declaration and then creating a set of background styles with semantically meaningful names:

```
.default h3 {
  background: #F6CE45;
}
.careers h3 {
  background: #F762E0;
}
.one_man h3 {
  font-size: 110%;
  background: #B18FD1;
}
.interviews h3 {
  font-size: 110%;
  background: #D7D493;
}
.profiles h3 {
  background: #C4DDB8;
}
```

Then, all you need to decide is the purpose for each box included in each column. Let's say you place a box to house the latest interviews. Add the interviews attribute to the existing box class, separating the two class names with a whitespace character:

```
<div class="box interviews">
  <h2>Latest Interview</h2>
  <div class="cbb">
    <h3>An Interview with Richard May</h3>
    content
  </div>
</div>
```

CS1

205

Suddenly, all instances of a level 3 heading inside this box take on the green background color (Figure 14). Exchange the word "interviews" for "default" and now all headings in that box have a yellow background. Remove the heading rule entirely, and headings have no background color at all. Notice that I'm also adjusting text sizes of some headings dependent on which section it is, by adjusting font-size. The world is my oyster here.

Figure 14. Controlling header background color using class combinations

Image classes and exceptions

Key to keeping markup lean is avoiding the use of extraneous divs and classes all over the place. By defining the behavior of certain tags in the CSS, you can cut down bloat significantly. In some cases this calls for a global definition, and in other cases it just requires a definition for a tag placed within a certain area of our page.

Default images

First, define rules common to *all* images on the page. It is then up to other styles to override these. By default, all images will have a 2-pixel border, and bottom and right margins of 5 pixels. They will all float left:

```
img {
  float: left;
  margin: 0px 0 2px 5px;
  border: 2px solid #C5BDBD;
}
```

Owned images

For any images in the default boxes—the pencil icons—I didn't want the 2-pixel border (Figure 15). So I set border to 0:

```
.default img {
  border: 0;
}
```

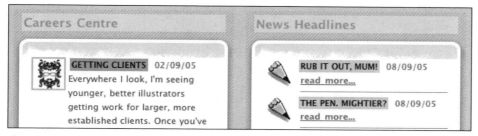

Figure 15. In the left box, the thumbnail is using the default image style. On the right, in the default box, the pencil icons have no border thanks to the .default img descendant selector.

Larger images

Larger images need class="mainImage" in the markup to set them apart. This is a small price to pay for layout control. For these larger images, I didn't want them to float, since that causes the image to be pushed to the left and everything else to the right in a two-column layout (Figure 16).

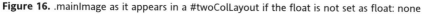

Figure 16. .mainImage as it appears in a #twoColLayout if the float is not set as float: none

So that can be fixed with float: none, which overrides the default img float declaration. Removing the float also means there is no need to clear the float and force the container to expand to hold it. Still, even if the image isn't floated, it will still produce a jumble of items (Figure 17).

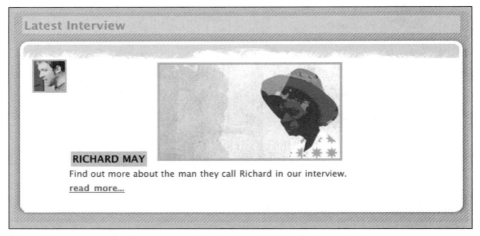

Figure 17. .mainImage as it appears in a #twoColLayout without display: block

So a top margin is declared to space the header and image apart, and also increase the border width slightly. Also, set it to display:block so that the image will force the header and other bits to appear below it in a one-column layout (Figure 18) and a two-column layout (Figure 19).

```
.mainImage {
  display: block;
  float: none;
  margin-top: 4px;
  border: 3px solid #C5BDBD;
}
```

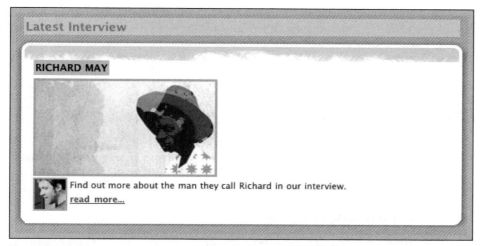

Figure 18. .mainImage as it appears in a #twoColLayout with display: block specified

Figure 19. .mainImage as it appears in a #threeColLayout layout

CS1

Thus, you always have complete control of .mainImage, illustrating how simple it is to make an exception to a blanket rule. Admittedly, you'll need to add class="mainImage" to the larger images to force this override, but it seems a small price to pay to cut out all the other divs. If certain images need special treatment, I recommend that these be the ones you use least, given that they'll require the extra XHTML.

Dealing with links

How could we look at advanced CSS without discussing checked-off visited links? To be honest, the technique is not that advanced, and using background images with link states has become increasingly common over the last 18 months. We'll also look at how to distinguish external links from links within your own site.

Understanding the sidebar links

Notice that the sidebar links are clickable for the whole sidebar width. This is because the CSS declaration display:block is used in conjunction with a set width, specifying a sensitive area longer than the actual link text.

Be aware here that any properties not declared for your sidebar links will be inherited from the default link states specified much earlier in the stylesheet.

Checked-off visited links

It's easy to show a user which links they have visited. Usually you would set the a:visited link class to a different text color to indicate this. Everybody does that, but using just one CSS background image, you can create an image trick to do this for you. As Figure 20 shows, *More Than Doodles* uses a checkmark to the right of all visited links, or an arrow appearing on hover to further entice the user to follow that link.

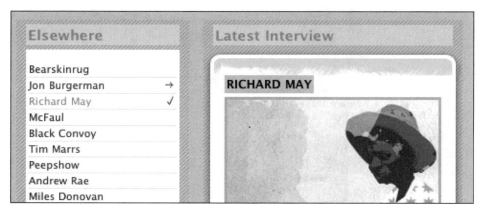

Figure 20. Checked-off visited links

First, create the background image. Be very careful to keep the dimensions as specified in Figure 21. You will use background-position to shift this image up and down by the appropriate number of pixels, showing a checkmark or an arrow as required. For example, the hover state specifies the image be moved up by 20 pixels, thus hiding the first 15-pixel bar and 5-pixel space of the image and making the bar with the arrow visible on rollover. For a visited link, everything moves up 40 pixels, making the bar with the checkmark viewable instead.

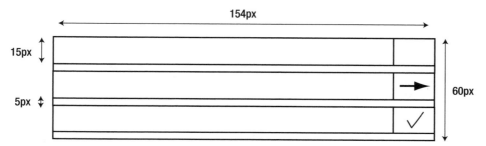

Figure 21. Dimensions for our checked-off links image

The CSS is pretty simple, and makes full use of the display:block and set width discussed earlier. Note that all list elements are owned by .cbSide:

```
.cbSide ul {
  list-style-type: none;
  margin-top: 0px;
  margin-left: 0;
  margin-bottom: 0;
  padding: 3px;
}

.cbSide li a:link {
  color:#333;
  line-height:150%;
  text-decoration:none;
  display:block;
  width:154px;
  border-bottom: 1px solid #EDEAEB;
  background: #FFF url(ticks.gif);
}

.cbSide li a:active {
  color:#333;
  line-height:150%;
  text-decoration:none;
  display:block;
  width:154px;
  border-bottom: 1px solid #EDEAEB;
  background: #FFF url(ticks.gif);
}
```

CS1

```
.cbSide li a:hover {
  color:#990000;
  line-height:150%;
  display:block;
  width:154px;
  border-bottom: 1px solid #EDEAEB;
  background: #FFF url(ticks.gif) 0px -20px;
  text-decoration:none;
}

.cbSide li a:visited {
  color: #999;
  text-decoration:none;
  line-height:150%;
  display:block;
  width:154px;
  border-bottom: 1px solid #EDEAEB;
  background: #FFF url(ticks.gif);
  background-position: 0 -40px;
}
```

One of the things I don't like about this method is the fact that I have to repeat the declarations for each link state. Ideally, the common values would all be placed within a .cbside li rule, but for one reason or another this resulted in an odd display in some browsers.

LAHV, not LVHA

It is widely accepted that CSS declarations for links should be arranged as link, visited, hover, active (or LVHA—"LoVe HAte"). I agree, but I like to have visited links show as checked off regardless of the hover state. This method goes against the expected behavior, but it's perfectly acceptable to change the order to achieve a desired effect. Thus, by organizing my link styles as LAHV (or "Let's All Have Vegetables") I can ensure that the visited state always has importance over the hover state. Therefore, on rollover, the checkmark remains and the arrow doesn't show.

Once you understand how the background-image and background-position properties are combining to create the effect, try resizing the image rows and adjust the CSS accordingly. For more information about this technique, and to copy the code and see it in action, visit www.collylogic.com/index.php?/weblog/comments/ticked_off_links_reloaded. Some designers have been very creative with this method, and remember you can make use of the whole background width, not just the far-right area. Go mad.

Highlighting external links

Here attribute selectors are used to identify the links that don't belong to our domain. The goal is to find a link that matches with the domain specified and ignore it. Likewise, any domains unrecognized by the CSS will be rendered with 10 pixels of padding to the right, into which is inserted our external link icon (Figure 22).

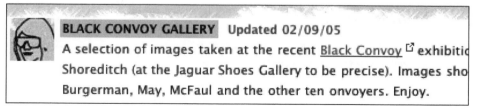

Figure 22. The external link to the Black Convoy website is clearly marked with an icon.

Here's how it works. First, notice that the action is targeted at any links within the content boxes that are combined with the default class, using an ID selector combined with a class selector—#box.default, Next, see that the link property is immediately followed by a declaration inside square brackets. This is the attribute selector, and for the first rule it is targeting all links that are absolute, hence the http://. Note that in that case, the padding and icon are attached to the link.

The second rule makes the exception for any links we specify; typically this will be those relating to the domain of the website.

The CSS itself might look a little alien at first:

```
.box.default a[href^="http:"] {
  background: url(external.gif) no-repeat right top;
  padding-right: 10px;
}
  .box.default a[href^="http://www.morethandoodles.com"],
  .box.default a[href^="http://morethandoodles.com"] {
  background-image: none;
  padding-right: 0;
}
```

Be warned that this method is currently only supported in Safari, Opera, OmniWeb, iCab, Konqueror, and Mozilla, but not IE. Although part of the CSS 2 specification, lack of implementation in IE means such methods are unfamiliar to many people. Microsoft has promised better support for attribute selectors with the forthcoming release of IE 7, which can come as some consolation to the weary developer.

CS1

Floated drop shadows (gallery)

The challenge here is to apply CSS to images to create the effect of a framed photograph placed on the page and casting its own shadow. It is an effect many people choose to apply in Photoshop prior to uploading an image, but this is not very forward thinking in that it would require all images to be reworked for future redesigns.

Casting the shadows

First, create the shadow image that will create the effect. It's massive, but this ensures that it can cope with any given image size (Figure 23).

Figure 23. Bottom-right corner of the drop shadow background image (cropped for this page)

The first task is to wrap all the appropriate images with the following markup:

```
<div class="img-wrapper">
<img src=" thumb.jpg" width="100" height="75" />
</div>
```

The .img-wrapper class places the drop shadow under the image, placing it bottom right, and moving the image 20 pixels from the top and 40 pixels from the right. It is defined as follows:

```
.img-wrapper {
  margin: 20px 40px 0 0;
  background: url(shadow.gif) no-repeat bottom right;
  line-height:0;
}
```

Next a class selector and descendant element selector are used to control the style and position of the image contained inside .img-wrapper. Here the border and padding is placed around the image. Note that as per the .mainImage style earlier in the chapter, I also need to differentiate this class from the default image classes, so I again specify float: none and so on:

```
.img-wrapper img {
  float:none;
  margin:0;
  background:#fff;
  padding:4px;
```

```
    border:1px solid #C5BDBD;
    position:relative;
    left:-5px;
    top:-5px;
}
```

Using relative positioning, the image is pulled up by 5 pixels and left by 5 pixels. This allows room for the bottom and right side shadow to appear. Padding of 4 pixels is applied to distance the 1-pixel border from the image itself, and the background color is set white to color the frame. The end result is an image with a perfect border, padding, and drop shadow.

Floating the images

On the *More Than Doodles* gallery page, I'm showing the nine latest images added to the gallery. Arranging these in rows could easily be achieved using good old table rows and columns, but think of the children. Instead, simply float the images next to each other, and they can force new rows based on the width of their container (Figure 24).

Figure 24. Floated drop shadow images

First, the following adjustment needs to be made to the image container:

```
.img-wrapper {
    float:left;
    margin: 20px 40px 0 0;
    background: url(shadow.gif) no-repeat bottom right;
    line-height:0;
}
```

Adding float: left will force the images to line up side by side rather than on top of each other, as long as there is enough available space. When there is no more space, they'll wrap to create a new line.

CS1

Summary

It goes without saying that *More Than Doodles* consists of many more techniques than I have been able to discuss in this case study, and that some of them may need a certain amount of tweaking for your own projects. That said, all the ones discussed are flexible and relatively problem-free.

The site is online at www.collylogic.com/morethandoodles/, and the source code is available for download at www.friendsofed.com, so feel free to copy and rip apart the XHTML and CSS to help come to grips with some of the methods.

CASE STUDY 2
TUSCANY LUXURY RESORTS

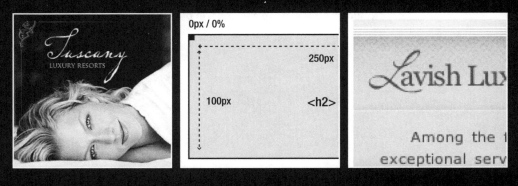

by Cameron Moll

Having astutely read the chapters in this book, you're now prepared to render living examples of the techniques Andy has presented. Simon and I have teamed up to produce two layouts that are both strong in aesthetics and solid in code. We've utilized a fair share of the methods covered in this book, while introducing additional flair of our own. You've already seen Simon's case study, so now it's time for me to share some other valuable techniques with you.

After you've finished this book, the onus will then lie with you to study all the techniques contained within, implement them in the projects you're involved in, and make the Web a better place for users from all walks of life. No pressure—we're confident you can do it!

In this case study you will learn about

- The fluid layout
- Alignment of elements using absolute positioning
- Background image techniques
- Image replacement
- Fluid imagery
- How to use a single list item for multiple elements

About this case study

Tuscany Luxury Resorts is a fictitious organization whose equally fictitious website was created expressly for this case study (Figure 1 shows the homepage). The CSS techniques employed in this case study, however, are anything but artificial. Each technique was carefully selected with the intent of providing you with an arsenal of advanced CSS techniques, most of which are quick to amaze and easy to implement, and have been thoroughly tested in real-world environments.

The goal of this case study is to demonstrate the ability to code fluid layouts, elegant background imagery, and complex menus without compromising aesthetics or having to resort to superfluous markup and code. In other words, we hope you walk away convinced that web standards don't restrict but rather enhance your ability to produce a successful website.

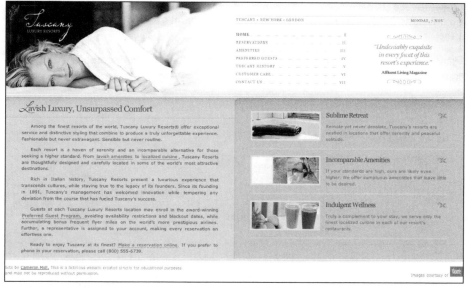

Figure 1. Tuscany Luxury Resorts homepage

The fluid layout

If we were to stand back and observe the visual evolution of the typical web layout from the early 1990s through today, we might summarize it as follows:

- Monospaced, ASCII goodness
- Text-only pages, default 100 percent width
- A few images, lots of text, 100 percent width
- More images, still lots of text, some width constraints
- Lots of images, lots of tables, lots of width/height constraints
- Flashy stuff flying everywhere, lots of width/height constraints
- Less flashy stuff, still lots of tables, lots of fixed widths
- Lots of fixed widths, fewer tables, some CSS
- Lots of fixed widths, CSS goodness

We've come a long way, haven't we? Gone is the archaic, text-only, 100 percent width legacy code, replaced with complex CSS trickery and fixed-width indulgence.

But what about 100 percent widths? Are they the bane of early web development, or a technique still worth considering? I presume full-width layouts naturally began to fall by the wayside as monitors increased in size and resolution, resulting in wide line lengths if no width constraints were in place. However, once schooled in the techniques described in this case study, you'll be armed to resurrect the full-width layout in style.

CS2

Full-width layouts have come to be known as *fluid layouts,* also referred to as flexible or liquid layouts. Whatever the term, they all denote a layout's ability to expand and contract as the browser width expands and contracts.

Tuscany Luxury Resorts employs a fluid layout in full glory. This is accomplished using six segments in the document's structure:

- Body
- Container
- Masthead
- Content
- Sidebar
- Footer

A wireframe for this underlying structure looks something like the one shown in Figure 2.

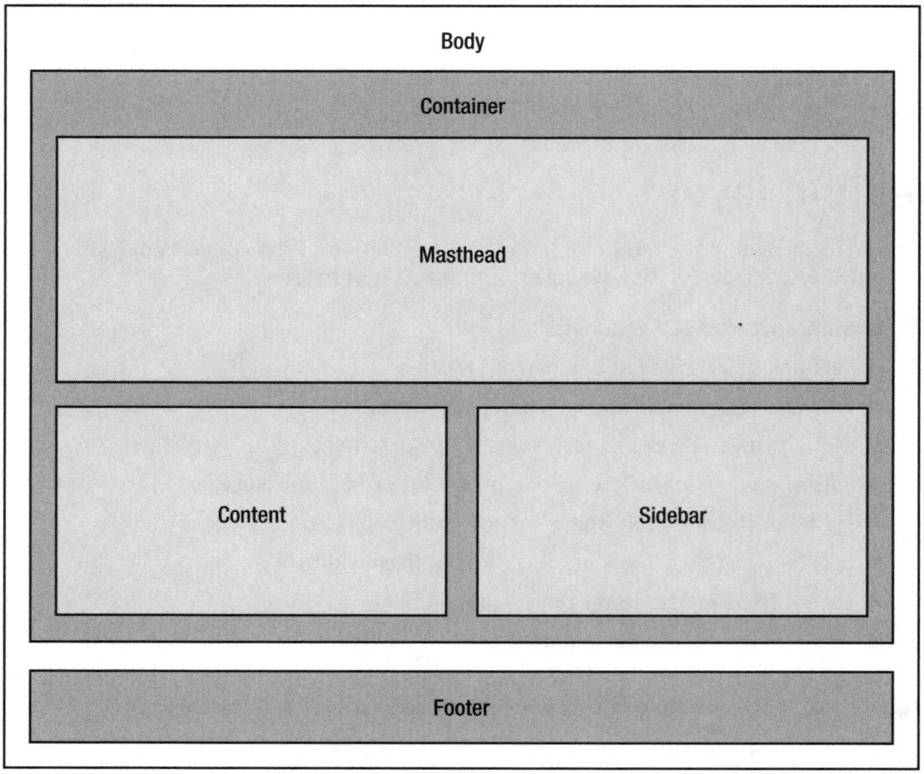

Figure 2. Wireframe for Tuscany Luxury Resorts

Body and container

To begin coding, start with the core element of your markup, the body element. Nothing special is required for the body when coding a fluid layout compared to a fixed one, but for Tuscany Luxury Resorts a margin and white background are needed to create the effect of having a white border around the layout:

```
body {
  margin: 10px;
  background: #FFF;
}
```

Create a containing div to house everything except the footer. Give it a selector ID of container:

```
<div id="container"></div>
```

Typically, if you were creating a fixed-width layout, you would specify width and margins, probably something like this:

```
#container {
  margin: 0 auto;
  width: 760px;
}
```

However, a fluid layout requires neither. In fact, the only reason you need a containing div is to control the background in the lower half of the page. You'll define styling for #container in the "Content and sidebar" section.

Masthead

I often refer to the top portion of a site containing logo, navigation, and other site-wide elements as the *masthead*, a term derived from the publishing world in reference to the date, logo, contact information, and editorial board of a publication. Though not a perfect application of the term in an online sense, it seems to be more appropriate than vague terms such as *header* or *top bar*.

On that note, add a div inside #container for the masthead:

```
<div id="container">
  <div id="masthead"></div>
</div>
```

Again, no special trickery in the CSS, aside from position: relative and a background image, both covered later in this case study:

```
#masthead {
  position: relative;
  background: #F7F7F4 url(../img/bg_repeat.gif) repeat-x;
}
```

CS2

221

I take that back—you do need a bit of trickery. Ideally you want the entire masthead to have a height of 246 pixels to properly contain all of its elements. If you were using a fixed height, your code would look like this:

```
#masthead {
  position: relative;
  background: #F7F7F4 url(../img/bg_repeat.gif) repeat-x;
  height: 246px;
}
```

However, as you'll learn later in this case study (see "'Bulletproofing' a Background"), you need to allow the entire #masthead element to be resized by those users who have difficulty reading at default text sizes. Therefore, convert your height from a fixed one to a more flexible one using an em value:

```
#masthead {
  position: relative;
  background: #F7F7F4 url(../img/bg_repeat.gif) repeat-x;
  height: 15.4em;
}
```

Now users can increase the text size without breaking the layout. This method isn't without flaw, however. Because you're using em instead of px, if for some bizarre reason users scale text *down* in size instead of *up*, the height of the masthead will be less than 246 pixels and things will begin overlapping. However, if users will be resizing, you can assume the greater number of them will be resizing text up, not down, and so leave the code as is.

Content and sidebar

While the lower area of the layout (Figure 3) utilizes several backgrounds, here we're concerned with the background used to create the appearance of two columns separating the main content ("Lavish Luxury, Unsurpassed Comfort" and everything beneath it) from the sidebar content ("Sublime Retreat," "Incomparable Amenities," and "Indulgent Wellness").

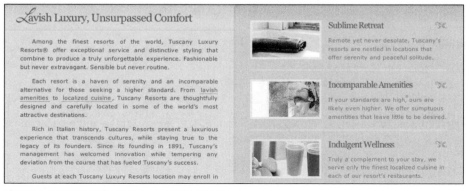

Figure 3. Content (left) and sidebar (right) areas

To accomplish this two-column effect, you'll use a technique called faux columns, which Andy has already covered in Chapter 7. However, there's nothing wrong with revisiting the technique here!

The technique is quite simple. First, use Photoshop (or similar program) to create a background image 1600 pixels wide by 10 pixels tall. Fill the left half of the image with a lighter background color (#E2E2D2) and the right half with a darker background color (#D6D6BF). I've also added a subtle drop shadow just to the right of the left half (see Figure 4).

0px ⟵—————————————————————————————————⟶ 1600px

Figure 4. Tile image, bg_container.gif, used for faux columns

In a moment you'll constrain the layout to expand only up to 1200 pixels, but a width of 1600px allows you to increase the layout width later on down the road without having to re-create the background image. In reality, you could create the faux column background as wide or as narrow as you please, as long as it fills the entire #container element.

Next, create two divs to act as the columns, one for the main content area and the other for the sidebar:

```
<div id="container">
  <div id="masthead"></div>
  <div id="content"></div>
  <div id="sidebar"></div>
</div>
```

Then, add your faux column background to #container:

```
#container {
  background: url(../img/bg_container.gif) repeat-y top center;
}
```

The value repeat-y instructs the background to tile only vertically, while top center tells it to tile starting at the top and centered on the page. The value top isn't really necessary, as for this particular background it doesn't matter if it tiles vertically from the top, center, or bottom of the page. However, the second value, center, is critical, as it centers the background *horizontally*, positioning the two columns evenly on the page.

You're probably wondering, "Why not just do a background in each column?" Alas, one of the frustrating features of CSS is that block elements stretch vertically only as far as the content within it. Therefore, if the content in the #content column were taller than the content in the #sidebar column, the background for #content would run all the way to the bottom while the background for #sidebar would stop short of it. Using faux columns trumps this issue and provides a way to make each column appear equal in height.

CS2

Fluid properties

Crucial to fluid layouts are widths that expand and contract based on the browser's width. To accomplish this effect, use percentage values (%) instead of px or em. Accordingly, percentage values are used in setting widths for the #content and #sidebar selectors. Each should fill half of the page (50 percent) horizontally, and the float property is used to align them adjacent to each other:

```
#content {
   float: left;
   width: 50%;
}
#sidebar {
   float: left;
   width: 50%;
}
```

But herein lies a problem. Internet Explorer has an issue with *tolerance* (the ability to calculate elements floated adjacent to one another). Two floated divs set to 50% are miscalculated as being too wide for the page, so IE stacks them on top of each other. But no worries—just change the width for #sidebar to 49.9% and you're good to go:

```
#content {
   float: left;
   width: 50%;
}
#sidebar {
   float: left;
   width: 49.9%;
}
```

It's important to note here that Safari doesn't like our decimal value and therefore rounds down the width value to 49%. This leaves a sizable gap just to the right of the sidebar area only in Safari. So we've fixed one problem (IE) but created another (Safari). If you and your users can live with the gap, leave it as is. If not, however, introduce a hack that presents a value of 49.9% to IE and a value of 50% to Safari:

```
#sidebar {
   float: left;
   width: 50% !important;
   width: 49.9%;
}
```

IE/Win will now process the second declaration of 49.9%, whereas Safari, Firefox, and Opera will process the first declaration of 50%.

Finally, wrap the content for each column in a shell:

```
<div id="container">
   <div id="masthead"></div>
   <div id="content">
```

```
      <div class="shell">Content goes here</div>
    </div>
    <div id="sidebar">
      <div class="shell">Content goes here</div>
    </div>
  </div>
```

The shell becomes necessary to add fluid pseudo-like padding on either side of the content, without affecting the tiled background that spans the full width of the content and sidebar areas:

```
.shell {
  margin: 0 auto;
  width: 85%;
}
```

Footer

Typically, every element of a layout is wrapped inside a containing block for the entire page, in this case #container. However, when using faux columns, I prefer to have the footer reside outside the containing block that has the faux column's background image in it. This is a surefire way of preventing the background image from tiling down the rest of the page.

Accordingly, add a div with an ID of footer just after #container:

```
<div id="container">
  <div id="masthead"></div>
  <div id="content"></div>
  <div id="sidebar"></div>
</div>
<div id="footer"></div>
```

The styling for the footer is rather simple, requiring only a background image and padding to round out the layout:

```
#footer {
  padding: 8px 0 1em;
  background: url(../img/bg_barbottom.gif) repeat-x top left;
}
```

CS2

Resolving fluid layout issues

To sing the praises of fluid layouts would be foolish without first confronting the problems they present. Naturally, the bulk of these issues are due to the fact that the width is resizable. An overly wide width, for example, will result in long line lengths, which tend to make onscreen reading a bit difficult. Conversely, a narrow width will eventually force undesirable soft breaks and overlapping.

To address these issues, the Tuscany Luxury Resorts site relies on min-width and max-width to define a minimum and maximum width for the entire layout. These properties are defined for both the #container and #footer ID selectors—the two primary containing blocks for the layout.

The initial code is rather simple:

```
#container, #footer {
    min-width: 740px;
    max-width: 1200px;
}
```

As 760px is a common value for fixed-width layouts, here you use 740px to account for the 10-pixel left and right margins in the body (760 – 10 – 10 = 740). This defines the minimum width for the layout.

The maximum width is set at 1200 pixels. This allows the layout to display full-width for screen resolutions up to 1280 pixels in width. Beyond that, the layout stops stretching, preventing unreasonable line lengths.

But there's a catch. Not surprisingly, IE 6 and below fails to offer support for min-width and max-width. There's a way around the issue, but it means using a proprietary extension:

```
#container, #footer {
    width: expression(document.body.clientWidth < 740? "740px" :
        document.body.clientWidth > 1200? "1200px" : "auto");
}
```

This JavaScript expression sets the width value to 740px if the body of the page is less than 740 pixels wide and to 1200px if it's wider than 1200 pixels.

Sadly, this proprietary extension invalidates the CSS. Therefore, we keep this code in a separate CSS file, ie.css. Also, we expect IE 7 to offer support for min-width and max-width—another reason to keep this hack separate from the master CSS so you can delete it later when it's no longer necessary.

Aligning elements using absolute positioning

In technical jargon, absolute positioning gives you freedom to precisely position an element anywhere on the page in relation to its containing block. Or, in layman's terms, it allows you to position a "child" element (e.g., p id="copyright-date") in relation to a "parent" element (e.g., div id="footer"). Although there are other values for the position property (static, relative, fixed), we'll cover only absolute positioning here.

Imagine coding a set of div, p, and strong elements as you normally do. Each will be positioned *in relation to the item before it in the markup flow*. Think of it as a game of Tetris, where each block must reside on top or to the side of the adjacent blocks already in the game.

In contrast, when coding the same set of tags with absolute positioning, each will be positioned *in relation to the containing block or parent element, regardless of markup flow.* Child elements can reside next to each other, they can overlap one another, or they can even be positioned anywhere outside the area of the parent element. Think of it as playing with Lego blocks, where each block can be stacked next to other blocks, on top of other blocks, or completely apart from the main group of blocks.

The top, bottom, left, and right properties determine positioning, while the z-index property determines stacking order, or the hierarchal order in which elements overlap one other.

Location properties (top, bottom, left, right)

Before we dive into location properties, let's be sure you understand a key point of positioning a location. The property and value of position: relative does not force a parent element to be positioned relative to another element, but instead forces any child elements to be positioned relative to the parent element (the one that's marked with position: relative).

Consider this example:

```
/* 'position:relative' tells any elements inside this h2
   to be positioned relative to it /*
h2 {
  position: relative;
  width: 250px;
  height: 100px;
}
```

This bit of code instructs any elements inside this heading to be positioned relative to the width and height of the h2. By default, all child elements are positioned relative to a parent element anyway. But you insert this bit of code so that you can force absolute positioning on the child elements and ensure they will be positioned in relation to the parent element.

CS2

The location properties for positioning an element are

- top
- bottom
- left
- right

Values for each of these properties are

- px
- em
- %

Any combinations of these properties and values are calculated in relation to the containing block or parent element. So, a location of bottom: 50px and left: 30px will position a child element 50 pixels from the bottom and 30 pixels from the left of its parent element. Also, values may be mixed, such as bottom: 50px and left: 3em.

Consider Figure 5, which demonstrates the width and height of the h2 above, as well as the values of the upper-left and lower-right corners.

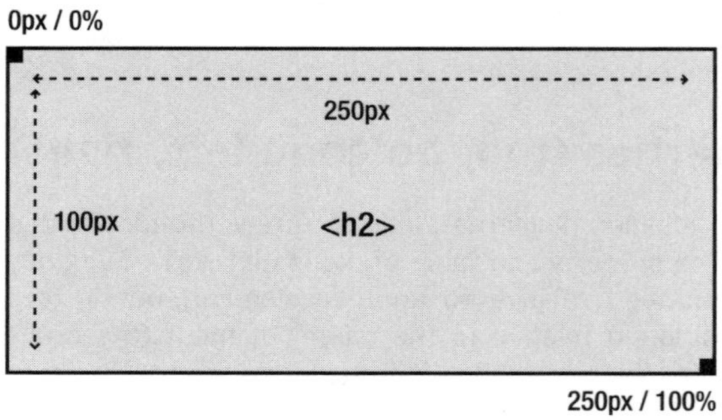

Figure 5. The h2 element, with its dimensions and corner values

The upper-left corner has a value of 0px or 0%, while the lower-right corner has a value of 250px or 100%. Any location inside the element is calculated based on those two corner values.

Putting this into practice, let's say we place a strong tag inside the h2. To position it absolutely, you would use the following:

```
/* This strong element will be positioned relative to the h2,
    with an absolute position of 0 pixels from the top and 10 pixels
    from the left of the header */
h2 strong {
  position: absolute;
  top: 0;
  left: 10px;
}
```

The location properties of top: 0 and left: 10px tell the strong element to be positioned 0 pixels from the top and 10 pixels from the left of the h2, as shown in Figure 6.

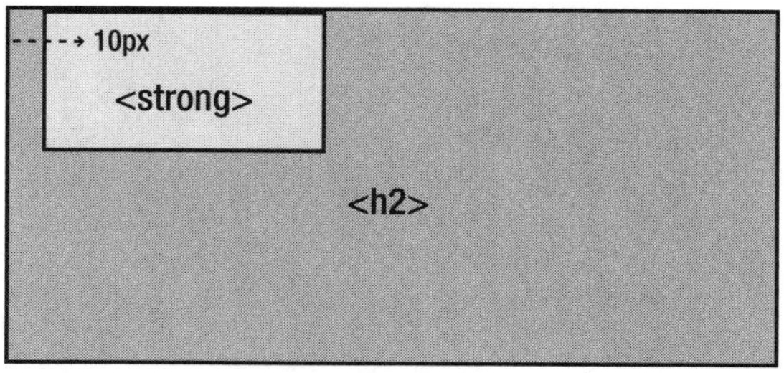

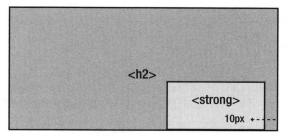

Figure 6. The strong element, positioned at the top left

We could have coded the same strong element with bottom: 0 and right: 10px and it would have been positioned as shown in Figure 7.

Figure 7. The strong element, positioned at the lower right

Stacking order (z-index)

The z-index property allows you to determine the stacking order of elements. The z is in reference to the z-axis, which tells us we're dealing not with left or right positioning (x-axis) or top or bottom positioning (y-axis) but with stacking and overlapping in a 3D sort of way—how each element stacks or overlaps the other elements within a containing block. This z-index is critical when elements overlap and the default markup flow with built-in defaults for stacking won't suffice, as is the case quite often when using absolute positioning.

Two values can be used with z-index:

- Integers (e.g., 0, 1, 2, 100)
- auto

The value auto is the default value, and you'll likely use this value only to override another style declared elsewhere in your CSS. Most of the time you'll use integers.

When using integers, the element with the higher z-index will appear on top or in front of elements with lower z-index values. Imagine holding a deck of face cards in your hand. If you were to count from 1 to 10 by placing the cards in a stack, the bottom card in the stack would be a 1 and the top card would be a 10. It's the same with z-index. An element with a value of 1 will always be beneath an element with a value of 10 within the same containing block.

CS2

229

For example, consider the following two elements:

```html
<div id="product">
  <div id="sale-price"></div>
  <div id="product-photo"></div>
</div>
```

with the accompanying CSS:

```css
#product {
  position: relative;
}
#sale-price {
  position: absolute;
  z-index: 2;
}
#product-photo {
  position: absolute;
  z-index: 1;
}
```

The rendered markup would place the element #sale-price with the higher z-index value on top of the element #product-photo, if the two were positioned to overlap one another.

However, take note that relativity comes into play so that stacking order is relevant only to child elements within a parent element. In the previous example, the parent element #product and its child elements (#product-photo, #sale-price) would be relative only to each other. They would be subject to stacking order for the entire page if z-index were used in other parent elements.

Confused? Don't be. We'll show examples of absolute positioning and z-index in two latter sections of this case study, and further information is available here:

- http://css-discuss.incutio.com/?page=AbsoluteLayouts
- www.stopdesign.com/articles/absolute/

Background image techniques

If you were to ask me what single style defines most of my work, the answer would likely be background images. They can be a powerful ally in enhancing the aesthetics of a site, and CSS makes it relatively easy to control background tiling and positioning.

While the homepage for Tuscany Luxury Resorts uses nearly 20 background images, we'll cover only a few here and allow you to explore the rest on your own:

- Dividing the top half of the page into three backgrounds
- "Bulletproofing" the h1 background image

Dividing the top in three

The masthead or top half of the page (often referred to as "above the fold") uses three images to produce the effect of a single background banner. Were this layout a fixed-width one, you could use a single background image and be done with it. However, the width of the Tuscany layout is fluid, and therefore the background needs to be split in three to accommodate.

This is done using an image at left (woman lying down), an image repeated horizontally the full width of the page, and an image at right (subtle gradient), as shown in Figure 8.

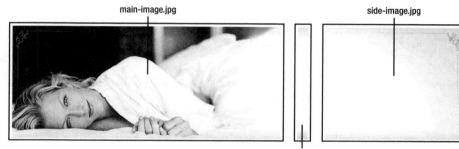

Figure 8. The three background images used to construct the top half

Accordingly, the markup uses three main div elements to control each background:

```
<div id="masthead">
  <div id="main-image"></div>
  ...
  <div id="side-image"></div>
</div>
```

Begin by coding the repeated background, which is the easiest of the three. This image is embedded in #masthead as follows:

```
#masthead {
 background: #FFF url(../img/bg_repeat.gif) repeat-x;
}
```

Three attributes combine to produce the desired effect:

- #FFF isn't really necessary for visual display, as the image bg_repeat.gif overrides it. However, it's included as a safety net, should images be disabled for any reason. It's always good practice to include background colors when background images are used and could potentially render content illegible if images are disabled (e.g., black text when the body background is also black).
- url(../img/bg_repeat.gif) references the image.
- repeat-x tells the image to tile only horizontally across the page and not vertically.

CS2

Next, code the images at left and right, but be aware the navigation menu, resort locations, and date stamp will all need to overlay the background. Thus, to accomplish this virtual layering of content and backgrounds, use absolute positioning and z-index instead of floats.

First, the side image (the subtle gradient):

```
#side-image {
   position: absolute;
   top: 0;
   right: 0;
   z-index: 1;
   width: 289px;
   height: 246px;
   background: url(../img/side-image.jpg) no-repeat;
}
```

The image is positioned flush with the top and right side of #masthead using top: 0 and right: 0, while no-repeat ensures the image won't tile across the page. The image naturally overlays bg_repeat.gif in #masthead due to the background stacking order. Additionally, a z-index of 1 ensures this image will stack beneath the image of the woman, should the browser's width be narrow enough that the two collide.

Next, the main image (the woman lying down):

```
#main-image {
   position: absolute;
   top: 0;
   left: 0;
   z-index: 2;
   width: 566px;
   height: 246px;
   background: url(../img/main-image.jpg) no-repeat;
}
```

The image is positioned flush with the top and left side of #masthead and without repeating, while a z-index of 2 stacks it above the side gradient image.

That's all there is to it. The three background images, with their individual repeat specifications and stacking order, combine to produce an elegant, fluid background. And in case you're curious, the flourishes in the upper-left and right corners were constructed using characters from the Nat Vignette One font family, available through MyFonts.com.

"Bulletproofing" a background

The subject of "bulletproofing" a layout is one Dan Cederholm covers at length in his book, *Bulletproof Web Design* (New Riders Press, 2005). While I've used a variety of his techniques in developing Tuscany Luxury Resorts, I'll cover just one briefly here.

The headline "Lavish Luxury, Unsurpassed Comfort" contains a repeated background along the bottom, as Figure 9 shows.

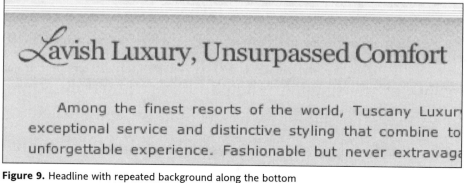

Figure 9. Headline with repeated background along the bottom

Without the background, the headline appears as shown in Figure 10.

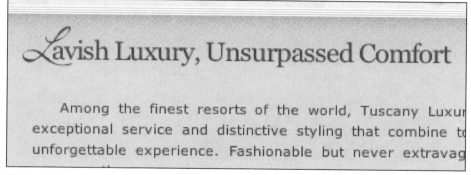

Figure 10. Headline without repeated background

CS2

The background adds a bit of flair and helps distinguish the headline from the rest of the body copy. If you were doing this with old-school tables and with a fixed layout, you could get away with embedding the background as one giant image to fill the entire headline. But you're new-school, and you're going to bulletproof that background.

The crux of bulletproofing is to make an element (div, h>, p, etc.) as flexible as possible so that it will stand up against any request for resizing and reshaping, no matter how tall the order.

So, the goal is to make your headline background as flexible as possible to tolerate any amount of short or long text, and, more importantly, to allow for user-controlled browser text resizing.

For starters, wrap the headline in a div with the selector #title:

```
<div id="title">
  <h2>Lavish Luxury, Unsurpassed Comfort</h2>
</div>
```

Under most circumstances, you could do away with the wrapper div and accomplish this technique with only the h2. However, you'll use another background in the h2 in the next section and therefore the wrapper div is necessary—that is, at least until the major browsers fully support CSS 3 with multiple backgrounds for a single element.

Here's the styling for the #title selector:

```
#title {
    background: url(../img/bg_hmain.gif) repeat-x bottom;
}
```

The attribute repeat-x instructs the background to repeat horizontally only, while bottom forces it to repeat along the bottom of the #title element instead of the top, which is the default setting. And now, if the text inside #title either spans two lines or is resized by the user, the background holds up and doesn't interfere with the text, as you can see in Figure 11.

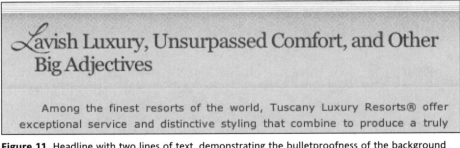

Figure 11. Headline with two lines of text, demonstrating the bulletproofness of the background image

This particular technique is more simple than most others covered in Cederholm's book, but the idea remains the same regardless of complexity: bulletproofing your site isn't a difficult task per se, but rather a shift from thinking about coding for fixed/one-size usage to thinking about coding for variable size usage and resizing.

Image replacement

Image replacement, covered in Chapter 3, is used twice in the Tuscany layout:

- The logo
- The initial cap in the headline "Lavish Luxury, Unsurpassed Comfort"

The basic technique is the same, but each requires specialized adaptation.

Logo image replacement

Three elements are required to code the logo (see Figure 12):

- Logo image
- Markup
- CSS

Figure 12. Tuscany logo image

Because the positioning of the logo is fixed, I've saved it as a simple GIF with transparency and a matte color similar to the section of the photo it overlays (black). I've used the lovely P22 Dearest typeface for the "Tuscany" type and Trajan Pro for "Luxury Resorts."

Whenever possible, code your logos using h1. This is because the name of the site is almost always the highest-ranking element in the overall markup structure of a page. Accordingly, begin as follows:

```
<h1>Tuscany Luxury Resorts</h1>
```

Note the text in the logo image is repeated in the h1. Not only is this a backup measure for those who browse with styles turned off (disabled users, some mobile users), but this typically helps with search engine rankings as well, as plain text inside an h1 tag is often given substantial consideration when determining the keyword ranking of a page.

Further, this h1 is somewhat all-encompassing. It houses the logo image as a background, it positions the logo absolutely on the page with top and left attributes, and it throws the backup plain text off of the displayable area of the page using text-indent:

```
h1 {
  margin: 0;
  position: absolute;
  top: 20px;
  left: 46px;
  z-index: 3;
  width: 126px;
  height: 87px;
  background: url(../img/logo.gif) no-repeat;
  text-indent: -9000px;
}
```

CS2

235

The width is the same as that of the logo image, and a z-index of 3 is used to ensure the logo appears on top of any other elements above the fold. We use the Phark image replacement method here (and for the rest of the case study) instead of the Gilder/Levin method or other IR methods due to transparency in the images.

You could stop coding at this point and walk away. However, let's take things a step further to accommodate a common usability request. A fair share of web users have come to expect a site's logo to be a link back to the homepage. To accomplish this, simply add an anchor tag to your markup:

```
<h1><a href="/">Tuscany Luxury Resorts</a></h1>
```

Then, add the following code to your stylesheet:

```
h1 a {
        display: block;
        height: 87px;
        background: url(../img/logo.gif) no-repeat;
}
```

Note the height and background image are repeated here. You can now remove the height from the h1 as duplication isn't necessary, but the background image needs to be repeated to avoid the flickering that often occurs in IE when a user mouses over the logo.

Initial cap image replacement

The elements used to code the initial cap in the headline "Lavish Luxury, Unsurpassed Comfort" (see Figure 13) are similar to that of the logo:

- "L" image
- Markup
- CSS

Figure 13. "L" image, coded using image replacement

This headline is second in importance in the overall markup structure, and therefore an h2 tag is used:

```
<h2>Lavish Luxury, Unsurpassed Comfort</h2>
```

Unlike the logo, you won't hide the full text, but rather only the first L. Wrapping the L in a strong tag will do the trick:

```
<h2><strong>L</strong>avish Luxury, Unsurpassed Comfort</h2>
```

We'll look at the strong styling in a moment, but the styling for the h2 looks like this:

```
#content h2 {
  position: relative;
  margin: 0 auto;
  padding: 25px 0 15px 25px;
  width: 85%;
  font: normal 2em Georgia, serif;
  color: #48546A;
  letter-spacing: -1px;
  background: url(../img/l.gif) no-repeat 0 .7em;
}
```

Aside from the typical margin, padding, and width attributes, two key attributes set the stage for properly displaying the initial cap:

- background: url(../img/l.gif) embeds the L image, no-repeat prevents it from tiling, and 0.7em positions it flush left and 0.7em from the top of the h2 (to approximate the baseline of the plain text).

- position: relative allows the strong tag to be positioned absolutely in the next step.

The styling for the strong tag looks like this:

```
#content h2 strong {
  position: absolute;
  left: -9000px;
}
```

Because the strong element isn't naturally a block element, you can't hide the plain-text L with text-indent (as you did with the logo) without first converting the strong tag to a block element using display: block. However, if you do so, the remaining plain text will soft break on a new line. So instead position the plain-text L absolutely, and then throw it off the page with a left position of –9000px. Problem solved.

CS2

Fluid imagery

The premise for this next technique is simple: the layout expands and contracts to accommodate browser width; shouldn't the imagery do the same?

To design for fluid imagery—that is, images that appear to expand and contract as browser width is resized—you need only to change the way you think about coding the images.

Typically, you would insert an image inline using the `img` element and a fixed width, as shown in Figure 14.

Full image

Image rendered
with img tag

Figure 14. Traditional image rendering with an img element

The markup is equally typical:

```
<img src="../img/hpic_bath.jpg" width="220" height="70"
  alt="Image of bath and towel" />
```

In contrast, when creating fluid imagery, you use a div element with a fluid width and embed the image as a background. Accordingly, if the div containing the background image has a fluid width, the image will need to fill the display area regardless of width. "Stretching" an image results in poor quality, and therefore the image is prepared to be wider than the dimensions of the div (see Figure 15).

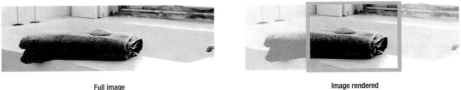

Full image

Image rendered
as div background

Figure 15. Fluid image rendering with the image as a div background

Essentially, the div "crops" the image and shows only a portion of it. The hidden portions of the image are revealed as the layout expands.

Coding a fluid image

First, begin with a div and class selector:

```
<div class="section_pic"></div>
```

The class selector section_pic will be repeated for each of the three featured images, with styling as follows:

```
.section_pic {
  float: left;
```

```
      margin-right: 1.25em;
      width: 34%;
      height: 70px;
      border: 4px solid #EBEBE5;
   }
```

Note the width is specified as a *percentage* rather than pixels. This allows the div to expand and contract as the layout does the same. Note also the height of the image won't be fluid, so a fixed height of 70px is specified.

An id is then added to each image div:

```
   <div class="section_pic" id="hpic1"></div>
```

The addition of id=hpic1 allows the image to be included as a background, specific to each div:

```
   #hpic1 {
      background: #E2E2D2 url(../img/hpic_bath.jpg) no-repeat
         center center;
   }
```

The image is centered both vertically and horizontally with center center, while no-repeat prevents the image from tiling regardless of browser width. Speaking of which, be sure to prepare the image with a width sufficient to cover the maximum width of your layout. As described in the first section of this case study, Tuscany Luxury Resorts will stretch up to 1200 pixels. Therefore, the images used are 220px in total width, which is plenty sufficient to fill the entire div when the browser is 1200 pixels wide or more.

Lastly, lest we forget disabled users and those who browse without full CSS support (e.g., some mobile users), include text that acts as a pseudo-alt description:

```
   <div class="section_pic" id="hpic1">(Image of bath and towel)</div>
```

We then throw the text off the page by adding text-indent:

```
   .section_pic {
     float: left;
     margin-right: 1.25em;
     width: 34%;
     height: 70px;
     border: 4px solid #EBEBE5;
     text-indent: -9000px;
   }
```

CS2

That wasn't difficult, was it? Again, it's more a mere shift in thinking, rather than a mastery of complex CSS techniques.

Using a single list item for multiple elements

In previous chapters you learned to use unordered lists whenever possible to code your navigation menus. However, writing clean code with a navigation menu like that of Tuscany Luxury Resorts can be a bit of a challenge (see Figure 16).

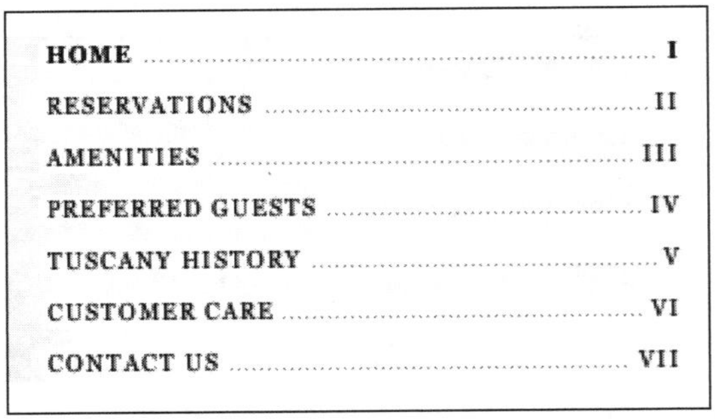

HOME	I
RESERVATIONS	II
AMENITIES	III
PREFERRED GUESTS	IV
TUSCANY HISTORY	V
CUSTOMER CARE	VI
CONTACT US	VII

Figure 16. Navigation menu for Tuscany Luxury Resorts

Note that each navigation item has three elements:

- Menu text (Home)
- Roman numeral (I)
- Dotted leader (....)

If you didn't care about clean markup, it would probably require less effort to code each of these elements as columns in a table, or to litter the markup with repeated periods (.) for the dotted leader. Instead, you'll wisely use a single li to code all three elements. The menu text is housed in an anchor (a) tag floated left, the Roman numeral in a span floated right, and the dotted leader as a repeated background image in the li.

Coding the menu

Begin with a simple unordered list:

```
<ul id="nav">
  <li><a href="/">Home</a></li>
  <li><a href="/reservations/">Reservations</a></li>
  <li><a href="/amenities/">Amenities</a></li>
  <li><a href="/preferred/">Preferred Guests</a></li>
  <li><a href="/history/">Tuscany History</a></li>
  <li><a href="/customer/">Customer Care</a></li>
  <li><a href="/contact/">Contact Us</a></li>
</ul>
```

Next, add Roman numerals wrapped in a span tag, and add <br /> to clear the floats you'll add in a moment:

```
<ul id="nav">
  <li><span>I</span> <a href="/">Home</a><br /></li>
  <li><span>II</span> <a href="/reservations/">Reservations</a>
     <br /></li>
  <li><span>III</span> <a href="/amenities/">Amenities</a><br /></li>
  <li><span>IV</span> <a href="/preferred/">Preferred Guests</a>
     <br /></li>
  <li><span>V</span> <a href="/history/">Tuscany History</a><br /></li>
  <li><span>VI</span> <a href="/customer/">Customer Care</a><br /></li>
  <li><span>VII</span> <a href="/contact/">Contact Us</a><br /></li>
</ul>
```

This is all of the markup required to generate the menu. All other styling will be controlled by the CSS. Note that the Roman numeral is placed *before* the menu text in the markup, even though it appears *after* the menu text when rendered by the browser. This is done to achieve the "table of contents" effect with styles enabled, while considering those browsing with styles disabled.

Now code the CSS. First, remove margin, padding, and list-style:

```
ul#nav {
  margin: 0;
  padding: 0;
  list-style: none;
}
```

Then specify styling for each li:

```
#nav li {
  margin: 8px 0;
  padding-top: 1px;
  font: .6em Georgia, serif;
  color: #777;
  text-transform: uppercase;
  letter-spacing: 1px;
  background: url(../img/bg_dotted.gif) repeat-x 0 77% !important;
  background-position: 0 61%;   /* Hack for Internet Explorer */
}
```

The background image is a simple dotted pattern repeated horizontally. Note its position at a vertical height of 77%, a few pixels shy of the bottom of the li. This allows you to hide the background behind the menu text and Roman numeral, to appear as if the dotted leader begins before and after each, respectively. Regrettably (and with no surprise), IE positions the background a bit lower, so we override the first position of 77% with a hack at 61%.

CS2

Position the menu text (wrapped in the anchor tag) at the left using a float. Add a white background, which will 1) hide the dotted background and 2) help with legibility when the browser width is small such that the navigation menu overlaps the background image of the woman. Padding is also added to artificially increase the height of the element to cover the dotted background the entire width of the menu text.

```css
#nav li a {
  float: left;
  padding: 1px 3px;
  background: #FFF;
  color: #777;
  text-decoration: none;
}
```

Position the Roman numeral (wrapped in a span) at the right using a float. Also similar to your styling for the menu text, a white background and padding are needed to hide the dotted background:

```css
ul#nav li span {
  float: right;
  padding: 1px 3px;
  background: #FFF;
}
```

Clear the floats for the menu text and Roman numeral using the <br /> tag added earlier:

```css
ul#nav li br {
  clear: both;
}
```

Finally, add specific selectors to each li to embolden the menu item of the current page. Here is sample markup for the Home menu item:

```html
<ul id="nav">
  <li id="nav-home"><span>I</span> <a href="#">Home</a><br /></li>
  ...
</ul>
```

The accompanying CSS is formatted as follows, with #home declared earlier in the body element:

```css
#home #nav-home {
  font-weight: bold;
}
```

(For additional explanation of this technique, see "Highlighting the current page based on the body class," in Simon's *More Than Doodles* case study.)

Figure 17 shows the final menu as shown in a browser. Figure 18 shows the same menu as it would appear if styles were disabled for the entire site.

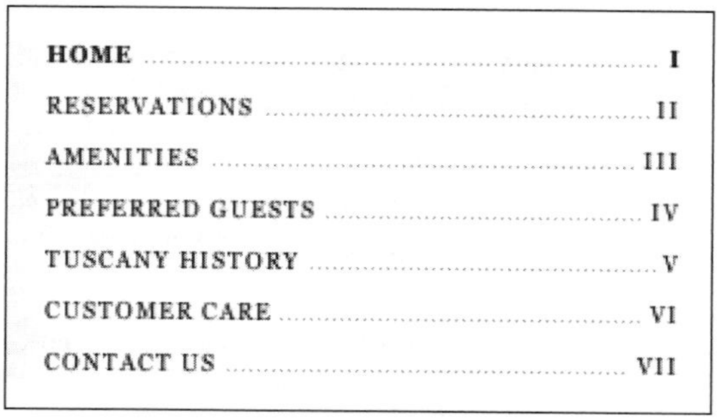

HOME	I
RESERVATIONS	II
AMENITIES	III
PREFERRED GUESTS	IV
TUSCANY HISTORY	V
CUSTOMER CARE	VI
CONTACT US	VII

Figure 17. Finished navigation menu

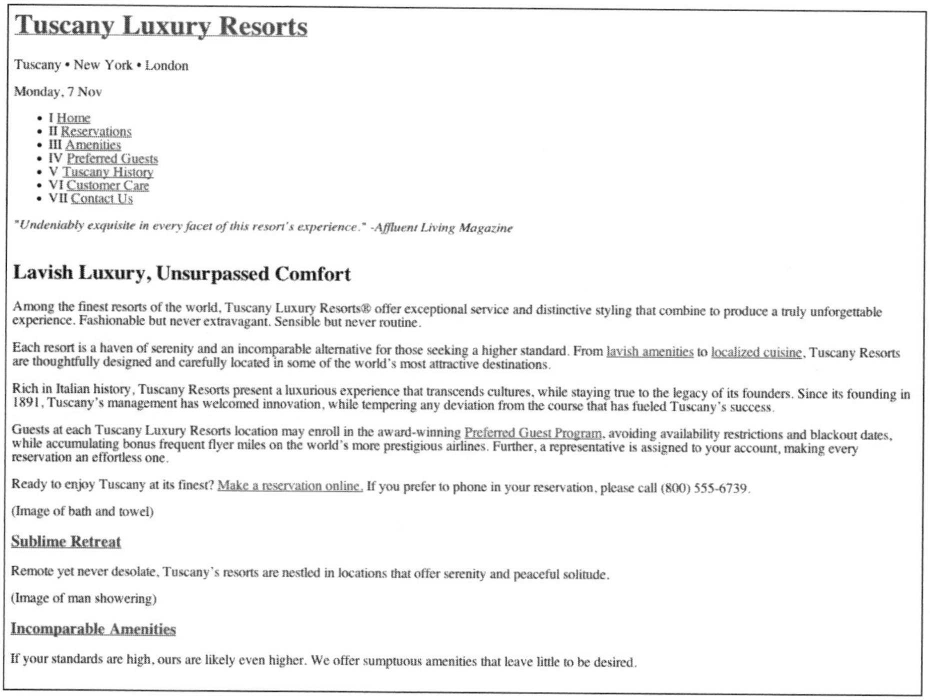

Tuscany Luxury Resorts

Tuscany • New York • London

Monday, 7 Nov

- I Home
- II Reservations
- III Amenities
- IV Preferred Guests
- V Tuscany History
- VI Customer Care
- VII Contact Us

"Undeniably exquisite in every facet of this resort's experience." -Affluent Living Magazine

Lavish Luxury, Unsurpassed Comfort

Among the finest resorts of the world, Tuscany Luxury Resorts® offer exceptional service and distinctive styling that combine to produce a truly unforgettable experience. Fashionable but never extravagant. Sensible but never routine.

Each resort is a haven of serenity and an incomparable alternative for those seeking a higher standard. From lavish amenities to localized cuisine, Tuscany Resorts are thoughtfully designed and carefully located in some of the world's most attractive destinations.

Rich in Italian history, Tuscany Resorts present a luxurious experience that transcends cultures, while staying true to the legacy of its founders. Since its founding in 1891, Tuscany's management has welcomed innovation, while tempering any deviation from the course that has fueled Tuscany's success.

Guests at each Tuscany Luxury Resorts location may enroll in the award-winning Preferred Guest Program, avoiding availability restrictions and blackout dates, while accumulating bonus frequent flyer miles on the world's more prestigious airlines. Further, a representative is assigned to your account, making every reservation an effortless one.

Ready to enjoy Tuscany at its finest? Make a reservation online. If you prefer to phone in your reservation, please call (800) 555-6739.

(Image of bath and towel)

Sublime Retreat

Remote yet never desolate, Tuscany's resorts are nestled in locations that offer serenity and peaceful solitude.

(Image of man showering)

Incomparable Amenities

If your standards are high, ours are likely even higher. We offer sumptuous amenities that leave little to be desired.

Figure 18. Tuscany Luxury Resorts with styling disabled

And that's it. Three elements, one `li`.

CS2

Summary

You've now successfully uncovered many of the techniques used to code Tuscany Luxury Resorts. The site is online at https://tuscany.cssmastery.com/, and the source code is available for download at www.friendsofed.com. There are plenty more—look under the hood, dive deeper into the code, and you just might find a few gems.

But the real beauty of what's demonstrated in this case study perhaps lies in the fact that the raw XHTML markup is just as solid as the aesthetic design. If all styling is disabled, users should have no difficulty reading and navigating the site (see Figure 18 in the previous section).

Though perhaps not beautiful to the web designer's eye, raw markup formatted cleanly is a real treat for screenreaders, mobile devices, and search engine listings. It's the best of both worlds—those with vision and full-featured browsers enjoy a rich visual experience, while those with limited vision or limited devices enjoy uncluttered, raw content.

INDEX